MASS AND THE SACRAMENTS

A Course in Religion
Book II

About This Series

Fr. John Laux, M.A. was a high school religion teacher who distilled the fruit of his many years of research and teaching into these fine high school religion books. At first glance, it might appear foolish to reprint books that were first published in 1928. But a reading of Fr. Laux's books will lay that thought to rest. For he had a rare talent of capsulizing the intricacies of our Catholic Faith and its theology into succinct, precise, learned and yet lively prose that is at once truly interesting and that all can easily understand. He is profoundly intellectual, yet always clear and easy. His writing, while aimed at the high school student, remains challenging and informative to the college student and the adult Catholic as well. But further, Fr. Laux writes in a virtually undated and almost undateable style, a style that is, one might say, classic and timeless, a style that truly befits his subject matter—the timeless teachings of our Ancient Church. For these reasons, the four books in this high school series are all works of rare genius, as also are his *Introduction to the Bible* and *Church History,* for they all possess these same qualities that make Fr. Laux such a pleasure to read and such a joy to study from.

Raphael

THE DISPUTÀ

ii

MASS AND THE SACRAMENTS

THE MASS, SEVEN SACRAMENTS, INDULGENCES, SACRAMENTALS

A Course in Religion
For Catholic High Schools and Academies

BOOK II

by

Fr. John Laux, M.A.

Late Instructor of Religion, Notre Dame High School, and Professor of
Psychology, Villa Madonna College, Covington, Ky.

*"And taking bread, he gave thanks, and brake;
and gave to them, saying: This is my body, which
is given for you. Do this for a commemoration
of me. In like manner the chalice also, after he
had supped, saying: This is the chalice, the new
testament in my blood, which shall be shed for you."*
—Luke 22:19-20

TAN BOOKS AND PUBLISHERS, INC.
Rockford, Illinois 61105

Nihil Obstat :   J. M. Lelen
                   Censor Librorum

Imprimatur: ✠ Francis W. Howard
                  Bishop of Covington, Kentucky
                  March 25, 1932

Copyright © 1934 by Benziger Brothers.

Originally published in 1928 by Benziger Brothers, New York, in an unillustrated edition. Republished in 1934 by Benziger Brothers in an illustrated edition, from which this present edition has been photographically reproduced complete and unabridged, with the addition of a few footnotes.

Copyright © 1990 by TAN Books and Publishers, Inc.

Library of Congress Catalog Card No.: 90-70439

ISBN: 0-89555-392-9

Cover illustration: St. Charles Borromeo (1538-1584) distributes Holy Communion to victims of a plague.

Printed and bound in the United States of America.

TAN BOOKS AND PUBLISHERS, INC.
P.O. Box 424
Rockford, Illinois 61105

1990

A Word to the Teacher

The need of some systematic presentation of the truths of our Holy Religion to boys and girls of our American Catholic High Schools has been felt by Catholic educators for a long time. The manuals now in use have been found to be either too technical or too simple, and the problem has been to prepare a text that would suit the needs of the growing mind, and, while enlisting the interest of the pupils in acquiring a knowledge of religious truths, would at the same time encourage the practice of virtue and cultivate a love for the Church.

The present *Course in Religion for Catholic High Schools and Academies* is an attempt to solve this problem. The general arrangement of the course is based, as far as possible, on the division and order of the larger Baltimore Catechism. The catechetical form of presentation has been abandoned, because, in the opinion of prominent educators, "it is conducive to memory work rather than to reasoning, encourages inefficient teaching, and makes almost no appeal to the interest of the pupil."

For practical purposes the work has been divided into Four Parts, each of which is bound and paged separately and provided with copious helps for study and review, a table of contents and an index.

The First Part embraces the mystery of the Trinity, the work of Creation, Redemption, Sanctification, and Consummation. It is introduced by a brief treatment of the nature, necessity, sources, and qualities of Faith. The Second Part treats of the Means of Grace: the Sacraments, the Sacrifice of the Mass, Indulgences and Sacramentals. Part Three is devoted to General and Special Christian Moral; Part Four to Apologetics.

The writer suggests that every pupil be provided with a copy of the New Testament, to be used throughout the course; a Student's edition of the Missal, to be used in connection with Part Two; and the *Imitation of Christ* as supplementary material for Part Three. It is presupposed that there is a well-stocked Religious Book Shelf in every High School Library.

The concluding words of Father Drinkwater's preface to his excellent little book of religious instruction *Twelve and After* are applicable to every textbook in Religion: "Let us remind ourselves that religion is not a book-and-writing matter. Such instruction as this book contains is very useful and in some ways necessary; but there are things even more necessary, such as plenty of singing, corporate prayer, both liturgical and unliturgical, and opportunities for personal service, not to speak of the more individual and interior practice of religion. If these more essential things are well managed, then the intellectual instruction will have all the more meaning and fruit. It should become the raw material of Catholic ideals. We can but build up our altar stone by stone and arrange our wood upon it as carefully as may be, and then pray for the fire of the Lord to fall in acceptance of the offering."

A word to the teacher of religion. The purpose of the teaching of religion must be the same in all our schools from the grades to the university—to form *religious characters,* to train men and women who will be ready to profess their Faith with firm conviction and to practice it in their daily lives in union with the Church.

This obvious purpose of all religious teaching imposes a twofold duty on the teacher of religion in the High School: to give his pupils a *fuller* and *more profound grasp of Christian Doctrine,* and to lead them on to the *intelligent use* of the helps that have been given us to lead Christian lives.

It is idle to dispute, as is sometimes done, whether the training of the intellect is more important than the training of the heart and the will; the imparting of religious knowledge, than the formation of religious habits. Both are of supreme importance. The will follows the intellect; but the intellect is also powerfully influenced by the will. Ignorance may sometimes be bliss, but never in religious matters. Well-instructed Catholics may become backsliders, but their number is small in comparison with those who are lost to the Church because their ignorance of Catholic teaching made them easy victims of the purveyors of false science, shallow philosophy, and neo-pagan morality. Religion requires that the *whole* man worship God with all his faculties and acts. The intellect must *believe* that which is true concerning God—

Faith; and the *will* must be directed to *do* those actions which are right and to avoid those which are wrong—*Morals.*

Catholic Action is today becoming a vital force throughout the world. The layman cannot effectively engage in Catholic Action unless he is well versed in the teachings of his faith and able at all times to explain and defend it. The type of layman, therefore, that is needed today is the type which Cardinal Newman asked for years ago when he said: "I want laymen, not arrogant, not rash in speech, not disputatious, but men who know their religion, who enter into it, who know just where they stand, who know what they hold and what they do not; who know their Creed so well that they can give an account of it; who know so much of history that they can defend it. I want an intelligent, well-instructed laity. I wish you to enlarge your knowledge, to cultivate your reason, to get an insight into the relation of truth to truth; to learn to view things as they are; to understand how faith and reason stand to each other; what are the bases and principles of Catholicism. Ignorance is the root of bitterness."

The great Cardinal's ideal of the Catholic layman may never be fully attained, but it is certainly worth striving after. It is only through such pious and enlightened laymen and laywomen, working with their bishops and pastors, that Catholic Action can be truly successful. It is the chief duty of our Catholic Educational System to place on the battlefield an army of laymen equipped to "fight the battles of the Lord."

THE AUTHOR.

CONTENTS

PAGE

CHAPTER I. The Sacraments in General

1. Nature of the Sacraments.................................... I
2. Number of the Sacraments.................................. 3
3. Division of the Sacraments.................................. 5
4. Effects of the Sacraments................................... 6
5. Administration and Reception of the Sacraments.............. 7

CHAPTER II. Baptism.. 12
    Rite of Baptism.. 21

CHAPTER III. Confirmation 26
    Rite of Confirmation....................................... 32

CHAPTER IV. The Holy Eucharist
    Introduction 35

A. THE REAL PRESENCE OF CHRIST IN THE EUCHARIST

1. Proofs of the Real Presence............................... 38
    a) The Words of Promise.............................. 38
    b) The Words of Institution........................... 40
    c) The Words of St. Paul.............................. 41
    d) Teaching and Practice of the Church................ 42

2. Transubstantiation 44
3. Eucharistic Adoration 46

B. THE HOLY EUCHARIST AS A SACRIFICE
    I. Nature of Sacrifice....................................... 49
    II. The Sacrifices of the Old Law........................... 51
    III. The Sacrifice of the New Law........................... 53
        a) The Sacrifice of the Cross...................... 53
        b) The Sacrifice of the Mass....................... 54
            1. Nature of the Mass........................... 54
            2. Institution of the Mass....................... 56
            3. The Sacrifice of the Mass in the Teaching and Wor-
               ship of the Church............................. 60
            4. The Four Ends of the Mass..................... 62
            5. The Fruits of the Mass........................ 62
            6. The Celebration of Mass....................... 66
            7. Assisting at Mass 68
            8. The Sacred Liturgy, or the Rite of the Mass......... 69
            9. The Language of the Mass...................... 73
            10. Some Notes on the Liturgy of the Mass............ 74

C. Holy Communion
   1. Nature and Necessity of Holy Communion.................... 83
   2. Dispositions for Receiving Holy Communion................ 87
   3. Effects of Holy Communion................................ 89

CHAPTER V. Penance

   1. Nature and Necessity of the Sacrament of Penance............. 95
   2. Contrition and Purpose of Amendment........................ 99
   3. Confession
      a) Necessity of Confession................................ 102
      b) Qualities of a Good Confession........................ 103
   4. Satisfaction 104
   5. Indulgences 105

CHAPTER VI. Extreme Unction 114
   Rite of Extreme Unction..................................... 117

CHAPTER VII. Holy Orders 121

CHAPTER VIII. Matrimony

   1. Marriage in Pre-Christian Times............................. 129
   2. Marriage in Christian Times................................. 130
   3. The Marriage Laws of the Church. Mixed Marriages........... 133
   Rite of Matrimony... 137

CHAPTER IX. The Sacramentals of the Church 139

**APPENDIX. The "Ordinary of the Mass" in Latin and English
with Rubrics and Explanatory Notes** 143

INDEX 197

MASS AND THE SACRAMENTS

A Course in Religion
Book II

CHAPTER I

The Sacraments in General

I. The Nature of the Sacraments

1. Means of Grace.—Without grace we can do no good work of ourselves towards our salvation. Hence the all-important question is, how can we obtain God's grace?

The principal means of obtaining grace are *Prayer* and the reception of the *Sacraments*. Prayer will be treated under the Ten Commandments; for the present it will suffice to point out the difference between prayer and the sacraments as means of grace:

a) The sacraments *produce* grace in us; prayer *obtains* it for us.

b) Through the sacraments we obtain those *special graces* for which they were instituted; through prayer we receive *all kinds of graces*, except those which are given only by the sacraments.

The word *sacrament* comes from the Latin word *sacramentum*, which the Romans used for any holy or sacred thing, such as forfeit money deposited in a temple or the military oath of allegiance. In the early Church it was applied to any religious object, rite, or ceremony which was hidden from the knowledge of the heathen; it was synonymous with *mystery*. In the course of time it received its present restricted meaning.

2. *A Sacrament is an outward or sensible sign instituted by Christ through which inward grace is imparted to the soul.* Hence three things are necessary for a sacrament:

a) An outward or sensible sign;

b) A corresponding inward or invisible grace;

c) Institution by Christ.

a) **The Outward Sign.**—An outward or sensible sign is something that can be perceived by one or other of the senses. Its purpose is to make something hidden known to us; thus a word, a movement of the hand, an inclination of the head makes known to us what is hidden in another's mind. *The outward signs of the sacraments make known to us the inward grace that is being produced in the soul.*

The outward sign of the sacraments is composed of two things, *matter* and *form*. The matter of the sacrament is the sensible thing or exterior act used in its administration, such as water, oil, bread and wine. The form consists in the words pronounced by the minister when he applies the matter, e.g., "I baptize thee in the name of the Father, and of the Son, and of the Holy Ghost."

To constitute a sacrament, the form must be united to the matter. "Take the word away," says St. Augustine, "and what else is baptismal water except ordinary water? but *add the words to the element and it becomes a sacrament*" (*In Joan. tract.* 80,3).

The matter of a sacrament is *remote* or *proximate*, according as we consider it in itself or in its actual application. Water in itself is the remote, the pouring of the water the proximate matter of the sacrament of Baptism.

b) **The Inward Grace.**—The outward signs of the sacraments do not merely signify grace, but actually impart the graces which they signify, unless we on our part put some obstacle in the way (Council of Trent, Session VII, Canon 6). When a priest pours water on the forehead of a child and pronounces the words, at that very moment the child is really cleansed from original sin and made holy and pleasing to God.

c) **Institution by Jesus Christ.**—No sensible things or outward signs have of themselves the power to produce inward supernatural grace, nor can any created being give such power to sensible things. If they have this power, it must have been given to them by God. He who merited grace for us, the God-Man Jesus Christ, attached to certain outward signs the power of imparting inward grace and sanctification to our souls. These signs have thus become the sacred channels through which flow to us the graces which Jesus Christ merited for us by His Passion and Death.

3. But why, it may be asked, should God bestow His supernatural favors upon us by means of outward signs and material symbols? The reason is because He adapts His methods to our nature. We are not pure spirits, but beings composed of body as well as of soul; so that even in our most spiritual operations we constantly make use of material and physical elements. Thus, when we wish to convey an intellectual idea to others we have to clothe it in language written or oral. In the same way God makes use of visible things as the vehicles of His invisible graces and blessings. We thus have *visible pledges* of the *invisible graces*.

There is another reason why God should convey His graces by visible signs, namely, to unite us all more closely together. "Since the sacraments are conferred under visible forms, we cannot receive them without giving public testimony of our faith, and of our fellowship with the millions of other Catholics spread throughout the world. We thereby prove ourselves to be members of the same Church, and sharers in the same benefits, and sheep of the same divine Shepherd."

4. Sacramental Ceremonies.—Christ gave His Church the power to administer the sacraments. Hence the Church also has the power to prescribe certain *ceremonies* and prayers, to be used before and after their administration. Their purpose is

a) To direct our attention to the graces received in the sacraments;

b) To prepare us for those graces;

c) To represent to us the dignity of the sacrament;

d) To increase our devotion and reverence.

Some of these ceremonies have Christ Himself as their author; others were instituted by the Apostles; others, again, by the Church at different times. As the ceremonies do not belong to the matter and form of the sacraments, they can be omitted or abbreviated in case of necessity.

2. NUMBER OF THE SACRAMENTS

1. The Council of Trent declared that there are seven, and only seven, sacraments instituted by Christ.—Baptism, Confirmation, Holy Eucharist, Penance, Extreme Unction, Holy Orders, and Matrimony.

In the case of four of the sacraments—Baptism, Holy Eucharist, Penance, Holy Orders—we know when Christ instituted them; Confirmation and Extreme Unction were administered by the Apostles; the sacramental character of Matrimony is clearly indicated in Holy Scripture.

The Greek Church, which separated from the Catholic Church in the ninth century, also recognizes seven, and only seven, sacraments. The Coptic, Armenian and Syrian Monophysites, who separated in the fifth century, have seven, and only seven, sacraments —a proof that the doctrine of seven sacraments was universally recognized in the Church at the time of their separation.

Lutherans admit only two sacraments, Baptism and the Eucharist. Luther at first also counted Penance among the sacraments, but later rejected it. When the Protestants of Germany sent a copy of their articles of faith to the Schismatic Patriarch Jeremias of Constantinople in the year 1573 for his approval, the Patriarch strongly objected to their tampering with the number of the sacraments. "There are seven sacraments," he replied, "no more and no less."

2. The Sacraments Supply Seven Great Needs in Man's Spiritual Life, which form a striking parallel to the needs of his bodily life.

a) In the first place, a man must be born into this world. But he needs a spiritual, no less than a natural, birth. In the sacrament of *Baptism* he is born into the Church, and becomes a child of God. *The spiritual life is received.*

b) But a child must grow and acquire strength, or it will never be able to hold its own in the battle of life. A similar need is felt

THE COUNCIL OF TRENT
After a sixteenth century engraving

by the newly born Christian in the spiritual order. The sacrament of *Confirmation* strengthens the soul and raises it from the weakness of childhood to the vigor of Christian manhood. *The spiritual life is strengthened.*

c) But even a grown-up person needs food and nourishment. The same is true of the adult Christian. Hence Christ instituted the *Holy Eucharist* to be the food and life of his soul. *The spiritual life is nourished.*

d) Man's body is subject to various maladies which call for a physician. Our souls, too, are subject to many spiritual diseases and require doctors and remedies. In the sacrament of *Penance* we consult our spiritual physician and are freed from our spiritual ailments. *The spiritual life is restored.*

e) When our last hour draws near and we have to die, the body requires special comfort and assistance. Our soul also stands in need of help and protection and confidence to battle successfully against the final assaults of the devil. The sacrament of *Extreme Unction* meets this special trial and danger, and helps our anxious soul to pass through the throes of death with calmness and resignation to God's holy will. *The spiritual life is cleansed from the remains of sin.*

f) Human society needs rulers, instructors, and teachers. So does the Christian society, which is the Church. Besides this, the members of the Church require men set aside to administer to them the means of grace and salvation. In the sacrament of *Holy Orders*, the power of ruling the people of God, of preaching the Gospel of Christ, and of administering the sacraments is propagated from generation to generation. *The human instruments of the spiritual life are perpetuated.*

g) The Church must spread and increase in the world; and children must be born to replace the thousands who daily become a prey of death. Now, as the welfare of the Church and of society depends on the way in which parents bring up their children, in the sacrament of *Matrimony* the union between husband and wife is blessed that they may sanctify themselves and people the Church of God with a succession of good Christians. *The spiritual life is extended.*

3. Division of the Sacraments

1. The Sacraments Admit of Several Classifications.—

a) Sacraments whose purpose is to *perfect the individual*: Baptism, Confirmation, Holy Eucharist, Penance, and Extreme Unction; and sacraments whose purpose is to *perfect society*: Holy Orders and Matrimony. The latter are also called sacraments of *free choice*, because no one is *obliged* to receive them.

b) Sacraments of the *living* and sacraments of the *dead*. The sacraments of the living are so called because, in order to receive them worthily, we must have spiritual life, that is, sanctifying grace. There are five sacraments of the living: Confirmation, Holy Eucharist, Extreme Unction, Holy Orders, and Matrimony. The sacraments of the dead are so called because, when we receive them, we either have not, or at least are not obliged to have, the life of grace. These sacraments are Baptism and Penance.

Occasionally a sacrament of the living may confer grace. For example, if a person in mortal sin, yet sincerely believing himself to be in a state of grace, were to receive a sacrament of the living with such attrition as is necessary to receive absolution, he would obtain the remission of his sin.

c) Sacraments that can be *received only once*, and sacraments that can be *received more than once*. Baptism, Confirmation, and Holy Orders imprint an indelible character (mark, seal) on the soul, and therefore cannot be repeated. The remaining sacraments do not imprint this indelible character, and may be received repeatedly. Baptism stamps the recipient indelibly as a *citizen of the Kingdom of Christ*; Confirmation, as a *soldier of Christ*; Holy Orders, as a *captain in the army of Christ*.

The indelible mark or character consists in a special consecration or dedication to God. This mark is not effaced by mortal sin, nor can it ever be removed from the soul: it will either add to our glory in Heaven, or to our misery in Hell.

St. Paul refers to this indelible character when he says: "God hath anointed us and hath *sealed* us and given us the earnest (i.e., the warrant or guarantee) of His Spirit in our heart" (2 Cor. 1,22).

St. Augustine calls Baptism, even when unworthily received, "a consecration and character of the Lord." St. John Chrysostom compares Confirmation to the mark burned into the flesh of the deserter by which he might always be known.

2. If we consider the sacraments according to their *importance*, we find that Baptism is the most important because it is necessary for all; Penance is necessary for those who after Baptism have fallen into mortal sin—it is the "second plank after the shipwreck"—; Holy Orders is necessary for the Church as such. The Holy Eucharist surpasses all the other sacraments in *dignity*, as is evident.

4. EFFECTS OF THE SACRAMENTS

1. The Sacraments Impart Grace ex opere operato (The Council of Trent).—This is a Latin expression and literally means "by the deed done," that is, in virtue of the sacramental act itself, if no obstacle be placed in the way, and not *ex opere operantis,* that is, not in virtue of the acts or the disposition of the recipient or the worthiness of the minister. All that is required is that the sacraments be validly administered and that the soul be properly disposed to receive them.

These spiritual dispositions are necessary in the recipient, not to cause or merit the grace of the sacrament, but to remove the obstacles or impediments to its entrance into the soul; for example, infidelity and attachment to sin. They are therefore *conditions,* not *causes,* of the sacramental grace, just as the opening of the door is a necessary condition to one's entrance into a room, but not the *cause* of the entrance.

2. That the sacramental act itself produces grace is clearly taught in Holy Scripture.—Our Lord told Nicodemus that we are *born again of water and the Holy Ghost* (John 3,5). And St. Paul writes to his disciple Timothy: "I admonish thee, that thou stir up the grace of God, *which is in thee by the imposition of my hands*" (2 Tim. 1, 6).

Protestants deny that the sacramental act itself produces grace; they maintain that we are justified by faith alone, and that the sacraments merely excite the faith or devotion of the recipient. But if faith alone justifies, how can little children be justified, and why baptize them?

3. The Sacraments Produce a Twofold Grace: *sanctifying grace* and special actual graces called *sacramental grace.*

Sanctifying grace is imparted by the sacraments if it does not already exist in the soul; if it already exists, it is increased.

With sanctifying grace is given the *right to special actual graces* which enable the recipient to obtain the end for which the sacrament was instituted. This sacramental grace is given according as circumstances demand, not merely at the time of the reception of the sacrament.

5. ADMINISTRATION AND RECEPTION OF THE SACRAMENTS

The sacraments cannot produce the effects intended by God unless they are validly administered and validly and worthily received.

1. Each Sacrament Has Its Proper Minister, i.e., the person who has the power of conferring it. The minister may be a bishop, or a priest, or, in some cases, a lay person. For the *valid administration* of a sacrament, the minister must have the *intention to do* *what the Church does,* and he must use the *matter and form* instituted by Christ. Neither sanctity, nor virtue, nor even faith, is necessary on the part of the minister.

The *Donatists* in the fourth century required the state of grace in the minister, and St. Cyprian (d. 258) and other African bishops maintained that Baptism administered by heretics was invalid. Both these opinions were condemned by the Church; and justly so, for the minister does not administer the sacraments by his own power, but by the power of Christ, whose instrument he is. He becomes the instrument of Christ by the sole intention of doing what Christ's Church does. St. Augustine says that "those who were baptized by Judas were baptized by Christ"; and that even if a murderer were to baptize, so long as the baptism was of Christ, it would be Christ Himself who baptized, for in every case the minister stands for the person of Christ. Even a sick doctor can heal his patients.

2. For the valid reception of the Sacraments, the following conditions are necessary:

a) The recipient must be still *alive* : the Church has power only over the living;

b) *Baptism* is a requisite for the reception of the other sacraments;

c) In the case of *adults,* the intention of receiving the sacraments is necessary; in the case of infants and idiots, such an intention is not required.

3. For the worthy reception of a Sacrament, the recipient must possess the dispositions necessary for gaining the grace of the sacrament. Hence before receiving a sacrament of the living, we must be in the state of grace; and before receiving a sacrament of the dead, we must have contrition for our sins, faith, etc.

Whoever deliberately receives a sacrament unworthily, commits a grievous sin, a *sacrilege.*

If an adult were to receive Baptism, Confirmation, Extreme Unction, or Matrimony unworthily but validly, the grace of the sacrament would not flow in upon his soul, but would remain, as it were, suspended until the obstacle was removed by an act of perfect contrition, or a good confession, or, in the case of Baptism, by eliciting an act of faith.

SUGGESTIONS FOR STUDY AND REVIEW

I. NATURE OF THE SACRAMENTS

1. Prepare a short paper to be read or delivered before the class on the *Nature of the Sacraments,* using the following outline:

Introduction:
- *a)* Without grace no salvation.
- *b)* God gives grace in answer to our prayers or through the reception of the *Sacraments.*
- *c)* Difference between Prayer and the Sacraments as means of grace.

Exposition:
- I. Various meanings of the word Sacrament. Its meaning here.
- II. Three essentials in every Sacrament:

    a) Outward Sign { Matter { Proximate / Remote } Form }

- *b) Inward Grace* "The Sacraments are *causes* of grace." "They impart the grace they signify."
- *c) Institution by Christ.* Why the Church cannot institute a Sacrament.
- III. Why Christ instituted visible signs to impart His grace.
- IV. Why *ceremonies* are added in the administration of the Sacraments.

Illustration: Paper-Money

On their accession to the throne, the Roman emperors used to throw money to the people. One of them once thought to throw them slips of paper signed by himself and showing sums of money more or less considerable, which the State would pay the bearer on presentation. The people, not realizing the value of these papers, despised them; but some, well advised, gathered up a large number of them, and became rich in a single day.

If a man can thus give value to what has no value in itself, how much more can God attach wonderful graces to common and simple elements, such as water and oil and human words!

2. Copy the following texts: John 20,22; Mark 7,33-34; John 9,6. What do they tell you about visible signs used to confer spiritual and corporal blessings? Does the Church still use these very signs in the administration of the Sacraments?

3. *Reading: Question Box*, pp. 228-230, and 235, "The Sacraments."

2-3. NUMBER AND DIVISION OF THE SACRAMENTS

1. *Seven,* a sacred and mysterious number. Quote examples from Scripture.
2. What does the Council of Trent define in regard to the number of the Sacraments?
3. Show that the doctrine of the Seven Sacraments has always been taught in the Church. How many Sacraments do the Protestants have? Why is it impossible for them to have any other Sacraments besides Baptism and Matrimony?

4. Show how the Seven Sacraments supply seven great needs in man's spiritual life.

5. Explain the following terms: "Sacraments of the Living," "Sacraments of the Dead," "Sacraments of Free Choice," "Sacraments that can be received only once."

6. Why are Baptism and Penance the most important Sacraments? Why is the Holy Eucharist the most excellent?

7. Write a short paper on *The Sacramental Character*, using the following outline:

    I. What is meant by a character, mark, or seal? Illustrate. Who was "marked" by God in the Old Testament? See Gen. 4,15.

    II. What do we mean by the Sacramental Character?

    III. St. Paul, St. Augustine, and St. John Chrysostom on the indelible mark imprinted on the soul by Baptism and Confirmation.

    IV. What special consecration or dedication to God is given by Baptism? by Confirmation? by Holy Orders?

    V. Why the Sacramental Character cannot be effaced in time or eternity. (A child, however rebellious, is still a child of its parents; a soldier, though a deserter, is still a soldier; a priest is "a priest forever.")

    VI. Value of the Sacramental Character in the next life.

    VII. Would it be a sacrilege to receive or confer Baptism, etc., knowingly a second time? Is "conditional Baptism" a second Baptism?

    VIII. Illustration: *Julian the Apostate.*

        "Twenty years after his Baptism the Emperor Julian renounced the faith and returned to paganism. Convinced that his Baptism and Confirmation had impressed a character upon his soul, he took every means in his power to rid himself of it. History says that he had the blood of victims offered to idols poured over his head, and that he made use of many other superstitious practices to efface the character he had received. Alas! in spite of his sacrilegious efforts, when the Angel's trumpet summons men to judgment, it will be as *Christian* that Julian the Apostate will arise and go forth to answer for the abuse of the abundant graces which the Sacraments brought to his soul."   —MASSILLON.

8. *Reading: Question Box*, pp. 232-235.

4-6. EFFICACY, ADMINISTRATION AND RECEPTION OF THE SACRAMENTS

1. Explain the words of the Council of Trent: "The Sacraments impart grace *ex opere operato*."

2. Copy the following texts: John 3,5; 2 Tim. 1,6; Acts 2,38; Rom. 6,3-4; Acts 22-16; John 6,54-59. What do these texts tell you about the efficacy of the Sacraments?

3. Do not Catholics attribute a *magical* effect to the Sacraments by believing that they confer grace of themselves (*ex opere operato*)? To answer this objection ask yourself, What is magic? and, Whence do the Sacraments derive their efficacy?

4. What twofold grace do the Sacraments produce? What is meant by *Sacramental grace*?

5. What is necessary in order that the Sacraments may produce the effects intended by God?

6. What is necessary for the *valid administration* of a Sacrament?

7. Why is neither sanctity, nor even faith necessary on the part of the minister for the *valid* administration of a Sacrament?

8. What is required for the *valid reception* of a Sacrament? For the *worthy reception* of the Sacraments?

9. What must a person do who has received Baptism, Confirmation, Extreme Unction, Holy Orders or Matrimony validly but unworthily? Must he apply to have these Sacraments repeated? Why not?

10. Can you list some *social advantages* of the Sacraments?

11. *Reading: Question Box*, pp. 236-238.

CHAPTER II

Baptism

1. Baptism is a sacrament in which, by water and the word of God, we are cleansed from all sin, re-born, and sanctified in Christ to life everlasting.

The word Baptism comes from the Greek, and means literally a *dipping in or under water*, or *washing* generally.

At the time of Christ converts to Judaism were baptized. The Baptism of St. John, which Our Lord also received, was not a sacrament, but an external profession of penance, to which the baptized added an oral confession of sins (Matt. 3,6). As it was no sacrament, it did not remit sin *ex opere operato,* but only *ex opere operantis.* We read in the Acts of the Apostles (19,5) that those who had received the baptism of John were afterwards baptized with the baptism of Christ.

2. The outward sign of Baptism consists in the washing with water and the words: "I baptize thee in the name of the Father, and of the Son, and of the Holy Ghost."

The remote matter of Baptism is pure natural water, as we learn from the Acts of the Apostles (8,36). Any liquid which can be regarded as no longer retaining the quality of water would not suffice. In conferring Baptism solemnly, that is, with all the prescribed ceremonies, *baptismal water* blessed on Holy Saturday or on the Vigil of Pentecost must be used.

The proximate matter consists in the application of the water either by *immersion,* that is, by dipping the person in the water; or by *aspersion,* that is, by sprinkling the person with water; or by *infusion,* that is, by pouring the water over the head or the body of the person. This last is the method now commonly used. According to the Roman Rite, the water should be poured over the head of the person three times.

When baptizing by aspersion or infusion, care must be taken that the water *flows* in some manner, otherwise there would be no *washing* or ablution. The water must also, for the same reason, reach the skin of the person; merely to moisten the hair or the clothes would not suffice.

Verrochio

ST. JOHN BAPTIZING OUR LORD

Fugel

THE APOSTLES PREACHING AND BAPTIZING

The form of Baptism consists of the words: "I baptize thee.*. . ." These words must be said *at the same time that the water is being poured and by the same person who pours it.* If it is doubtful whether a person has been baptized at all or validly baptized, the words "If thou art not baptized" are pronounced before the form.

In the *Didache*, an early Christian manual written before the end of the first century, we find the following instruction on Baptism: "Baptize in the name of the Father, and of the Son, and of the Holy Ghost in living (i.e., flowing) water. If you have no living water, use other water. If you cannot baptize in cold water, do so in warm water. If you have neither, pour water three times over the head in the name of the Father, and of the Son, and of the Holy Ghost. Before Baptism the minister as well as the person to be baptized, and others too, if they can, should fast; but you must command the person who is to be baptized to fast for one or two days before the Baptism takes place."

3. That Christ Instituted the Sacrament of Baptism is clear from His command to baptize all nations. "All power is given to Me in heaven and earth. Going, therefore, teach all nations, baptizing them in the name of the Father, and of the Son, and of the Holy Ghost" (Matt. 28,18-20). But we cannot state with certainty the exact time when He instituted it. St. Augustine, St. Gregory, and St. Thomas are of the opinion that its institution took place at the time of Our Lord's baptism by St. John. We there see the matter defined and sanctified, the form intimated by the manifestation of the three Divine Persons, and the supernatural effects of baptism signified by the heavens opening, as they are opened to us when we receive the sacrament.

4. The ordinary minister of Baptism is a bishop or priest. The *extraordinary minister* is a deacon delegated for the purpose by the bishop or the parish priest. *In case of necessity,* any person, even a heretic or a pagan, can baptize validly, provided he or she baptizes in the way required by the Church, and with the intention of doing what the Church does.

5. The effects of Baptism may be summed up as follows:

a) Baptism *blots out not only original sin*, but, in the case of adults, *all actual sins also committed before Baptism.* "Do penance, and be baptized every one of you for the remission of your sins, and you shall receive the gift of the Holy Ghost" (Acts 2,38). Adults must, of course, have at least imperfect contrition for their sins.

*The complete "form," or words for administering Baptism are these: "I baptize thee in the name of the Father and of the Son and of the Holy Ghost."
—*Editor*, 1990.

b) It remits *all punishment due to sin*. Whoever dies immediately after Baptism goes straight to Heaven, says the Council of Trent.

c) It confers on all who receive it worthily *sanctifying grace*, and infuses into the soul the three Theological Virtues, the four Cardinal Virtues, and the Gifts of the Holy Ghost. St. Paul says of the baptized: "You are washed, you are sanctified, you are justified in the name of our Lord Jesus Christ, and the Spirit of our God" (1 Cor. 6,11).

d) It confers *sacramental grace* which gives us a right to those actual graces that are necessary to preserve the spiritual life, to fight against the inclination to evil, and to fulfill the duties of a Christian.

e) It imprints on our soul an *indelible character*, a spiritual mark or seal, which distinguishes us from all who are not Christians, and which prevents the sacrament from being received more than once.

f) It makes us *members of Jesus Christ and of His holy Church*, and therefore sharers in the Priesthood of Christ, a "kingly Priesthood"; it gives us a right to receive the other sacraments, and to all the blessings of the Church. "Know you not that your bodies are the members of Christ?" (1 Cor. 6,15.) "He [Christ] has made us to our God a kingdom and priests" (Apoc. 5,10).

Because every one who is validly baptized belongs to the Church, we say of Protestants who become Catholics that they *return* to the Church.

Although Baptism cleanses us from original sin, we are still subject to some of the effects of original sin, such as bodily infirmities, sufferings, death, and concupiscence, or the inclination to sin. These *penalties* of original sin remain during this life for our trial and merit, but they disappear at the resurrection of the body.

6. Baptism is the most necessary of all the sacraments, because without it no one can be saved. "Unless a man be born again of water and the Holy Ghost, he cannot enter the Kingdom of Heaven" (John 3,5).

7. Infant Baptism.—In modern times various Protestant sects, especially the *Baptists*, have rejected *infant Baptism*.

It is true that in the early ages persons often put off their own

THE CONFERRING OF BAPTISM IN THE CATACOMBS

Baptism or that of their children, except when they were in danger of death, from a dread of losing sanctifying grace. Still, the Catholic doctrine that children are to be baptized may be inferred from *Holy Scripture* and is abundantly justified by *tradition*.

a) We read of the Apostles baptizing whole families, which naturally included also the little children (Acts 16,34). The very fact that Christ promised His Kingdom to little children (cf. Luke 18,16 with John 3,5) shows that He did not mean to exclude them from the sacrament of regeneration.

b) The early Fathers are explicit in their testimony. Origen says that infant Baptism is "an apostolic institution." And St. Irenaeus writes: "Christ came to save all—all, I say, who through Him are *born again to God*, infants and little ones, boys and young men, and the aged." An African Council under St. Cyprian declared that infants should be baptized as soon as possible after birth.

God has not revealed to us what becomes of those children who die without Baptism. They are certainly not condemned to hell. Some theologians say that they live in a place of natural happiness called the *Limbo of Children*.

8. Substitutes for Baptism.—When one who believes cannot receive the Baptism of water, the sacrament may be supplied by the *Baptism of Desire* or the *Baptism of Blood*.

Baptism of Desire is an act of perfect contrition combined with an ardent wish, either explicit or implicit, to receive Baptism. A person who does not know the necessity of Baptism, but wishes to do all that is required for salvation, is said to have an *implicit* desire of Baptism. "Every one that loveth is born of God" (1 John 4,7).

St. Ambrose says of the Emperor Valentinian II, who was murdered before he could receive Baptism: "As others are cleansed by their own blood, so this man was cleansed by his piety and his ardent desire."

Baptism of Blood is martyrdom suffered for the sake of Christ. "He that shall lose his life for Me shall find it," says our Divine Lord. The Baptism of Blood remits all punishment due to sin. "It would be an insult," says St. Augustine, "to pray for the martyrs."

9. Since Baptism is necessary for salvation, *infants should be baptized as soon as possible after birth*. Except when in danger of death, an infant should not be baptized without the permission of a parent or guardian. Children who have attained the age of reason must give their consent before they can be baptized. Children of non-Catholic parents may be baptized if one of the parents consents and if there is a reasonable hope of their being brought up as Catholics.

10. Ceremonies of Baptism.—There are many *beautiful and instructive ceremonies* connected with the administration of Baptism. They are all very ancient. In the early Church they were used only at the solemn Baptism of adults. The ones now customary before the administration of the sacrament were then used at the *reception of Catechumens* (i.e., applicants for Baptism) ; the others at the Baptism itself.

Before receiving Baptism the candidate renounces Satan, and all his *works* (sin), and all his *pomps* (the spirit and vanities of the world by which Satan blinds men and entices them to sin), and promises to believe firmly all the truths of the Catholic Church, and to lead a new life pleasing to God. On the other hand, God promises him His grace and eternal salvation. These mutual promises are called the *Covenant of Baptism*. The promises made by the person to be baptized are called the *Baptismal Vows*.

In the case of little children the *sponsors* pronounce these vows in their name. They thus become, as it were, the spiritual parents of the children and take it upon themselves to see that the baptismal promises are duly carried out. If the natural parents neglect their duty in this respect, it is the duty of the *god parents* to see that their *god children* are instructed in the Catholic religion. Hence they must be good Catholics themselves.

There must be at least one sponsor of either sex; if two are chosen, they must not be of the same sex. Sponsors must be over fourteen years old. The minister of Baptism and the god parents contract a spiritual relationship with the person baptized. This spiritual relationship forbids marriage between the persons thus related.

Sponsors at the Baptism of children are mentioned as early as A.D. 200 by Tertullian. The name of an Angel or a Saint is given to the child (or the adult) in Baptism in order that it may have an intercessor with God and an example for imitation.

Ceremonies before Baptism. In the early Church when an adult applied for Baptism, the priest made the *Sign of the Cross* upon his forehead and put a few grains of *blessed salt* upon his tongue as an emblem of Christian wisdom. By this ceremony the applicant became a *catechumen*, or official candidate for reception into the Church. During the weeks immediately preceding Baptism, the catechumen was required to present himself repeatedly in the church. Each time the priest *laid his hand upon the catechumen's head,* and an *Exorcist* prayed over him in the name of the Blessed Trinity to deliver him from the power of the devil.

All these ceremonies still take place at the Baptism of infants in the vestibule or at the door of the church, to show that Baptism alone gives the right to entrance.

The child is then brought into the church and carried to the font, the sponsors reciting aloud with the priest the *Creed* and the *Our Father*. The priest *anoints the child's ears and nostrils with spittle* saying, in imitation of Our Lord when He cured the deaf and dumb man: *Ephpheta*—which is, be thou opened, to signify that by the grace of Baptism his spiritual senses are opened to the doctrine of Christ.

After having, through the sponsors, renounced the devil and all his works and all his pomps, the child is *anointed with the oil of the catechumens* on the breast and between the shoulders in order that he may be able to bear the yoke of Christ. Then the priest asks concerning his belief in the Articles of the Creed, and if he will be baptized.

Then follows the *act of Baptism.*

Ceremonies That Follow the Act of Baptism. The crown of the child's head is anointed with *Chrism,* to signify that he is now a Christian, that is, an anointed of God. A white linen cloth is laid on his head with the words: "Receive this white garment, and see thou carry it without stain before the judgment seat of Our Lord Jesus Christ that thou mayest have life ever-lasting." The priest next gives the child or the sponsor a *lighted candle,* a symbol of the light of faith and of good example.

In the early Church the Baptism of the catechumens took place on Holy Saturday. The neophytes wore the white garment which they received on this occasion until the first Sunday after Easter, which was on this account called *Dominica in Albis,* White Sunday. This custom is alluded to in the noble hymn still used in the Vespers of Low Sunday:

Ad regias agni dapes	Now at the Lamb's high royal feast
Stolis amicti candidis,	*In robes of saintly white we sing,*
Post transitum maris rubri	Through the Red Sea in safety brought
Christo canamus Principi.	By Jesus our immortal King.

If the ceremonies have been omitted, as is the case in lay Baptism or Baptism by a priest when there is danger of death, they must be supplied afterwards in the church.

SUGGESTIONS FOR STUDY AND REVIEW

BAPTISM

1. Develop, in your own words, the following brief summary of the Church's teaching on Baptism:

   I. *The word "Baptism".*—The Baptism of St. John.—The Sacrament of Baptism.

   II. *The Institution by Christ:* John 3,5; Matt. 28,18-20. When was it instituted?

   III. *Essentials in the Administration of Baptism:*
   1. The *Matter:* Washing with water. Three ways.
   2. The *Form,* or words used.
   3. The *Minister:* (a) ordinary; (b) extraordinary; (c) in case of necessity.
   4. The *Recipient:* all men, infants, adults, idiots, etc.

   IV. *Effects of Baptism:*
   a) remits *all* sin. Acts 2,38;
   b) remits all penalties due to sin;
   c) bestows grace, sanctifying and sacramental, and the infused virtues;
   d) imprints an indelible mark;
   e) makes recipient a member of Christ and of the Church ("initiation").

   V. *Necessity of Baptism:* (a) for salvation; (b) for the reception of the other Sacraments. John 3,5; Matt. 18,19; Mark 16,16; Acts 2,37.

   VI. *Substitutes for Baptism:* (a) Baptism of Desire; (b) Baptism of Blood. Holy Innocents. Martyrs. Matt. 10,32 and 39; 1 John 4,7.

   VII. *Conditional Baptism.* Baptismal Name. Sponsors. Baptismal Vows. Ceremonies of Baptism (*See below*).

2. The text of the ceremonies prescribed by the Roman Ritual for the Baptism of Infants is subjoined. Read it very carefully; you will learn more about the Sacrament of Baptism than by reading a whole theological treatise. Note the beautiful symbolism of the rites, and the majestic words which accompany them.

THE BAPTISM OF INFANTS

Ceremonies before Baptism

The Priest, vested in Surplice and Violet Stole, meets the child and the sponsors at the door of the church and asks the following questions, which the sponsors answer together:

Priest. N., what dost thou ask of the Church of God?

Sponsors. Faith.

P. What doth Faith give thee?

S. Life everlasting.

P. If, therefore, thou wilt enter into life, keep the commandments. Thou shalt love the Lord thy God with all thy heart, and with all thy soul, and with all thy mind, and thy neighbor as thyself.

The Priest then gently breathes three times upon the face of the infant and says once:

Depart from him, thou unclean spirit, and give place to the Holy Ghost, the Paraclete.

Thereupon he makes with his thumb the Sign of the Cross upon the forehead and upon the breast of the child, saying:

Receive the Sign of the Cross both upon the forehead and also upon the heart; take unto thyself the faith of the heavenly precepts, and be in thy manners such that now thou mayest be the temple of God.

Let us pray.

Mercifully hear our prayers, O Lord, we beseech Thee; and with Thy perpetual power guard this Thine elect, N., signed with the seal of the Cross of the Lord: that, being faithful to these ordinances of Thy great majesty, he may, by keeping Thy commandments, deserve to attain the glory of the regeneration, Through Christ our Lord. *R.* Amen.

He then lays his hand upon the infant's head and says:

Let us pray.

Almighty, everlasting God, Father of our Lord Jesus Christ, look graciously down upon this Thy servant, N., whom Thou hast graciously called unto the beginnings of the faith: drive out from him all blindness of heart: break all the toils of Satan wherewith he was held: open unto him, O Lord, the gate of Thy loving kindness, that, being impressed with the sign of Thy wisdom, he may be free from the foulness of all wicked desires, and in the sweet odor of Thy precepts may joyfully serve Thee in Thy Church, and grow in grace from day to day. Through the same Christ our Lord. *R.* Amen.

The Priest then blesses the salt, which, after it has been once blessed, may serve for the same purpose on other occasions:

I exorcise thee, creature of salt, in the name of God, the Father Almighty, and in the love of our Lord Jesus Christ, and in the power of the Holy Ghost. I exorcise thee by the living God, by the true God, by the all-holy God, by the God who hath created thee for the preservation of the human race, and hath appointed thee to be consecrated by His servants for the people coming unto the faith, that in the name of the Holy Trinity thou mayest become a saving sacrament to put the enemy to flight. Wherefore we pray Thee, O Lord our God, that sanctifying Thou mayest sanctify this creature of salt, and blessing Thou mayest bless it, that, unto all who receive it, it may become a perfect cure, abiding in their hearts, in the name of the same our Lord Jesus Christ, who shall come to judge the living and the dead, and the world by fire. *R.* Amen.

He then puts a little of the salt into the mouth of the infant, saying:

N., receive the salt of wisdom; may it be to thee a propitiation unto everlasting life. *R.* Amen.

Priest. Peace be with thee.

Resp. And with thy spirit.

Let us pray.

O God of our fathers, O God the Author of all truth, vouchsafe, we humbly beseech Thee, to look graciously down upon this Thy servant, N., and as he tastes this first nutriment of salt, suffer him no longer to hunger for want of heavenly food, to the end that he may be always fervent in spirit, rejoicing in hope, always serving Thy name. Lead him, O Lord, we beseech Thee, to the laver of the new regeneration, that together with Thy faithful, he may deserve to attain the everlasting rewards of Thy promises. Through Christ our Lord. *R.* Amen.

I exorcise thee, thou unclean spirit, in the name of the Father, and of the Son, and of the Holy Ghost, that thou go forth and depart from this servant of God, N.; for He Himself commands thee, accursed outcast, He who walked upon the sea, and stretched forth to the sinking Peter His right hand.

Therefore, accursed devil, acknowledge thy sentence, and give honor unto the true and living God; give honor unto Jesus Christ, His Son, and unto the Holy Ghost; and depart from this servant of God, N., because him hath God and our Lord Jesus Christ vouchsafed to call unto His holy grace, and blessing, and the font of Baptism.

Here he makes with his thumb the Sign of the Cross upon the infant's forehead, saying:

And this Sign of the holy Cross, which we place upon his forehead, do thou, accursed devil, never dare to violate. Through the same Christ our Lord. *R.* Amen.

Immediately laying his hand upon the infant's head, he says:

Let us pray.

O holy Lord, Father Almighty, Eternal God, Author of light and truth, I implore Thine everlasting and most just goodness upon this Thy servant, N., that Thou wouldst vouchsafe to enlighten him with the light of Thy wisdom: cleanse him and sanctify him: give unto him true knowledge, that, being made worthy of the grace of Thy Baptism, he may hold firm hope, right counsel, holy doctrine. Through Christ our Lord. *R*. Amen.

After this, the Priest lays the end of his stole upon the infant, and admits him into the church, saying:

N., Enter thou into the temple of God, that thou mayest have part with Christ unto life everlasting. *R*. Amen.

As soon as they have entered the church, the Priest, while approaching the font, says, in a loud voice, along with the Sponsors the Apostles' Creed and the Our Father. Before reaching the baptistry, he says:

The Exorcism

I exorcise thee, every unclean spirit, in the name of God the Father Almighty, and in the name of Jesus Christ, His Son, our Lord and Judge, and in the power of the Holy Ghost, that thou depart from this creature of God, N., which our Lord hath deigned to call unto His holy temple, that it may be made the temple of the living God, and that the Holy Ghost may dwell therein. Through the same Christ our Lord, who shall come to judge the living and the dead, and the world by fire. *R*. Amen.

The Priest then moistens his thumb with spittle from his mouth and touches the ears and the nostrils of the infant. While touching first the right ear and then the left, he says:

EPHPHETA, that is to say, Be opened.

Then he touches the nostrils, saying:

For a savor of sweetness.

And he adds:

And do thou, O devil, begone! for the judgment of God is at hand.

Then, addressing by name the person to be baptized, he asks:

N., dost thou renounce Satan?

Sponsors. I do renounce him.

P. And all his works?

S. I do renounce them.

P. And all his pomps?

S. I do renounce them.

The Priest then dips his thumb into the Oil of Catechumens and anoints the infant upon the breast and between the shoulders, in the form of a Cross, saying:

I anoint thee with the oil of salvation in Christ Jesus, our Lord, that thou mayest have life everlasting. *R*. Amen.

Here the Priest lays aside the violet stole, and puts on another of white color. With cotton or some like material he wipes his thumb

and the parts anointed. Addressing by name the child to be baptized,
he asks, the sponsors answering:

N., dost thou believe in God, the Father Almighty, Creator of
heaven and earth?

S. I do believe.

P. Dost thou believe in Jesus Christ, His only Son, our Lord, who
was born, and who suffered for us?

S. I do believe.

P. Dost thou also believe in the Holy Ghost, the Holy Catholic
Church, the Communion of Saints, the forgiveness of sins, the resurrection of the body, and life everlasting?

S. I do believe.

Then, addressing by name the child to be baptized, the Priest says:
N., wilt thou be baptized?

Sponsors. I will.

Then the godfather or the godmother, holding the infant (if both
sponsors are present, the godmother holds the infant resting on her
right arm, and the godfather places his right hand on or under the
infant's shoulder), the Priest takes the baptismal water in a small
vessel or pitcher, and pours it thrice in the form of a Cross on the
head of the infant; and at the same time, he pronounces the words
once only, distinctly and attentively, saying:

N., I baptize thee in the name of the Father (*he pours the first time*),
and of the Son (*he pours the second time*), and of the Holy Ghost
(*he pours the third time*).

But if there is a doubt whether the child has been baptized before,
this form is used:

N., if thou hast not been baptized, I baptize thee in the name of the
Father, and of the Son, and of the Holy Ghost.

He then dips his thumb in the Holy Chrism and anoints the infant
upon the crown of the head in the form of a Cross, saying:

May Almighty God, the Father of our Lord Jesus Christ, He who
hath regenerated thee by water and the Holy Ghost, and given thee
remission of all thy sins, anoint thee with the Chrism of salvation,
in the same Jesus Christ our Lord, unto life everlasting.

R. Amen.

P. Peace be with thee.

R. And with thy spirit.

He then wipes his thumb and the part anointed with cotton or some
like material, and puts upon the head of the infant a white linen cloth,
saying:

Receive this white garment, which mayest thou bear without stain
before the judgment seat of our Lord Jesus Christ, that thou mayest
have life everlasting. *R.* Amen.

Thereupon he gives the child or the godfather a lighted candle, saying:
Receive this burning light, and keep thy Baptism so as to be without
blame: keep the commandments of God, that when the Lord shall come

to His nuptials, thou mayest meet Him together with all the Saints in the heavenly court, and mayest live forever and ever. *R.* Amen.

Lastly he says:

N., go in peace, and the Lord be with thee.

R. Amen.

3. *Reading: Catechism of the Council of Trent,* Part II, The Ceremonies of Baptism Explained (Ed. Donovan, pp. 133-137).

A. D'Alès, *Baptism and Confirmation,* pp. 112ff.: "Substitutes for Baptism."

St. Francis de Sales and the Baptismal Font.—St. Francis de Sales would often lead his young companions to the parish church and place them round the sacred font where in infancy they had been baptized. "See," he would say, "this is the spot that should be dearer to us than any other, for here it was we were made children of God." Then they would say together the "Glory be to the Father" in thanksgiving for God's mercy, and, kissing the font on bended knee, disperse for their games.

CHAPTER III

Confirmation

1. Confirmation is a sacrament by which we receive the Holy Ghost with His sevenfold gift, and are made perfect Christians and soldiers of Christ. It takes the second place in the order of the sacraments, because its object is to strengthen and complete the life of grace received in Baptism.

Confirmation (Latin *Confirmatio*) is so called from its principal effect, namely, spiritual strength. It is also called *imposition of hands, sealing, unction, chrism, sacrament of the Holy Ghost.*

2. That Confirmation was instituted by Christ is proved from Holy Scripture and Tradition.

a) From Holy Scripture we learn that Christ promised the Holy Ghost to His followers (John 15,26; Acts 1,8) and that the apostles imparted the Holy Ghost by prayer and the imposition of hands. In the Acts of the Apostles (8,14-17) we read that Peter and John went to Samaria to lay their hands upon those who had been baptized that they might receive the Holy Ghost. Since the apostles were not the authors, but merely the dispensers of the mysteries of God (1 Cor. 4,1), there can be no doubt that it was by command of Christ that they performed this ceremony with which inward grace was connected.

b) *Tertullian*, who lived in the second century, thus speaks of Confirmation: "The body is anointed that the soul may be sanctified, the body is signed that the soul may be fortified, the body is overshadowed by the imposition of hands that the soul may be illumined by the Holy Ghost."

St. Cyprian, who was martyred in 258, writes: "What took place in Samaria still takes place with us; those who have been baptized in the Church are presented to the rulers of the Church, and through our prayer and the imposition of our hands receive the Holy Ghost and are made perfect with the seal of the Lord." And St. Augustine, the greatest Doctor of the Church, says: "The Sacrament of Chrism is just as holy as Baptism."

3. Confirmation is administered in the following manner:

The bishop extends his hands over all who are to be confirmed and prays that the Holy Ghost may come down upon them.

He next places his right hand on the head of each candidate and at the same time makes the Sign of the Cross with Holy Chrism upon the forehead of each one, saying: "I sign thee with

Feuerstein

VENI, SANCTE SPIRITUS

the Sign of the Cross and I confirm thee with the Chrism of salvation, in the name of the Father, and of the Son, and of the Holy Ghost."*He then gives the one who has been confirmed a slight blow on the cheek, saying: "Peace be with thee." In conclusion he gives the episcopal blessing to all in common.

The ceremony of the *slight blow on the cheek* is first mentioned in the twelfth century. It is probably an imitation of the slight blow on the shoulders with the flat blade of the sword which marked the conferring of

*This is the traditional "form," or set of words, used to administer the Sacrament of Confirmation. —*Editor,* 1990.

knighthood in the Middle Ages. By Confirmation we become knights of Christ and must be ready to suffer persecution and reproach for the name of Jesus (Acts 5,41).

4. The remote matter of Confirmation is *holy chrism,* a mixture of oil of olives and balsam solemnly blessed by the bishop every year at Mass on Holy Thursday. The *proximate matter* is the anointing of the forehead with the chrism, and the imposition

Führich

STS. PETER AND JOHN CONFIRMING IN SAMARIA

of the hands of the bishop. The *form* consists of the words used by the bishop during the anointing.

Oil was used in ancient times by the athletes as an ointment to promote bodily vigor; hence it aptly signifies the inward strength which we receive through Confirmation for the combat against the enemies of our salvation. *Balsam* possesses the power of preserving things from corruption, and thus signifies that he who has been confirmed receives the grace of preserving himself from the corruption of the world; its *fragrance* indicates the sweet odor of virtue which those ought to send forth who have been confirmed.

5. The ordinary minister of Confirmation is a bishop.— Any priest may, however, with special permission from the Pope, administer this sacrament, but he must use chrism blessed by a bishop. In the Churches of the Eastern Rites, Confirmation has been given by priests for many centuries; in the Western Church priests receive this power only exceptionally.

6. All who have been baptized can be confirmed.—It is customary, however, in the Latin Church to administer the sacrament only to those who have come to the use of reason, for it is only then that the temptations set in which the sacrament of Confirmation helps us to overcome.

© Benziger Brothers

A BISHOP CONFIRMING

7. The Sacrament of Confirmation is not absolutely necessary for salvation; but it would be a sin to neglect to receive it through carelessness, indifference, or contempt. Especially in our day and in our country this sacrament is greatly needed, because the dangers threatening faith and virtue are constantly on the increase. We know from Holy Scripture and Church history how eager the early Christians were to receive this great sacrament of the Holy Ghost.

8. As Confirmation is one of the sacraments of the living, the recipient must be in the state of grace to receive it worthily. If a person were to receive it in mortal sin, he would commit a sacrilege, and would not receive the grace of the sacrament until he removed the obstacle thus put in its way by a good confession or an act of perfect contrition.

We should prepare ourselves with great care for the reception of this sacrament. It is our Pentecost, and it comes only once for each one of us. The Blessed Virgin and the disciples prepared for the first coming of the Holy Ghost by a nine days' retreat (Acts 1,13-14).

9. A sponsor is required at Confirmation just as at Baptism. This custom owes its origin to the fact that for many centuries Confirmation was administered immediately after Baptism. A sponsor in Baptism should not again discharge this office for the same person in Confirmation unless Confirmation immediately follows Baptism. Only a practical Catholic who has been confirmed may be chosen as sponsor. Parents may not act as sponsors for their children, nor husbands for their wives, nor wives for their husbands. If there is only one sponsor, he must be of the same sex as the person to be confirmed. There should be one sponsor for each candidate, but in many places one man acts as sponsor for all the males, and one woman for all the females. A spiritual relationship arises between the sponsor and the one confirmed, but since Pentecost, 1918, no matrimonial impediment results from this relationship.

10. The principal effects of Confirmation may be summed up as follows:

a) As a sacrament of the living, Confirmation produces an *increase of sanctifying grace.*

b) The special *sacramental grace* of Confirmation is *strength* to profess our faith, and *fortitude* in the combat against the enemies of our salvation.

c) The *indelible character* which this sacrament imprints on the soul is that of *soldier of Christ,* who must be ready, if need be, to make the supreme sacrifice for his "Captain Christ."

The gifts of tongues and of prophecy, which often accompanied the sacrament of Confirmation in the early Church, continued as long as they were necessary for the good of the Church; but, as they were meant, not for the benefit of those who received them, but for others, they ceased when they were no longer necessary for the spread of the Gospel.

We should pray frequently and earnestly that the Gifts of the Holy Ghost may be increased within us. Every one should know by heart and often repeat the *Veni, Sancte Spiritus,* the hymn sung by the Church on the Feast of Pentecost. In the Middle Ages it was known as the "Golden Sequence." It is justly regarded as one of the masterpieces of sacred Latin poetry. Dr. Trench, a Protestant writer, considers it the loveliest of all Latin hymns.

VENI, SANCTE SPIRITUS

Veni, Sancte Spiritus,
Et emitte caelitus
Lucis tuae radium.
Veni, pater pauperum,
Veni, dator munerum,
Veni, lumen cordium.

Consolator optime,
Dulcis hospes animae,
Dulce refrigerium.
In labore requies,
In aestu temperies,
In fletu solatium.

O lux beatissima,
Reple cordis intima
Tuorum fidelium.
Sine tuo numine
Nihil est in homine,
Nihil est innoxium.

Lava quod est sordidum,
Riga quod est aridum,
Sana quod est saucium.
Flecte quod est rigidum.
Fove quod est frigidum,
Rege quod est devium.

Da tuis fidelibus,
In Te confidentibus
Sacrum septenarium.
Da virtutis meritum,
Da salutis exitum,
Da perenne gaudium.

Holy Spirit, come and shine
On our souls with beams divine,
    Issuing from Thy radiance bright.
Come, O Father of the poor,
Ever bounteous of Thy store,
    Come, our hearts' unfailing light.

Come, Consoler, kindest, best,
Come, our bosom's dearest guest,
    Sweet refreshment, sweet repose.
Rest in labor, coolness sweet,
Tempering the burning heat,
    Truest comfort of our woes.

O divinest light, impart
Unto every faithful heart
    Plenteous beams from love's bright flood.
But for Thy blest Deity,
Nothing pure in man could be,
    Nothing harmless, nothing good.

Wash away each sinful stain;
Gently shed Thy gracious rain
    On the dry and fruitless soul.
Heal each wound and bend each will,
Warm our hearts, benumbed and chill,
    All our wayward steps control.

Unto all Thy faithful just,
Who in Thee confide and trust,
    Deign the sevenfold gift to send.
Grant us virtue's blest increase,
Grant a death of hope and peace,
    Grant the joys that never end.
—Translated by FATHER AYLWARD, O.P.

SUGGESTIONS FOR STUDY AND REVIEW

1. Recall what you learned about the Holy Ghost in Part I of this Course
in Religion:
    1) The Holy Ghost is true God like the Father and the Son.
    2) He proceeds from the Father and the Son.
    3) As God, He is everywhere; as the "Lifegiver," He is in a special
    manner in the Church and in the souls of the just.
    4) He appeared on earth in the form of a dove and in the form of
    tongues of fire.
    5) He teaches the Church through the Pope and the Bishops.

6) He sanctifies the Church especially through the Sacraments.

7) He rules the Church invisibly till the end of time.

8) He enlightens and sanctifies the soul and dwells in it as in His temple.

2. Copy the following texts: John 14,16; 15,26; 16,7; 7,38-39; Acts 2,4; 2,38; 8,14-18; Eph. 1,13; 1 Cor. 12,30; 1 John 2,20 and 27. Show from these texts

1) That Christ promised that those who believed in Him would receive the Holy Ghost.

2) That this promise was fulfilled the first time on Pentecost Day.

3) That the Pentecostal gift was intended for all Christians.

4) That Confirmation is conferred only on those who have been baptized.

5) That special gifts, such as healing, speaking with divers tongues, prophesying, etc., did not always accompany Confirmation in the early Church.

3. Briefly summarize the teaching of the Church on Confirmation under the following headings:

1) Nature and Institution.

2) Matter and Form.

3) Minister.

4) Recipient.

5) Necessity.

6) Sponsors.

7) Effects.

4. How is the Sacrament of Confirmation administered according to the Roman Rite? The following excerpt from the *Roman Pontifical* will give you the completest answer to this question.

The Sacrament of Confirmation

Standing with his face towards the persons to be confirmed, and having his hands joined before his breast (the persons to be confirmed kneeling, and having their hands also joined before their breasts), the Bishop says:

May the Holy Ghost descend upon you, and may the power of the Most High preserve you from sin. *R.* Amen.

Then, signing himself with the Sign of the Cross, from his forehead to his breast, he says:

V. Our help is in the name of the Lord.

R. Who hath made heaven and earth.

V. O Lord, hear my prayer.

R. And let my cry come unto Thee.

V. The Lord be with you.

R. And with thy spirit.

Then, with hands extended towards those to be confirmed, he says:

Let us pray.

Almighty and eternal God, who hast vouchsafed to regenerate these

Thy servants by water and the Holy Ghost, and hast given unto them forgiveness of all their sins: send forth from heaven upon them Thy sevenfold Spirit, the Holy Comforter.

R. Amen.

V. The Spirit of Wisdom and Understanding.

R. Amen.

V. The Spirit of Counsel and Fortitude.

R. Amen.

V. The Spirit of Knowledge and Piety.

R. Amen.

Fill them with the Spirit of Thy Fear, and sign them with the Sign of the Cross of Christ, in Thy mercy, unto life eternal. Through the same our Lord Jesus Christ, Thy Son, who liveth and reigneth with Thee in the unity of the same Holy Ghost, God, world without end. Amen.

The Bishop then inquires separately the name of each person to be confirmed, who is presented to him by the godfather or godmother, kneeling; and having dipped the end of the thumb of his right hand in the Holy Chrism, he says:

N., I sign thee with the Sign of the Cross,

Whilst saying these words he makes the Sign of the Cross, with his thumb, on the forehead of the person to be confirmed, and then says:

And I confirm thee with the Chrism of salvation. In the name of the Father, and of the Son, and of the Holy Ghost. *R*. Amen.

Then he strikes him gently on the cheek, saying:

Peace be with thee.

When all have been confirmed, the Bishop wipes his hands with bread-crumbs and washes them over a basin. In the meantime the following Antiphon is sung or read by the clergy:

Confirm, O God, that which Thou hast wrought in us, from Thy holy temple which is in Jerusalem.

R. Glory be to the Father, etc.

Then the Antiphon "Confirm, O God" is repeated; after which the Bishop, laying aside his miter, rises up, and standing towards the Altar, with his hands joined before his breast, says:

O Lord, show Thy mercy unto us.

R. And grant us Thy salvation.

V. O Lord, hear my prayer.

R. And let my cry come unto Thee.

V. The Lord be with you.

R. And with thy spirit.

Then, with his hands still joined before his breast, and all the persons confirmed devoutly kneeling, he says:

Let us pray.

O God, who didst give to Thine Apostles the Holy Ghost, and didst ordain that by them and their successors He should be given to the rest of the faithful; look mercifully upon our unworthy service; and grant that the hearts of those whose foreheads we have anointed with holy Chrism, and signed with the Sign of the Holy Cross, may, by the same Holy Spirit coming down upon them and graciously abiding within them, be made the temple of His glory. Who with the Father and the same Holy Ghost, livest and reignest, God, world without end. *R.* Amen.

Then he says:

Behold, thus shall every man be blessed that feareth the Lord.

And, turning to the persons confirmed, he makes over them the Sign of the Cross, saying:

May the Lord bless you out of Sion, that you may see the good things of Jerusalem all the days of your life, and may have life everlasting, *R.* Amen.

---

5. Write a composition on the hymn *Veni Creator Spiritus:*

    DIVISION :

    > I. We invite the Holy Ghost to come into our hearts (stanza 1).
    > II. Titles of honor of the Holy Ghost (stanzas 2-3).
    > III. Petitions to the Holy Ghost (stanzas 4-6).
    > IV. Praise of the Most Blessed Trinity (stanza 7).

    EXPLANATIONS :

    > Why is the Holy Ghost called *"Creator Spirit"*? See Gen. 1,2.
    > *"Paraclete."* A Greek word which means "one who is called to your side to help you and comfort you." John 14,16.
    > *"Gift of God." "Living Spring."* John 4,10, and 4,14; and cf. John 7,37-39.
    > *"Fire,"* and *"Love."* Matt. 3,11; Luke 12,49; Acts 2,3; John 15,9; Rom. 5,5.
    > *"Spiritual Unction."* Think of the Sacraments; which one in particular? Oil symbolizes strength.
    > *"Sevenfold Gift."* The Seven Gifts of the Holy Ghost. "Finger of God's right hand." Power of God. See Luke 11,20 and Matt. 12,28.
    > You will find the Latin text and an English translation of this splendid hymn in any hymn book.

6. *Readings:*

    a) Cardinal Manning, *Internal Mission of the Holy Ghost,* pp. 343-362, "Devotion to the Holy Ghost."

    b) A. D'Alès, *Baptism and Confirmation* (Herder), pp. 175-178, "Effects of Confirmation."

    c) Katherine Byles, *Confirmation; God's Forgotten Gifts* (Paulist Press Pamphlet).

    d) Father Lasance, *Come Holy Spirit* (Benziger).

CHAPTER IV

The Holy Eucharist

INTRODUCTION

1. Definition and Dignity.—The Sacrament of the Holy Eucharist is the Body and Blood of Our Lord Jesus Christ under the appearances of bread and wine.

Of all the sacraments instituted by Christ the Holy Eucharist is the greatest and holiest, for

a) It does not merely *give grace* to those who receive it worthily, but it *contains the Author and Source of all grace*, Jesus Christ Himself;

b) It does not merely exist while it is being administered, like the other sacraments, but it is something lasting, and continues to exist as long as the appearances remain unchanged.

c) It is not only a *sacrament*, but also a *sacrifice*.

2. Various Names Are Given to This Sacrament.—In Holy Scripture it is called the *Breaking of Bread* (Acts 2,42) and the *Lord's Supper* (1 Cor. 11,20). The early Christians called it the *Eucharist*, that is, Thanksgiving, because at its institution Our Lord gave thanks to His Eternal Father, and because a long and solemn prayer of thanksgiving formed the main part of the celebration of the Lord's Supper. Very ancient, too, is the name *Sacrament of the Altar*. It is so called because the mystery of the Holy Eucharist, which is both a sacrament and a sacrifice, is effected on our altars. The word *Holy Communion* aptly expresses the principal effect of the Holy Eucharist, viz., union with Christ. We call it the *Holy Viaticum*, that is, food for the journey, when it is administered to us at the end of our earthly pilgrimage to strengthen us for our passage to eternity. The expressions *Bread of Angels* and *Heavenly Bread* are Scriptural allusions to the manna of old, which was a type of the Holy Eucharist (John 6,50ff.).

3. The principal Types or Figures of the Holy Eucharist in the Old Testament were:

35

A TABLE ALTAR

A mosaic in the Basilica of St. Vitalis, Ravenna, showing the sacrifice
of Abel and of Melchisedech

a) The *sacrifice of Melchisedech*, "the priest of the most high
God," who offered up bread and wine (Heb. 5,6).

b) The *Paschal Lamb*, which was offered to God, slain, and
eaten whole (1 Cor. 5,7).

c) The *Manna*, the miraculous bread of the Israelites during
their forty years' sojourn in the desert (John 6,32).

d) *Isaac*, the beloved and only-begotten son of Abraham, whose
willing sacrifice on Mount Moria was typical of the Sacrifice of
Christ on Calvary.

In figuris praesignatur,	In the figures contemplated,
Cum Isaac immolatur	'Twas with Isaac immolated,
Agnus Paschae deputatur:	By the Lamb 'twas antedated,
Datur manna patribus.	In the Manna it was known.
	–From the Hymn *Lauda Sion*.

4. The Holy Eucharist is a Sacrament because it combines
within itself all the conditions required for a sacrament: the outward sign, the inward grace, and the institution by Christ.

a) The *matter* of the Holy Eucharist is wheaten bread and
wine of the grape. A little water is mixed with the wine because
Christ Himself most probably did so at the Last Supper, and also
because blood and water flowed from the sacred side of Christ on
the Cross. The Greek Church uses leavened bread; since the ninth
century the Latin Church uses unleavened bread. Either kind of
bread is valid. It is merely a matter of Church discipline.

The *form* of the Sacrament consists in the words of Christ:

Schnorr

ABRAHAM'S SACRIFICE OF ISAAC
As Abraham is about to slay his son, an angel stays his hand.

"This is My Body, this is My Blood,"*which the priest as the representative of Christ pronounces over the bread and wine in the Mass.

b) The *inward grace* conferred by the Holy Eucharist is Christ Himself, the Author of all graces, who gives Himself to us to be the life and food of our souls and to perfect our union with Him. "He that eateth My Flesh and drinketh My Blood abideth in Me and I in him" (John 6,57).

c) Christ instituted the Holy Eucharist on the eve of His Passion at the end of the Last Supper. While they were yet at table, He took bread in His sacred and venerable hands, and blessed, and broke, and gave to His disciples, saying:"Take ye and eat; this is My Body." In like manner, taking the chalice, He gave thanks, and bade them all drink of it, saying: "Drink ye all of this; for this is My Blood of the New Testament, which shall be shed for many unto the remission of sins" (Matt. 26,28). And He concluded with the words: "Do this for a commemoration of Me" (Luke 22,19).

*See page 196 for this note. —*Editor,* 1990.

5. "Do This for a Commemoration of Me."—By this command Christ gave to the Apostles and their successors, the bishops and priests of the Church, the power to do as He Himself had done,—the power to change bread and wine into His Body and Blood. Hence, bishops and priests alone can validly consecrate. Bishops and priests are also the ordinary ministers charged with dispensing the Holy Eucharist to others. Deacons may, however, with the permission of the bishop, exercise this function. At present this permission is given only in special cases of necessity.*

6. Christ Instituted the Holy Eucharist for a Threefold Purpose.—

A) To be always *really present* with us, not only as God, but also as Man;

B) To offer Himself through us in the *Holy Sacrifice of the Mass*;

C) To nourish our souls in *Holy Communion*.

A. The Real Presence of Christ in the Eucharist

1. Proofs of the Real Presence

1. Against the so-called reformers of the sixteenth century the Council of Trent declared that "in the most Holy Sacrament of the Eucharist, there is *truly, really*, and *substantially*, the Body and Blood, together with the Soul and Divinity, of Our Lord Jesus Christ." Jesus Christ is *truly* present, not merely under a sign or symbol; He is *really* present, not merely in virtue of our belief or imagination; He is *substantially* present, not merely by His power and grace.

2. We know that Jesus Christ is really present in the Holy Eucharist

a) From the words of *Promise*;

b) From the words of *Institution*;

c) From the words of *St. Paul*;

d) From the constant *teaching* and *practice of the Church*.

a) THE WORDS OF PROMISE

Christ did not institute the Holy Eucharist without preparing His disciples for so marvelous a gift; a whole year before His death He had promised to give them His Flesh to eat and His Blood to drink. It was the day after the miraculous multiplication of the loaves. By this miracle He had given proof of His almighty

*This was true when Fr. Laux wrote. Presently deacons are used extensively. —*Editor*, 1990.

power, and the following night He had proved to His disciples that He was superior to the laws of nature by walking upon the sea. The crowds had followed Him to the other side of the lake and looked to Him for further signs. In reply He spoke to them in the Capharnaum synagogue a discourse in which He clearly manifested His intention of instituting the Holy Eucharist. Taking up the suggestion of the Jews that He should give them bread from Heaven as Moses did, He announced to them that He would give them a more excellent Bread still, a living Bread, the true Bread of Life that cometh down from Heaven, of which the manna was but a figure. And when the Jews begged Him: "Lord, give us always this bread," He said to them: *"I am the Bread of Life:* he that cometh to Me shall not hunger, and he that believeth in Me shall never thirst. I am the Living Bread which came down from Heaven."

He then went on to tell them in the most unmistakable terms that He would give Himself as the food of men: "The Bread that I will give is My Flesh for the life of the world." The Jews took scandal at these words, and asked: "How can this man give us His Flesh to eat?" But Jesus said to them: "Amen, amen, I say unto you: except you eat the Flesh of the Son of Man, and drink His Blood, you shall not have life in you. He that eateth My Flesh and drinketh My Blood hath everlasting life, and I will raise him up at the last day. *For My Flesh is meat indeed, and My Blood is drink indeed.* He that eateth My Flesh, and drinketh My Blood, abideth in Me and I in him. As the living Father hath sent Me, and I live by the Father, so he that eateth Me, the same also shall live by Me. This is the Bread that came down from Heaven. Not as your fathers did eat manna, and are dead; he that eateth this Bread shall live forever."

These words must be taken literally, not metaphorically, for

1. The Jews understood them literally. Their conduct proves this: "They strove among themselves, saying: How can this man give us His Flesh to eat?"

2. The disciples understood them literally; they said: "This saying is hard, and who can hear it?"

3. Jesus wished them to be literally understood, for

a) Although the Jews and the disciples took offense at His words, He did not explain them away, but solemnly declared: "**My Flesh is meat indeed, and My Blood is drink indeed**"; He went even further and threatened to exclude from eternal life those who would refuse to eat His Flesh and drink His Blood: "Unless you eat the Flesh of the Son of Man, and drink His Blood, *you shall not have life in you;*"

b) To His Apostles, He gave no other choice than either to believe His words or to leave Him. He said to them: "Will you also go away?"

c) If Christ had not intended His words to be understood literally, He would either have used different words or explained His words as a figure of speech, as He did on other occasions.

b) THE WORDS OF INSTITUTION

What our Divine Savior promised in the Synagogue at Capharnaum, He fulfilled a year later in the Cenacle at Jerusalem.

At the Last Supper Jesus took bread, blessed it, and broke and gave it to His disciples, saying, "Take ye, and eat: this is My Body." After that, in like manner, He took the chalice with wine in it, blessed and gave it to His disciples, saying, "Drink ye all of this: this is My Blood. Do this for a commemoration of Me."

These words, too, must be taken in their literal sense.

1. Our Lord wanted His Apostles to understand them literally, for after saying, *This is My Body*, He added the words, *which is given for you*; and to the words, *This is My Blood*, He added the words, *which shall be shed for you.* Now, Jesus gave His *real* Body for us and shed his *real* Blood for us; therefore what He gave His disciples was also His real Body and His real Blood.

THE CENACLE AT JERUSALEM

2. In the Synagogue at Capharnaum Jesus had promised, as we have seen, to give His followers His Flesh to eat and His Blood to drink. He did not keep His promise, if the words of the institution are not literally understood.

3. Jesus knew when He uttered them that they would be taken in their literal sense, and that, by the great body of the faithful, divine worship would be paid to His Body and Blood under the appearances of bread and wine to the end of time. If He wished His words to be understood in a metaphorical or figurative sense, He should have said so. If He is not really present in the Eucharist, He Himself has led His Church into error and caused her to be guilty of the abominable crime of idolatry for all these centuries. Even to think of such a thing would be blasphemy.

c) THE WORDS OF ST. PAUL

If Christ's words "This is My Body, this is My Blood" were to be understood in a figurative sense, the Apostles would not have taken them literally. And yet we find that St. Paul, writing to the Corinthians about twenty-four years after the Last Supper, uses words that also clearly express a true and real presence of Christ's Body and Blood in the Holy Eucharist. He says: "The Chalice of Benediction which we bless, is it not the communion of the Blood of Christ? and the Bread which we break, is it not the partaking of

Rembrandt

ST. PAUL

the Body of the Lord?" (1 Cor. 10,16.) And in another place he says: "Whosoever shall eat this bread, or drink the chalice of the Lord unworthily, shall be guilty of the Body and Blood of the Lord" (1 Cor. 11,27).

d) TEACHING AND PRACTICE OF THE CHURCH

The faith of the Church in the Real Presence is evident (1) **from the testimony of the Fathers,** (2) **from the Discipline of the Secret,** (3) **from the paintings in the Catacombs,** and (4) **from the testimony of the pagans.**

1. *St. Ignatius of Antioch,* writing on his way to martyrdom at Rome (A.D. 107), says: "The *Docetes* abstain from the Eucharist because they do not confess that the Eucharist is the Body of Our Savior Jesus Christ." The Docetes taught that Christ's body was merely a phantom or appearance, hence there could be no question of the presence of a real body of Christ in the Eucharist.

St. Justin, Martyr (d. 165) says in his *First Apology,* addressed to the Emperor Antoninus Pius and the whole Roman people: "We do not receive these things (i.e., the Eucharistic bread and wine) as common bread and drink, but we have learned that the food and drink, made a Eucharist by a word of prayer that comes from Him, by change are the Flesh and Blood of the Incarnate Jesus." He then goes on to describe the Mass of his time, which was the same as ours in its main points.

THE "FRACTIO PANIS"
From the Catacomb of Priscilla

St. John Chrysostom, the *Doctor Eucharistiae*, speaks in still clearer terms: "How many of you say: I should like to see His face, His garments, His shoes. You do see Him, you touch Him, you eat Him. He gives Himself to you, not only that you may see Him, but also to be your food and nourishment."

St. Augustine writes: "Christ held Himself in His hands when He gave His Body to His disciples, saying: This is My Body. *No one partakes of this Flesh before he has adored it.*"

For a thousand years no heretic dared to impugn the belief of the Church in the Real Presence of Christ in the Eucharist. It was assailed for the first time in the eleventh century by Berengarius, the head of a school at Tours in France. He taught that after the Consecration the bread and wine are still present, and that Our Lord's Body is present in some spiritual manner. Later on he admitted his error and died in communion with the Church.

2. Another important witness for the belief of the early Church in the Real Presence is the so-called *Discipline of the Secret.*

During the third and fourth centuries there prevailed in the Church the practice of gradually initiating the catechumens into the more important Christian rites and teachings, and of secrecy in speaking and writing of them. The Holy Eucharist was mentioned only in the vaguest terms by preachers when addressing the catechumens. Even in their private letters the Popes and Bishops of those days refrained from speaking of the Canon of the Mass and the Act of Consecration.

Writing to Decentius, Bishop of Gubbio in Umbria, Pope Innocent I (401-417) says: "You say that some priests give the Kiss of Peace to the people or to each other before the mysteries are consecrated, whereas the Peace is certainly to be given after all those things *which I may not describe.*" Origen refers to the Eucharist as a "certain holy body." St. Epiphanius says of Jesus: "He took *that* and giving thanks said: This is My *that.*"

A very ancient Greek inscription discovered at Autun in France in 1839 reads as follows: "Take the food sweet as honey of the Saviour of the holy ones and eat it hungrily, holding the fish in thy hands." These words were intelligible to Christians, among whom the *fish* meant "Jesus Christ, Son of God, Savior," but mere jargon to those outside the Church.

It would have been foolish and childish to speak of the Holy Eucharist in this way unless it had been regarded as a great and holy mystery, the mystery of the Real Presence of Christ under the appearances of bread and wine. There was no danger of profanation on the part of the unbaptized if there was nothing sacred to be profaned, if the bread and wine remained bread and wine.

3. The *frescoes in the Catacombs* also testify to the belief of the early Christians in the Real Presence. In the Catacombs of St. Calixtus there is a painting on the wall dating from the second century, showing a party of Christians at the Breaking of Bread. On the table we see a fish and some small loaves. On the left side of the table a man is standing, who represents Christ or a priest consecrating the bread. A woman on the right is thanking with uplifted and outstretched arms for the wonderful gift of God to men, the Bread which came down from Heaven to become the food of God's children. "The Eucharistic meaning of the painting is proved from the actual place it occupies in the chapel, between two other scenes emblematic of Baptism and the Eucharist, and quite close to the painting of Abraham's sacrifice of Isaac."

4. Even the *pagans* testify to the faith of the Church. Among the crimes attributed by them to the Christians, the most abominable was that in their mysterious meetings they killed children, drank their blood, and ate their flesh wrapped in bread. The Eucharistic rite, distorted reports of which had reached the pagan world, alone can explain how such a calumny could have arisen and been believed.

2. Transubstantiation

1. What is Transubstantiation?—What Jesus took into His "holy and venerable hands" at the Last Supper was bread and wine; what He gave to His disciples was His Body and His Blood, for He said: "This is My Body; This is My Blood." Bread and wine were consequently changed into the Body and Blood of Christ. But the change took place only in regard to the *substance* of the bread and the wine; the *appearances* remained the same.

By the *appearances* (also called *species* and *accidents*) of bread and wine, we mean everything about them that is perceived by the senses, for instance, shape, color, taste, smell; by *substance* we mean the thing in itself, stripped of its appearances. Since appearances or accidents cannot exist without a substance to hold them up, as it were, the appearances of bread and wine after the Consecration are miraculously preserved without their substances by God's almighty power.

The change or conversion of the entire substance of the bread into the substance of the Sacred Body of Christ, and of the entire substance of the wine into His Precious Blood, is called, since the Fourth Lateran Council A.D. 1215, *Transubstantiation.*

A EUCHARISTIC PROCESSION ON THE PLAZA OF SAN MARCO, VENICE

2. Luther and his followers denied Transubstantiation; they maintained that Christ is present in the Holy Eucharist *in,* *with,* and *under* the substance of bread and wine. This teaching was condemned by the Council of Trent.

That a real *change* does take place follows from the words of Christ. He did not say: *In,* or *with,* or *under* this bread is My Body; but: *This is My Body.* If the substance of bread or wine had been present in any way whatever when Christ spoke these words, He would have uttered a falsehood.

The Fathers of the Church often use the expressions that bread is *made,* or *becomes,* or is *changed into,* the Body of Christ. "In Cana of Galilee," says St. Cyril of Jerusalem, "Christ changed water into wine, and shall we think Him less worthy of credit when He *changes* wine into His Blood?" The most ancient liturgies use the same expressions.

3. Christ Entirely Present Under Each Species.—*In virtue of the words of consecration* the bread is changed into the Body, and the wine into the Blood of Christ. But since Christ in Heaven is living and immortal, His Body and His Blood, His Soul and Divinity cannot exist apart. Therefore He must be entirely present under each species just as He exists in Heaven—with Flesh and Blood, with Body and Soul, with His Manhood and Godhead.

4. Christ is present in the Holy Eucharist sacramentally, that is, He is present wherever the sacramental species are. His Sacred Presence fills every particle, even when the Sacred Host is divided. No division takes place except in the sacramental species. The following considerations will make this clear:

a) At the Last Supper each one of the Apostles received and partook only of a portion of the sacred species, and yet each one received the entire Christ.

b) Before the Consecration the substance of bread and wine was entirely present in every part of the species; in the same manner the entire substance of the Body and Blood of Christ is present under every part of the species after Consecration.

This truth is brought out very clearly in one of the stanzas of the *Lauda Sion,* the great hymn of St. Thomas Aquinas for the Feast of Corpus Christi:

Fracto demum Sacramento	When at last the Bread is broken,
Ne vacilles, sed memento,	Doubt not what the Lord hath spoken:
Tantum esse sub fragmento,	In each part the same love-token,
Quantum toto tegitur.	The same Christ our hearts adore;
Nulla rei fit scissura:	For no power the Thing divideth—
Signi tantum fit fractura:	'Tis the symbols He provideth,
Qua nec status, nec statura:	While the Saviour still abideth
Signati minuitur.	Undiminished as before.

3. Eucharistic Adoration

1. Christ is present under the species of bread and wine as long as the species themselves continue to exist and not merely, as Luther maintained, at the moment of Communion.

This follows from the words of institution. When Christ gave the consecrated Bread to His disciples, He said: This *is* My Body, and not: This will be My Body at the moment when you receive it.

From the earliest times it was customary to carry the Blessed Sacrament to the sick, and in times of persecution to keep it in private houses; people even took it along with them when they went on a journey. "No one is richer," says St. Jerome, "than he who carries the Body of Christ in a little wicker basket and His Blood in a glass."

2. Since Christ is *permanently present* in the Holy Eucharist, and not merely at the moment of Holy Communion, **we are bound**

Zurbarán

ST. THOMAS AND ST. BONAVENTURE
St. Thomas coming one day to visit St. Bonaventure, asked him in what books he had learned his sacred science. Pointing to his crucifix the latter replied: "This is the source of all my knowledge."

to adore Him under the sacramental species. "The *duty of adoration* arises from the *fact*, not from the *manner*, of His presence. We adore Christ in the Holy Eucharist as He is—with His Godhead and Manhood. Both are alike the object of our adoration, whilst the Divinity alone is the *reason* for our adoration" (Wilmers).

Adoro te devote, latens Deitas,	Devoutly I adore Thee, hidden Deity,
Quae sub his figuris vere latitas;	That beneath these figures hidest verily;
Tibi se cor meum totum subjicit	Subject is my spirit wholly to Thy sway.
Quia te contemplans totum deficit.	For in contemplating Thee it faints away.

3. Devotion to the Holy Eucharist was always the chief and central devotion of the Church, but it was not until the thirteenth century that it found expression in outward forms other than those used in the celebration of Mass.

In the year 1264 Pope Urban IV, at the suggestion of Bl. Juliana, an Augustinian nun of Liège in Belgium, established the Feast of *Corpus Christi* (The Body of Christ), to be observed by the whole Church on the Thursday after Trinity Sunday. The Mass and Office of the feast were composed at the Pope's request by St. Thomas Aquinas, and include the beautiful hymns *Lauda Sion, Pange Lingua, Verbum Supernum,* and *Sacris Solemniis.* He wrote another hymn, the *Adoro Te,* for private devotion. St. Thomas is the greatèst theologian of the Church, and his hymns contain an admirable summary of the Catholic doctrine on the Holy Eucharist.

4. After the institution of the Feast of Corpus Christi, **processions and exposition** of the Blessed Sacrament became common. The *Forty Hours' Exposition,* one church following another throughout the city, was introduced at Rome in the sixteenth century as a prayer against the dangers from the Turks. About the same time *Benediction* began to be given with the Blessed Sacrament; it grew out of the practice of evening devotions to the Blessed Virgin with a short exposition of the Blessed Sacrament added to give greater solemnity. The *O Salutaris* and *Tantum Ergo* sung at Benediction are parts of St. Thomas' hymns for the Corpus Christi Office.

5. A very popular and widespread devotional exercise in honor of the Blessed Sacrament is the **Holy Hour.** Once every week or every month pious persons meet in church to adore for a whole hour the Lord of Hosts hidden under the species of bread. Prayers are said in common and hymns are sung by those assembled. The priest, kneeling in the sanctuary, takes the lead. "Could you not watch one hour with me?" Our Lord said to His Apostles in the garden of Gethsemane. In view of this complaint and to make up for the outrages Jesus suffered in His bitter Passion, the "Holy Hour" has been introduced.

Wherever the Blessed Sacrament is reserved in the Tabernacle, a lamp is kept burning before it day and night as an emblem both of the burning love of the Sacred Heart of Jesus and of our own faith and love. (Eucharistic Congresses, Perpetual Adoration.)

6. The real and continual presence of Christ in the Holy Eucharist is altogether *consistent with the character of Christianity* and *satisfies the deepest yearning of the human heart.*

a) Under the Old Dispensation, which, as St. Paul says, "had a shadow of the good things to come" (Heb. 10,1), God dwelt in a cloud over the Ark of the Covenant. God was present in a figure. This figure is realized on our altars, where God dwells really and truly as the Word Made Flesh.

b) Man feels within him a longing to have God near him, and, as far as may be, in visible form. "As the hart panteth after the fountains of water, so my soul panteth after Thee, O God" (Ps. 41,2). This demand of the human soul is met, as far as that is possible in our present state, by the Holy Eucharist: God Himself dwells amongst us visibly, but in such a manner that we still have the full merit of faith. We can truly say with the Psalmist: "My heart and my flesh rejoice in the living God" (Ps. 83,3).

B. THE HOLY EUCHARIST AS A SACRIFICE

Christ instituted the Holy Eucharist, not only in order to be with us always under the sacramental species, but also in order to offer Himself for us in the Holy Sacrifice of the Mass. The Holy Eucharist is not only the greatest of all the Sacraments; it is also the most perfect of all sacrifices.

I. Nature of Sacrifice

Sacrifice comes from the two Latin words, *sacer*, "sacred," and *facere*, "to make." Hence it means something made sacred, something consecrated and offered to God.

1. Noe's Sacrifice.—After Noe had left the Ark, he built an altar to the Lord and, taking of all cattle and fowls that were clean, offered holocausts (i.e., whole burnt-offerings) upon an altar. And the Lord was pleased with his offering (Gen. 8,20-22).

By killing and burning the animals, Noe withdrew them from the service of men and gave them entirely to God. He *immolated* them. His purpose in doing this was, in the first place, to honor God as the sovereign Lord of all things and to dedicate himself to Him; secondly, to acknowledge by the blood-stained condition of his gift his own sinfulness as well as his intention to make reparation, and his desire for pardon.

In What a True Sacrifice Consists.—From what Noe did we can see:

a) There must be a *visible gift*;

b) The gift must be offered to God, and for this purpose it must be immolated, must be made a *victim*, but not necessarily by the person who offers it;

c) The offering or *oblation* must be made by an authorized person or persons;

d) The *purpose* of the gift must be a *religious* one: to pay honor and glory to God, to make reparation for sin;

e) The gift must be accepted by God.

A sacrifice may, therefore, be defined as "the visible token of our inward self-dedication to God in the shape of a gift meant primarily by its removal from profane use and its transference into God's dominion to testify to our own religious consecration, and secondarily to bespeak by its blood-stained condition the acknowledgment of our guilt, along with the intention of repairing it in some way and the desire of being pardoned" (M. de la Taille).

2. The principal purpose of sacrifice is, as we have seen, to give honor and glory to God. But, since the fall of man, every sacrifice presupposes sin, and it is therefore also offered up to make satisfaction or expiation for sin. As adoration includes thanksgiving, and petition is necessarily bound up with expiation, we speak of a fourfold purpose of sacrifice: *adoration, thanksgiving, expiation,* and *petition.*

From the definition of a sacrifice it follows that it can be offered to God alone, and that it is the highest form of worship that can be paid to Him.

In a *broader sense* sacrifice includes every religious act by which we offer ourselves to God. In this sense prayer, almsgiving, obedience, contrition, acts of self-denial, are sacrifices. "Sacrifice to God is an afflicted spirit" (Ps. 50,19).

3. *All nations* of the earth, whether in historically remote or in more recent times, whether civilized or uncivilized, have always looked upon sacrifice as the most appropriate means of paying adoration and homage to God. All religions, except pure Buddhism, Islamism, and Protestantism, recognize sacrifice as an integral part of their worship.

The ancient Egyptians and Babylonians, Greeks and Romans killed cattle, hogs, and fowls, poured wine upon the ground, and burnt incense. The Chinese sacrifice oxen, sheep, and pigs. Even human sacrifices were offered by some pagan nations. The Phoenicians and Chanaanites immolated children to their god Moloch, and it is said that the number of human victims slaughtered yearly by the pagan Mexicans amounted to many thousands.

II. The Sacrifices of the Old Law

1. The Hebrews had never fallen into the abomination of human sacrifices except at rare intervals when they were infected by the surrounding paganism. Their father, Abraham, had been called out of heathenism by God, and they had the story of Abraham and Isaac to show them that God did not want human sacrifices. But He did want other sacrifices, and on Mt. Sinai He strictly commanded them and through Moses gave minute directions as to the manner in which they were to be offered.

There were *unbloody sacrifices*, such as the first fruits, also bread, oil, and wine. But the chief sacrifices were *bloody*: the offerer brought his goat, ox, or sheep, laid his hand on it to show that he gave it God, and its throat was cut; then the priest sprinkled the blood round the altar, and the victim was entirely burnt (holocaust) or partly burnt and partly eaten by the priests or by the offerer and his friends at a common meal (sacrificial banquet).

2. The sacrifices of the Old Law, especially that of the **paschal lamb** and the yearly **sacrifice of atonement,** were typical of the great sacrifice that the Redeemer was to offer on Calvary.

The *paschal lamb*, a lamb without blemish, was offered to God, slain and eaten at a family meal every year in remembrance of the deliverance out of the Egyptian slavery. On the great *Day of Atonement* the high priest laid both his hands upon the head of one of the goats which were to be offered up for the sins of the people, confessing at the same time the iniquities of the Children of Israel, and praying that they might light upon the head of the animal; then the goat was driven out into the desert, to express symbolically that the sins of the people were taken away out of God's sight (scapegoat). The high priest then sacrificed a heifer for his own sins and a goat for the sins of the people and sprinkled the blood of the victims on the Ark and the pavement in the Holy of Holies.

Since these sacrifices were only types and figures of the unspotted Sacrifice of the New Law, from which they derived their efficacy, they were not to last longer than the Old Law itself. They foreshadowed an event—Christ's death on the Cross for the sins of the whole world—and when that event had happened, they lost their meaning, their reason for existing.

Dirk Bouts

THE PASCHAL LAMB (Ex. 12, 8-11)

"And they shall eat the flesh that night roasted at the fire, and unleavened bread with wild lettuce. You shall not eat thereof any thing raw,
nor boiled in water, but only roasted at the fire: you shall eat the head
with the feet and entrails thereof. Neither shall there remain any thing of
it until morning. If there be any thing left, you shall burn it with fire.
And thus you shall eat it: you shall gird your reins, and you shall have
shoes on your feet, holding staves in your hands, and you shall eat in
haste: for it is the Phase (that is the Passage) of the Lord."

In his famous prophecy of the "seventy weeks of years," the
Prophet Daniel clearly foretold the very time when the sacrifices
of the Old Testament should cease. "And He shall confirm the

covenant with many in one week, and in the half of the week the *victim and the sacrifice shall fail*" (Dan. 9,27).

III. The Sacrifice of the New Law

The Sacrifice of the New Law took the place of the sacrifices of the Old Law; the *One Sacrifice* supplanted the *many*; the *shadow* was followed by the *reality*. This new and true sacrifice is the *Sacrifice of the Cross* and its continuation, the *Sacrifice of the Mass*.

a) THE SACRIFICE OF THE CROSS

1. The Sacrifice of the Cross the Most Perfect Sacrifice.— The Sacrifice of the New Law is the Son of God Himself, who, by His death on the Cross, offered Himself to His Heavenly Father in our stead and "obtained everlasting redemption" for us (Heb. 9,12).

The sacrifice of Christ on the Cross is called a sacrifice of redemption, because by it He ransomed us from the slavery of sin. It was the most perfect sacrifice that could be offered, because it fulfilled in the most perfect manner the conditions essential to a sacrifice:

a) It was worthy of God's majesty, for it was the sacrifice of the Son of God, who was both the Priest and the Victim;

b) It was a fit and proper sacrifice for man's sins, for it involved the offering of a human body—of a body specially fashioned, as St. Paul remarks, for that sacrifice;

c) The sacrifice was an expression of the most perfect and absolute submission to God's holy will;

d) The sacrifice was accepted by the Father.

2. But all sacrifice was not to cease with the death of Christ on the Cross, for

a) Sacrifice is the most perfect visible expression of the adoration we owe to God. All religions have sacrifices; hence Christianity, the one perfect religion, must also have a true sacrifice;

b) The New Law is the fulfillment of the Old Law. The sacrifices of the Old Law were types and figures of a perpetual sacrifice in the New Law. Therefore we must conclude that the Christian religion must have a perpetual sacrifice;

c) A perpetual sacrifice was not only prefigured in the Old Law; it was also expressly foretold by God: "I have no pleasure in your sacrifices, saith the Lord of hosts; I will not receive a gift of your hands. For from the rising of the sun even to the going down, My Name is great among the Gentiles, and in every place there is sacrifice, and there is offered to My Name a clean oblation" (Mal. 1,11). As this sacrifice cannot be of less value than the sacrifice of the Cross, it follows that, if Christianity is to have a sacrifice at all, the sacrifice which Christ offered once on the Cross must be continued to the end of time.

The *Holy Sacrifice of the Mass* is this perpetual renewal and continuance of the Sacrifice of the Cross.

b) THE SACRIFICE OF THE MASS

1. *Nature of the Mass*

The word "Mass" comes from the Latin *missa*, a later form for *missio* (like *repulsa* from *repulsio, collecta* from *collectio*) and originally meant merely "dismissal." In the first ages of the Church, after the Gospel and the sermon, the catechumens were admonished by the deacon to leave the church; this was called the *missa,* or dismissal of the catechumens. At the end of the Holy Sacrifice the deacon said to the faithful: *Ite, missa est—* "Go, it is your dismissal"; this was called the *missa,* or dismissal of the faithful. Thus, we see that the Eucharistic part of the service began and ended with a *missa,* and in the fourth century this part was itself called the *missa.* It was used in this sense for the first time, as far as we know, by St. Ambrose, who relates in one of his letters that after the dismissal of the catechumens he began the celebration of the Mass: *Missam facere coepi.* Later on, the word Mass was applied to the *whole* liturgical service.

1. The Mass Is a Real Sacrifice because it has all the conditions required for a true sacrifice:

a) The *Victim* is Jesus Christ Himself under the appearances of bread and wine;

b) The *oblation* takes place at the Consecration, when Christ, at the words of the priest: *This is my Body—This is my Blood,** becomes present on the altar under the separate species of bread and wine. The separate species represent the death of Christ, the separation of His Blood from His Body;

c) By this most perfect oblation God is adored and honored in the most perfect manner, and the fruits of the Sacrifice of the Cross are applied to our souls.

The Mass is, therefore, in the words of St. Peter Canisius, "both a representation, at once holy and living, and an offering,

*See the note for page 37 on page 196. —Editor, 1990.

Copyright, Benziger Brothers

THE MYSTERY OF FAITH

"For as often as you shall eat this bread and drink the chalice, you shall show the death of the Lord," (I Cor. 11: 26.)

*bloodless yet actual, of the Passion of the Lord and of the blood-
stained sacrifice which was offered for us on the Cross."*

"The Mass, while picturing, also offers to God the Sacrifice
of the Cross. That is offered which is represented. Christ's
death is represented; Christ's death is offered. Hence the Sacrifice of the Mass is the same as the Sacrifice of the Cross: the
same Victim, the same Priest; only the manner of offering is
different: blood-stained on the Cross, bloodless on our altars"
(M. de la Taille).

2. An Objection Answered.—But, it may be objected, how
can the Mass be a real sacrifice of the Body and Blood of Christ?
Is it not absurd to think of Christ as a victim, something slain,
immolated? He is the glorified Christ in Heaven, who, as St. Paul
says, "dieth now no more." And yet if there is no real victim,
how can there be a real sacrifice?

We answer: Christ offered Himself on the Cross as a victim
to atone for our sins, and God accepted His sacrifice. God took
the price of our sins, paid by Christ, into His hands, as it were,
and there keeps it forever. Hence Christ is a victim even now;
He is the perpetual victim, *hostia illa perpetua,* as St. Thomas
calls Him. "In Heaven He is a victim, no less than He was on
the Cross. But if He is a victim already, then He has not got to
be turned into a victim by the priest at Mass. He has not to be
slain or immolated or changed in any way." When He becomes
present on our altars by the Consecration, He becomes present as
the *victim of our salvation.*

Panem, vinum in salutis	The bread and wine we consecrate
Consecramus hostiam.	Into the victim of salvation.

2. *Institution of the Mass*

1. When the priest consecrates the Body and Blood of Christ,
He offers up to God the Victim of the Passion, the "Sacrifice of
our Ransom," as St. Augustine says. How is that? Simply because
by pronouncing the words of consecration he is doing the same
thing which was done by Christ before him. He is carrying out the
command given to the Apostles and their successors by Christ
Himself at the Last Supper: *Do this for a commemoration of Me.*

"Do *this*," Christ said, that is, "Do the same that I have done.
I have offered My death; you shall offer My death." But did

Dirk Bouts

THE LAST SUPPER

Christ at the Last Supper offer up to God His Passion and Death for the redemption of mankind? How can we doubt it? "This is My Body," He says, "which is delivered up for you; this is My Blood which is shed for you unto the remission of sins." This is certainly death—death put before us in a symbol by means of the sacramental separation of the Blood from the Body. "Our Lord had His death before Him at that moment, and He was pledging Himself in the chalice of His own Blood to shed that Blood to the last drop upon the Cross. As our great High Priest 'according to the order [i.e., the likeness] of Melchisedech' He was making His One Offering for the sins of the world. This One Offering was completed and carried out on the Cross." The sacrifice which Christ offered at the Last Supper and the sacrifice of the Cross are not two sacrifices, but one and the same sacrifice.

By the words: "Do this for a commemoration of Me" He gave His Apostles and their successors not only the *power*, but the *command* also, to do what He Himself had just done. He made them priests and thereby perpetuated the Sacrifice of our Redemption in His Church.

"If any one say that by the words 'Do this in commemoration of Me,' Christ did not make His apostles priests, or did not ordain that they and other priests should offer His Body and Blood, let him be anathema" (Council of Trent, Sess. XXII, Can. 2).

2. The sacrifice which Our Lord offered at the Last Supper cannot be separated from His Sacrifice on the Cross; neither can the Sacrifice of the Mass be separated from the Sacrifice of the Cross. In the Mass the priest does what Christ did at the Supper, only with this necessary difference:

a) The priest's offering is connected with Christ's Passion and Death as things of the past, whereas Christ's offering at the Supper pointed to the Cross as a thing of the future.

b) At the Mass is commemorated that sacrificial death which at the Last Supper Christ was anticipating.

c) Christ's sacrifice was not finished till He died on the Cross; ours is ended with the Eucharistic celebration.

d) At the Supper Christ offered alone; in the Mass we join with Him in offering; we offer under Him and by His commission.

e) At the Supper Christ offered up His Passion and Death for the remission of our sins; in the Mass the fruits of His Passion and Death are applied to our souls.

3. Hence the Sacrifice at the Last Supper, the Sacrifice of the Cross, and the Sacrifice of the Mass are not three sacrifices, but the selfsame Sacrifice.—And thus the objection raised against the Mass by the Lutherans and Calvinists, that it is a "belittling of Christ's one only sacrifice of propitiation," falls to the ground. "By One Sacrifice," says St. Thomas, "Christ cleansed forever them that are sanctified. And if it be objected to this that we offer daily, I reply that we do not offer other than that which Christ offered for us, namely, His Blood. Hence ours is not another sacrifice, but is the commemoration of that Sacrifice which Christ offered, as we read in Luke: *This do for a commemoration of Me.*"

The following plan will help the reader to grasp the all-important truth that the Sacrifice of the Mass is a true sacrifice, substantially the same as the Sacrifice of the Cross.

Essentials of a Sacrifice	The Sacrifice of the Cross	The Sacrifice of the Mass
1. A visible gift.	Jesus Christ.	Jesus Christ, the "Eternal Victim."
2. Immolated, i.e., made a victim.	Immolated on the Cross.	His death truly represented by the dual Consecration.
3. Offered to God alone by an authorized person (priest).	Offered Himself to His Father at the Last Supper.	Offers Himself through His Church by the priest and the faithful.
4. For the religious purpose of *a*) adoration, *b*) thanksgiving, *c*) expiation, *d*) petition.	To give honor and **glory** to God, to expiate the sins of the world, and to merit the grace of salvation for mankind.	To give honor and glory to God, and to apply the fruits of His Passion and Death to our souls according to our dispositions.
5. In the hope that it will be accepted by God.	His oblation was accepted by the Father, as is manifest from His Resurrection and Ascension.	By accepting the Sacrifice of the Cross, God also accepted the Sacrifice of the Mass, which is a continuation of the Sacrifice of the Cross.

3. *The Sacrifice of the Mass in the Teaching and Worship of the Church*

The Church has always believed the Mass to be a true sacrifice and the center and soul of her worship.—

1. St. Paul speaks of a permanent sacrifice in the Christian Church, when he says: "We have an *altar* whereof they have no power to *eat* who serve the tabernacle," that is, the Jews (Heb. 13,10). By this altar only the Sacrifice of the Mass can be meant, for there is no other altar whereof Christians can eat.

In another place the same Apostle calls Holy Communion a *Sacrificial Banquet,* which he could not do if the Mass were not a sacrifice: "The things which the heathens sacrifice, they sacrifice to devils, and not to God, and I would not that you should be made partakers with devils. You cannot drink the *chalice* of the Lord and the chalice of devils; you cannot be partakers of the *table* of the Lord and of the table of devils" (1 Cor. 10,21). The "table of devils" refers to idolatrous sacrifices; hence the "table of the Lord," placed in such sharp contrast to it, also refers to a sacrifice.

In the First Epistle to the Corinthians (11,24-26) St. Paul relates the institution of the Holy Eucharist at the Last Supper. After quoting the words of Christ: "This do ye in remembrance of Me," he adds: "For as often as you eat this bread and drink of the cup, you proclaim the death of the Lord, until He come." The Apostles are to do what Christ has done, and therefore to present His Body and Blood in a sacrificial state. Unless the Mass is a sacrifice, they cannot proclaim the Lord's death, because the mere partaking of His Body and Blood does not do so.

2. In the *Didache,* the earliest Christian work after the New Testament, we read the following exhortation to the faithful: "Every Sunday of the Lord, having assembled together, break bread and give thanks, having confessed your sins, that your *sacrifice* be pure; for it is the sacrifice of which the Lord hath said: In every place and at every time a clean oblation shall be offered to My Name."

In the second century St. Justin Martyr writes: "Of the *sacrifice* which we offer in every place, that is, of the bread and chalice of the Eucharist, Malachias has prophesied."

St. Irenaeus, who died in 202, says: "Jesus taught a new

THE MASS OF ST. GREGORY

Christ appears to the Saint with the instruments of His Passion, showing the reality of His presence on the altar after the Consecration.

sacrifice which the Church received from the Apostles and offers throughout the whole world."

The ancient *Liturgies* (Mass Books), reaching back to the third and fourth centuries, contain directions and prayers for the celebration of Mass which evidently suppose the belief that it is a true sacrifice.

The *oriental sects* which fell off from the Church in the fifth century have retained the belief in the Holy Sacrifice of the Mass.

Thus, we see that the so-called reformers of the sixteenth century placed themselves in direct opposition to the teaching and practice of the whole Church from the time of the Apostles when they rejected the Sacrifice of the Mass. By doing so, they destroyed the center, the very soul of Christian worship.

Julius Wellhausen, the famous Protestant Biblical scholar, being asked what was the difference between the Lutheran and the Catholic divine service, replied: "The Lutheran service is the same as the Catholic service, except that its *heart* has been cut out."

4. *The Four Ends of the Mass*

There are four things we owe, as creatures, to God: *adoration, satisfaction* for sin, *thanksgiving* for favors received, and *petition.* These were the ends for which the sacrifices of the Old Law were offered; they must also be the ends of the Sacrifice of the Mass, which has taken the place of the sacrifices of the Old Law. The sacrifices of the Old Law could discharge the fourfold duty of man to God only in an imperfect manner, but in the Mass this is done in the most perfect manner, because the Victim offered to God in the Mass is not a lamb or a goat, but Jesus Christ, the Son of God.

The Sacrifice of the Mass, being the same as the Sacrifice of the Cross, is in a special manner a sacrifice of *propitiation.* As such it obtains for us, according to the teaching of the Church, the grace of repentance, and contrition for the forgiveness of our sins, as well as the remission of the temporal punishment we deserve for them.

5. *The Fruits of the Mass*

1. By the *fruits of the Mass* we mean the effects which it produces *for us,* in as much as it is a sacrifice of *propitiation* and *impetration.*

From the nature of the Mass it is evident that its value or fruit is *infinite* if we regard the *gift* offered; but *finite,* limited, if we regard the *offering* of the gift. The fruit of each Mass is therefore proportioned to the dispositions, that is, the degree of holiness, of those who offer it.

2. Who are the offerers of the Mass?—There is, in the first place, the *Church*; secondly, the *priest,* the public minister of the Church; thirdly, the *faithful,* who contribute materially to the

THE PATEN OF ST. BERNWARD

From the so-called *Guelph Treasure* of the House of Brunswick-Lüneburg, 12th century. Silver, partly gilded and nielloed. The inscription along the edge reads: EST CORPUS IN SE PANIS FRANGITUR IN ME. VIVET IN ETERNUM QUI BENE SUMIT EUM. In the rounded arches the four Cardinal Virtues and the symbols of the four Evangelists are alternately engraved and nielloed. The inscription round the inner circle reads: HUC SPECTATE VIRI. SIC VOS MORIENDO REDEMI. In the center Christ thrones on the rainbow as the Prince of Peace and the *Salvator Mundi*

Sacrifice by the offering of stipends, and, lastly, the *faithful who assist at Mass.**

a) The *Church,* under Christ, is the offerer of every Mass. The Sacrifice is made by the Church by means of the priest, as the Council of Trent teaches. The Church is the Mystical Body of Christ, one and inseparable into parts. Hence, whoever offers up the Sacrifice does so as a member of that Body. No sacrifice

*All of these, of course, offer the Mass only in and with Christ, who is the primary "Offerer," that is, the Chief Priest in every Mass. —*Editor,* 1990.

is ever offered to God except on the part of the whole Church, that is, by all the faithful who compose the Church. This is clear from the words of the Canon of the Mass: *Te igitur* and *Memento, Domine. . .*

But, it may be objected, how can the faithful be *offerers* of the Sacrifice unless they share in the *sacerdotal character*?

We answer that the whole Church is endowed with the sacerdotal character, that she is a "royal priesthood," composed of all those whom Christ has redeemed. "He has made us to our God a kingdom and priests" (Apoc. 5,10). All who are baptized participate in the life and power of Christ, who was Victim and Priest. St. Jerome calls Baptism the "priesthood of the laity"; and St. Augustine says: "We call all Christians priests, because they are members of the one Priest, Christ."

We should always be mindful of this our sublime dignity; we should try to realize more and more that the Masses which are being celebrated throughout the world are being offered by us as members of the Mystical Body of Christ, and that the fruit of these Masses is increased or diminished by the degree of holiness which we possess. What an encouragement for us always to live in the state of grace and to sanctify ourselves continually in order to make the fruits of the Mass more abundant.

b) Besides being the offering of the whole Church, the Mass is in a very special manner the *offering of the priest*. As the minister of Christ, he has the power derived from Christ of Consecration, of changing the bread and wine into the Body and Blood of Christ. As the minister of the Church, he offers up the infinite Victim in her name. Hence his participation in the Sacrifice is the most intimate given to any human being. The Sacrifice can be said, in a sense, to belong to him. He has the power of applying the Mass to some particular intention.

c) Next to the priest in their share in the sacrifice come those who by their contributions to the support of the Church and the priest make the sacrifice possible. The *stipend offerers* can be truly said to provide the bread and wine for the sacrifice, and, therefore, to put God Himself, as it were, under an obligation to them. The priest must offer the Mass for their intentions and mentions their names in the Canon of the Mass. Stipend offerers in a wider sense are all the faithful who contribute to the support of their Church; hence the pastor is obliged to say Mass for them on Sundays and holy-days.

d) After the stipend offerers, those most closely associated with the priest in the Mass are the *faithful who assist at it*. They take an active part in the sacred rite. The Mass becomes, as it were, the special privilege of the group or family present. Those present at Mass may be compared to St. John and the holy women who were near the Cross on Calvary.

That those who assist with devotion at Mass are in a very special manner offerers of the Holy Sacrifice is evident from the prayers of the Mass, especially from the *Orate, fratres,* the *Hanc igitur,* and the *Unde et memores.*

Thus, we see that all the members of the Church participate in the Sacrifice of the Mass, "but the closer one is to the mystery, the more does one ally oneself with Christ and share the fruits of the Mass: first by right of order and dignity the priest, then the stipend offerers, next the congregation, and last the body of the faithful who, when in grace, are never far from Calvary and the risen Victim."

3. The Mass may be offered (*a*) for *all the living,* and not merely for the faithful, but also for heretics and infidels, pagans and schismatics, in order to obtain their conversion; (*b*) for the *relief of the souls in Purgatory,* that God may be pleased to shorten the time of their expiation. A Mass for the poor souls always benefits them, but we do not know how much of the value of the Mass it is God's will to apply to them; (*c*) *to honor the Saints* and to obtain their intercession for us. We ask them "to plead for us in Heaven while we celebrate their memory on earth." Mass is never offered *to* the Saints, but only *in their honor.* "What priest," asks St. Augustine, "standing at the altar near the bodies of the holy martyrs, has ever said: We offer to thee, Peter, Paul, Cyprian?"

As early as the second century we already hear of Masses being said in honor of the holy martyrs on the anniversaries (*natalicia*) of their death. The *Memento* of the Saints in the Canon of the Mass is also very ancient.

6. *The Celebration of Mass*

1. Every priest rightly ordained can *validly* say Mass. Hence, a Mass said by a priest who is an apostate from the Faith or excommunicated by the Church is as real a sacrifice as that said by the most saintly priest. Yet, the faithful are not allowed to assist at the Mass of one who is publicly known as a heretic or schismatic.

2. Although it is the priest who says the Mass, it must be remembered that the faithful really join him in offering the Sacrifice, and that he offers it in the name of the Church. Before the Preface he turns to the people and says: *"Orate, fratres, ut meum ac vestrum sacrificium acceptabile fiat apud Deum Patrem omnipotentem"*—"Brethren, pray that my sacrifice and *yours* may be acceptable to God, the Father Almighty."

3. The Holy Sacrifice may be celebrated every day except on Good Friday. On this day the Host consecrated on Holy Thursday is consumed by the priest, but no sacrifice is offered since no consecration takes place. On Holy Thursday and Holy Saturday there should be only one Mass, and that a solemn one, in each church.

4. The same priest is allowed to say only one Mass a day, except on All Souls' Day and on Christmas, when he may say three Masses. On Sundays and holy-days of obligation a priest may, with the permission of the bishop, say two Masses when the needs of the people require it. When a priest says two Masses on the same day, he may take a *stipend* (i.e., an offering for a Mass) only for one Mass, except on Christmas Day.

5. In the early days of the Church, Mass was said in the evening, after the example of Our Lord at the Last Supper. At present it may be said at any time from dawn to midday.* In winter it may be said an hour or two before dawn. In some places permission is given to begin Mass an hour after midday. On Christmas a Mass may be said in each church at midnight.

6. Mass should be celebrated only in churches that are blessed or consecrated, or in chapels that are blessed. Exceptionally it may be said in a private room, in the open air, on a vessel, or in a train, but only with the proper permission and on an altar stone.

7. Priests who have charge of souls are obliged to celebrate Mass themselves or supply a substitute on all Sundays and holy-days of obligation in order to give those who are entrusted to their care an opportunity of complying with the precept of the Church. On these days and on all feast days which were once holy-

*This was true when Fr. Laux wrote. Presently, however, Mass may be said at any time. —*Editor*, 1990.

days of obligation, the pastor must apply the fruits of the Mass to his people; he may not take a stipend for these Masses.

8. Priests who are not pastors are bound to say Mass several times a year. If they do not say Mass on Sundays and holy-days of obligation, they are obliged to assist at Mass just like the faithful.

9. From the moment a priest accepts a *stipend* (an offering for a Mass) he is bound under pain of mortal sin to say Mass according to the intention of the donor, and within a reasonable time if no special day has been agreed upon. The stipend for each kind of Mass (low Mass, high Mass, solemn Mass) is fixed by the statutes of the diocese or by legal custom.

Dirk Bouts

THE SACRIFICE OF MELCHISEDECH (Gen. 14, 18)

7. Assisting At Mass

1. When we consider what the Mass is—the most sacred, solemn and sublime act of religious worship that we can perform, the most pleasing to God and the most advantageous to our souls —we can readily see what esteem and veneration we should have for it, and with what reverence, attention, and devotion we ought to assist at it. One Mass *assisted at with real devotion* is of such inestimable value that, if we could but realize it, we would certainly not be content with our one Mass of obligation on Sundays and holy-days.

2. There are various ways of assisting at Mass with profit, but they may all be reduced to two: *prayer* and *meditation.*

a) **The method of prayer** consists in uniting our prayers to those of the priest at the altar. Suitable prayers are found in every good prayer book, but the best book to use is certainly the Missal in the original Latin or in some English translation. If we say other prayers than those in the Missal, such as the Rosary, the various Litanies, or prayers before Communion, we must always remember to join ourselves to Our Lord's Sacrifice at the Consecration.

b) **The method of meditation** consists in meditating on *Our Lord's Passion,* the different circumstances of which are represented by the Mass. "Nothing is easier than to unite ourselves during the Holy Sacrifice with the suffering Saviour. What we hear and see there reminds us of bonds and prison bars, of judgment seats, of Golgotha, of the Cross; of the Saviour's wanderings to and fro, from one judge to the other, of His long martyrdom, of His Precious Blood, of the separation of His Soul from His Body. The sacred vestments, the altar, the inclinations, the genuflections, the outstretched arms,—all speak to us of Christ's Passion and Death. Follow the priest with open eye and ear and heart, and he will bring you from Gethsemane to Calvary and from Calvary to the stillness of the Sepulcher" (Doss, *Thoughts and Counsels*).

We can also direct our attention to the four ends of Mass: adoration, expiation, thanksgiving, and petition.

> "Adore till the Gospel;
> Give thanks till the bell;
> Till Communion ask pardon;
> Then all your wants tell."
> —FATHER RUSSELL.

3. Never forget that the fruits of the Mass depend in great measure on the devotion of the participants.—Those who assist at the Holy Sacrifice offer with the priest, are co-sacrificers with him. They should therefore be filled with a true spirit of sacrifice, take part in the sacrificial action by joining in the congregational singing and in the prayers said in common, and share in the *Sacrificial Banquet* by actually or spiritually receiving Holy Communion.

The Saints of God could never understand how anyone could assist at Mass without devotion. "When you see how the Lord is offered up," says St. John Chrysostom in his beautiful book on the Priesthood, "and how the priest stands and prays at the Sacrifice, can you still believe that you are amongst men and standing on the earth?"

8. *The Sacred Liturgy, or the Rite of the Mass*

Liturgy (from the Greek *leiturgia*) meant at first any public service. In the Greek translation of the Bible it is used for the public service of the Temple. In Christian use it first meant any service in church, then specially the Eucharistic service; a meaning which it still has in the Eastern Churches. When we speak of the holy or sacred liturgy, we mean the Mass. But we also use the word liturgy for the *rite* of the Mass, that is, for the ceremonies, prayers, and functions of the Mass, and we say that the liturgy or rite of the Mass differs in various parts of the world, although the Mass itself is *essentially* the same everywhere.

The Essentials of the Mass, i.e., those things without which the Mass would not be the Mass, were given to us at the Last Supper. Christ took bread, gave thanks, blessed, and broke it, said over it the words of Institution, and gave it to His Apostles to eat. Then He took the chalice of wine, again gave thanks, said the words of Institution over it and gave it to His Apostles to drink. In conclusion He told them to do what He had done, in memory of Him. Prayer of thanksgiving, Consecration of bread and wine by the words of Institution, consumption of the consecrated species—these are the essential elements of the Holy Eucharist as a Sacrifice. The prayers and ceremonies of our present Mass gradually grew out of this simple rite. We can distinguish several stages in this growth:

1. The *first Christians* were mostly converts from Judaism. Hence it was quite natural for them to begin their assemblies with a sort of Christianized synagogue service. This consisted, as we know from various texts of the New Testament, of readings from the Bible, sermons on what had been read, singing of psalms and hymns, public recitation of prayers, collection of alms for the poor, etc. Then followed the Eucharist proper. There were as yet no fixed prayers for this part of the service, the celebrant "giving thanks" in words chosen by himself.

The Eucharistic service was often preceded by the *agape*, or love-feast, which was a supper eaten in common, in memory of the Last Supper; but this led to disorders, as we learn from St. Paul (1 Cor. 11, 18-22), and the love-feasts gradually died out.

2. *St. Justin Martyr,* writing about the year 150, gives us a detailed description of the Eucharistic service at Rome in his time. It does not differ much from the rite used in the Apostolic Age. There were lessons from the Scriptures, a sermon by the bishop, a long prayer said by all, standing, for all kinds of people, and the Kiss of Peace was given. Then bread and wine with water were brought to the altar and received by the bishop. After a long Eucharistic prayer, the Consecration took place, consisting of a prayer in memory of Our Lord's Passion, and the words of Institution. The people answered *Amen,* and received Communion under both kinds. Deacons carried the Blessed Sacrament to those who were unable to be present. At some time during the service a collection for the poor was taken up.

3. The oldest complete text of the Mass is found in the so-called *Apostolic Constitutions,* the work of an Eastern writer of the fourth century. It is no doubt a copy of the text of the Mass used in the great city of Antioch and other parts of Syria. A résumé of the text will be given below.

4. The fifth century brings a great change in the liturgy of the Mass. There is still the same general outline, but we have a number of rites which differ from one another in various details, especially in the number, length, and arrangement of the prayers and ceremonies. They may be roughly divided into the *Eastern* and *Western Rites.*

To the *Western Rite* belong:

a) The *Gallican rite* once used in Gaul, Spain, North Italy, Britain, and Africa; it disappeared gradually since the eighth century, except for two remnants: the *Ambrosian rite,* still used at Milan, and the *Mozarabic* at Toledo in Spain.

b) The *Roman rite,* according to which Mass is celebrated today in most of the countries of the world. A few modifications of the Roman rite introduced in the Middle Ages by some religious orders and in some dioceses still linger on.

The *Canon* of the Roman Mass was revised by St. Gregory the Great and has not been changed since. For many centuries there was no one Mass-book, but a different book for the celebrant, the deacon, the lector, the choirmaster, etc. The Mass was always a high Mass. In the eleventh century *low Mass,* a shortened form of high Mass, was introduced, and in consequence the various Mass-books had to be put into one, which was called the *Missale.* The Missal received its present form from Pope St. Pius V, in 1570.*

The liturgies of the East and West agree in this, that both divide the Mass into two distinct parts: the *Mass of the Catechumens*—our Mass up to the Offertory—and the Mass of the Faithful; and that in both the Consecration is the climax of the Eucharistic service and Holy Communion the conclusion.

The difference between the present liturgy of the Mass and the liturgy of the fourth century can be seen best by placing the Roman rite and the rite handed down in the *Apostolic Constitutions* in parallel columns.

MASS ACCORDING TO THE ROMAN RITE	MASS ACCORDING TO THE APOSTOLIC CONSTITUTIONS
I. Mass of the Catechumens	
1. Prayers at the foot of the altar, first incensing of the altar.	
2. Introit.	
3. Kyrie.	
4. Gloria.	
5. Collects.	
6. Epistle, Gradual (Tract, Sequence), Gospel, Sermon.	Se- Readings from Scripture, Prayers for the Catechumens, the penitents, etc. Sermon, dismissal of the Catechumens and penitents.
7. Credo.	

---

*See page 196 for this note. —*Editor,* 1990.

Mass according to the Roman Rite (Cont'd)   *Mass according to the Apostolic Constitutions (Cont'd)*

II. Mass of the Faithful

I. OFFERTORY

1. Offertory Antiphon.
2. Prayer for the offering of bread and wine. Incensing of the offerings and the altar.
3. Lavabo.
4. Second prayer for the offerings.
5. Secrets.

Prayers of the faithful (all standing towards the East) for the whole world, the Church, the benefactors, the afflicted, their enemies, all non-Christians, the infants, their own welfare.
Kiss of Peace.
Offertory.

II. THE CANON

1. Preface.
2. Sanctus.
3. Three commemorations:
   a) the Church,
   b) the living,
   c) the Saints.
4. Prayers before the Consecration.
5. Consecration and Elevation.
6. Commemoration of Jesus.
7. Two oblation prayers.
8. Three commemorations:
   a) the dead,
   b) ourselves,
   c) all nature.
9. Second elevation.

1. Preface.
2. Sanctus.

Prayer before Consecration.
Consecration.
Commemoration of Jesus.
Invocation of the Holy Ghost.
Various intercessions. The Blessing is given by the bishop.

Elevation.

III. COMMUNION

a) *Preparation*

1. Pater Noster.
2. Prayer for peace.
3. Breaking of the Host.
   Pax Domini.
4. Agnus Dei.
5. Prayer for peace.
   Kiss of peace.

b) *Communion*

1. Two prayers before Communion.
2. Domine non sum dignus.
3. Communion of the priest under both kinds.

All present receive Communion under both kinds.
During Communion, Psalm 33, "I will bless the Lord at all times," is sung.

c) *Thanksgiving*

1. Two prayers of thanksgiving.
2. Communion Antiphon.
3. Post-Communion.

1. Prayers of thanksgiving.
2. Various petitions.

d) *Conclusion*

1. Dismissal.
2. Blessing.
3. Last Gospel.

Dismissal of the faithful

9. *The Language of the Mass*

During the first two centuries the liturgical language at Rome was Greek. During the next two centuries Greek and Latin were used side by side. Then Latin supplanted Greek altogether. Since most of the west-nations were evangelized from Rome, Latin became the liturgical language of the whole Western Church.

The advantages of having one liturgical language, and that an unchangeable one, are obvious:

a) The use of the same language throughout the Church promotes the unity and union of its members.

b) The liturgy would have lost much of its sublime and venerable character if, in the course of time, as often as the words of a living language would change their meaning or become obsolete or trivial, the Church would have to substitute new ones. (Compare the language of Chaucer, and even of Shakespeare and Milton, with our present English.)

c) Wherever a Catholic goes, the language of the Church makes him feel at home, whereas non-Catholics are strangers as soon as they leave their own country.*

d) If the Mass were said in every country in the vernacular, priests traveling in foreign lands would either have to know many languages or carry their own Missals with them if they wished to say Mass.

e) The Mass being a sacrifice, and not merely a form of prayer or a sermon, it is not necessary to understand all the words

---

*This was the case until the 1960's, when the vernacular was introduced, for Latin was still in universal use at the time Fr. Laux wrote, and the Latin Rite is found throughout the world. —*Editor,* 1990.

said by the priest in order to take part in the service. Even though the Mass were said in the vernacular, most of our churches are so large that the people could hardly understand the words spoken by the priest at the altar.

f) We never hear the faithful complain that the use of the Latin tongue detracts in any way from their devotion.

g) Not only the Roman Catholic Church, but the Russian, Greek, Armenian, Chaldean, and other Eastern Churches celebrate the liturgy in a tongue distinct from the vernacular. In Egypt, for example, the Christians speak Arabic, while the liturgical language is partly Greek, partly Coptic. To this day the Jews use Hebrew in their synagogue service, although it is a dead language. Even the pagan Romans retained in their public religious rites the old Latin words and forms after they had become unintelligible to the majority of the people.

10. *Some Notes on the Liturgy of the Mass**

1. The essence of the Mass consists in the Consecration, by which Christ becomes present on the altar under the appearances of bread and wine and is offered to the Heavenly Father as a ransom for our sins. The *Offertory* is merely the dedication of the sacrificial gifts, not the sacrifice itself. The priest's *Communion* under both species is more important than the Offertory; it is an *integral part* of the sacrifice, the sacrificial banquet, without which the sacrifice would not be complete. The Offertory, Consecration and Communion are the *principal parts* of the Mass, but the center and climax of the holy action is the Consecration.

2. We distinguish several kinds of Masses:

a) *Solemn Mass—Missa solemnis—*with deacon, sub-deacon and a choir. For about a thousand years there was no other kind of Mass.

b) *Low Mass—Missa privata—*an abridged solemn Mass, in which the celebrant supplies the parts of the deacon and the sub-deacon. There is no singing; Mass-servers answer all the prayers. Low Mass is unknown in the Eastern Rites.

c) *High Mass—Missa cantata—*which is really a low Mass with singing as at solemn Mass.

d) *Pontifical Mass,* which has certain special ceremonies whose

* For complete text and rubrics with explanatory notes of the Ordinary of the Mass, also the furniture and articles on altar and in sanctuary, see Appendix (page 144).

purpose is to express the greater dignity of the bishop. A Pontifical High Mass still keeps the old distinction between the Mass of the Catechumens and the Mass of the Faithful; the bishop remains at his throne during the first part and goes to the altar only at the Offertory.

3. The Introit (Lat. *introitus*, entrance) was originally the processional psalm sung by the choir as the celebrant and his assistants advanced to the altar. At high Mass it is now sung whilst the celebrant says the prayers at the foot of the altar. The Introit is the first of the variable parts of the Mass, changing according to the Sunday or feast. The different Masses in the Missal are named after the first word (or words) of the Introit. Thus a Mass for the Dead is called *Requiem*, the Mass of the Sacred Heart, *Miserebitur*. Some Sundays are still called after the first word of the Introit, e.g., *Laetare Sunday*, the fourth Sunday in Lent.

4. At solemn Mass the altar is **incensed** before the celebrant reads the Introit. Incense was used both by Jews and pagans in their sacrifices but it was not introduced into Christian worship until the fourth century. The Romans used incense as a sign of

A Pontifical Mass

honor and carried it before high dignitaries. In the Bible it is a symbol of prayer.

5. Kyrie eleison, *Christe eleison* are *Greek phrases* meaning "Lord have mercy, Christ have mercy." They are the only Greek formulas in the Mass. The Kyrie eleison was introduced into Rome from Antioch in the fifth century; the Christe eleison, which is not found in the Eastern liturgies, was added by St. Gregory the Great. It seems that at one time a long Litany formed the opening of the Mass—as is still the case on Holy Saturday and the Vigil of Pentecost—and that the Kyrie eleison is all that is left of this litany.

6. The Gloria in excelsis is the translation of a very old Greek hymn. It was introduced into the Roman liturgy from the East. At first it was used on Christmas day only. Being a hymn of joy, it is always omitted on days of penance and in Masses for the dead.

7. The Collect is the first of the three special prayers sung or said by the celebrant, the other two being the *Secret* and the *Post-communion*. The word *collecta* is late Latin for *collectio*, and means "gathering" or "assembly." Originally it was the prayer said when the people were assembled before the Mass began: *oratio ad collectam populi*, i.e., "prayer at the gathering of the people." Before saying this prayer, the celebrant greets the faithful with the words *Dominus vobiscum*. "He is about to speak to God in their name, so first he, as it were, presents himself to them." Instead of *Dominus vobiscum*, "The Lord be with you," a bishop says, *Pax vobis*, "Peace be with you." The answer of the people: *Et cum spiritu tuo*, "And with your spirit," is a Semitism and simply means "And with you." The celebrant says the Collect standing with uplifted hands, the old attitude of public prayer.

8. The Gradual, the chant between the Epistle and the Gospel, is so called because it used to be sung from the steps (Lat. *gradus*) of the *ambo*, or platform near the altar from which the Gospel was read. Some churches had two ambos, a smaller one for the Epistle and a larger one for the Gospel and the sermon. The ambo is the precursor of our pulpit.

The Gradual is followed by the **Alleluia,** a Hebrew ejaculation of joy: "Praise the Lord." From Septuagesima till Easter and in all Masses for the dead we have a *Tract* instead of the Alleluia.

AMBOS IN CHURCH OF SAN CLEMENTE, ROME

The name means something sung *in uno tractu,* i.e., straight through without an answer by the people.

9. At Easter, Pentecost, and Corpus Christi, on the two feasts of the Seven Sorrows of the Blessed Virgin, and in Masses for the dead a hymn is sung after the Gradual. Because this hymn *follows* the Gradual it is called a **sequence** (Lat. *Sequentia,* from *sequor,* follow). The first writer of sequences was Notker Balbulus, monk of St. Gall in Switzerland (9th century). There were hundreds of sequences in the Missals of the Middle Ages. In our present Missal only the following five are found: Victimae Paschali, Veni Sancte Spiritus, Lauda Sion, Stabat Mater, and Dies Irae—all masterpieces of Sacred Poetry.

10. During the reading or singing of the Gospel all stand up as a mark of respect for the words of Christ. At solemn Mass the Gospel book is incensed, because it is a symbol of Christ Himself.

11. The custom of preaching after the Gospel is as old as the Mass. St. Paul preached a very long sermon at a Eucharistic

CIBORIUM DOVE   EUCHARISTIC DOVE

In the Middle Ages, before tabernacles were introduced, the Blessed
Sacrament was reserved in such receptacles.

service (Acts 2,11), and St. Justin Martyr says: "When the
reader has finished, the bishop warns and exhorts us to follow
these glorious examples." Preaching is therefore by no means a
modern addition to the Mass, but an element of the sacred liturgy
from the very beginning.

12. The Creed did not always have a place in the Mass. The
Apostles' Creed was used from the earliest times, and is still used,
as a profession of faith before Baptism. Of the many Creeds
drawn up at different times the most famous is the one made by
the Council of Nicaea in the year 325. It was modified and expanded by the Council of Constantinople in the year 381; still
later the word *filioque* was added. In the Mass the Creed appears
first in Spain towards the end of the sixth century as a protest
against the Arian heresy. From Spain it spread over France and
Germany. It was not said at Mass in Rome till 1014, when it was

inserted at the request of the Emperor Henry II. It is often omitted, but never on Sundays and the feasts of Our Lord, the Blessed Virgin, and the Apostles.

13. After the Gospel (or the Creed), the celebrant turns to the congregation and says: *Dominus vobiscum*, and then: *Oremus*, "Let us pray." But no prayer follows, and he immediately says the Offertory Psalm with folded hands. "This beginning without a continuation remains as a relic and an indication of the place of the old *Prayers of the Faithful*." (See above in the outline of the Mass according to the Apostolic Constitutions.)

14. At the Offertory the people formerly brought bread and wine to the altar; part of their offering was used for consecration and Communion, the rest was kept for the poor. Our collection of money at the Offertory and the practice of giving stipends for Mass still represent the old offering of bread and wine by the faithful. The Offertory prayers are all later additions to the Mass.

15. After the Offertory the celebrant washes his hands, as a sign of respect and as a symbol of the purity of soul required for offering up the sacred mysteries. During the washing the priest recites a portion of the 25th Psalm. From the first word of this Psalm the ceremony is called the **Lavabo**—"I will wash."

16. The Orate, fratres (Pray, brethren) is the celebrant's request for the prayers of the faithful before the most solemn part of the Mass begins. It is said in a low voice, because the choir is still singing the Offertory Psalm. For the same reason the celebrant also says the next prayer in a whisper—hence called the *Secret* prayer. The Secret ends with the words *Per omnia saecula saeculorum*, sung or said aloud to warn the faithful that the Preface is about to begin.

17. The Preface, with its short dialogue at the beginning, is one of the primitive elements of the Mass, and is really part of the Canon, with which it forms one long prayer whose dominant note is thanksgiving—*Eucharist*. In the Roman rite it is called Preface (*Praefatio*), because it is regarded as the Introduction to the Canon.

For many centuries there was a special Preface for nearly every feast; all but eleven of these were dropped when Pius V revised the Missal. In recent years three new ones have been added: for St. Joseph, for Requiems, and for Christ the King. In all Prefaces there are two leading ideas: thanksgiving to God for the Incarna-

tion and other benefits, with special allusions to the occasion of the
Mass, and then calling on the angelic host to join us in praise.

18. The Sanctus, with the *Benedictus,* is a continuation of
the Preface, and is found in all the liturgies. The simplest *Sanctus* chant, e.g., in Requiems, continues the melody of the Preface.

19. The part of the Mass which begins after the Sanctus and
ends with *per omnia saecula saeculorum* just before the *Pater
Noster* is called the **Canon,** i.e., the norm or rule, because it is the
fixed, unchangeable form according to which the Sacrifice is offered up. In our Missals the text of the Canon is always preceded
by a picture of the Crucifixion. That the Canon has come down
to us from very ancient times is clearly shown by the fact that the
Saints mentioned in it all belong to the first four centuries. St.
Leo the Great and St. Gregory the Great added a few phrases to
the original text; since then no change has been made.*

20. The Words of Consecration, with those which immediately precede them, do not exactly correspond to the Scriptural
narrative, although the sense is absolutely the same. Perhaps our
present text goes back to the time before there were any written
Gospels.**

21. The Elevation of the Host and the Chalice was introduced into the Mass in the twelfth century; up to that time there
had been only the simultaneous elevation of the Host and Chalice
before the Pater Noster, which we now call the "little elevation."
Pius X granted an indulgence to all who look at the Blessed Sacrament when it is elevated and say "My Lord and my God."

22. The Pater Noster was put in its present place by St.
Gregory the Great; with it begins the third part of the Mass, the
Communion. It is introduced by a clause begging God to permit
us to say it and ends with the so-called *embolism,* an expansion
of the petition to deliver us from evil. Both of these additions are
very beautifully worded in our Missal.

23. At the Last Supper Our Lord took bread and *broke* it.
From the very beginning the **"breaking of the Bread"** formed
an element of the Mass, and is found today in all the Rites.
Shortly after the Pater Noster the celebrant breaks the Host into
three parts; the two larger ones he places on the paten for his own
Communion, and drops the smallest one into the Chalice.

24. The Agnus Dei, the threefold petition to the Lamb of

*See page 196 for this note.
**See page 196 for this note. —*Editor,* 1990.

THE ELEVATION OF THE HOST
From a 14th century manuscript

God for mercy and peace, was originally sung to fill up the time while the Consecrated Bread was being broken for the Communion of the people.

25. The Agnus Dei is followed by a prayer for peace and the **Kiss of Peace,** a sign of fellowship and unity. In the Roman rite it is given only at solemn Mass, and is exchanged only between the celebrant and the clergy. The prayer for peace and the Kiss of Peace are omitted in all Requiem Masses, because these were originally private Masses.*

26. During the distribution of Holy Communion a psalm or sacred hymn used to be sung by the choir. One of these hymns, sung by the monks of Bangor in Ireland (6th century), has come down to us:

Sancti venite,	Approach, ye just, and take
Corpus Christi sumite,	The Body of the Lord;
Sanctum bibentes	Your thirst of spirit slake
Quo redempti sanguinem.	With his dear Blood outpoured.

27. Domine, non sum dignus. . . . "O Lord, I am not worthy. . . ." Origen, St. John Chrysostom, St. Augustine, and

---

*In the *Novus Ordo* Mass, a handshake is exchanged at the time of the "Kiss of Peace." —*Editor,* 1990.

many other Fathers of the Church point out how suitable these words of the centurion are for Holy Communion. They are beautifully paraphrased in the well-known hymn:

> O Lord, I am not worthy
>   That Thou shouldst come to me,
> But speak the word of comfort,
>   My spirit healed shall be.
>
> I'm longing to receive Thee,
>   The Bridegroom of my soul,
> No more by sin to grieve Thee,
>   Or fly Thy sweet control.

28. The Prayers at the Communion of the people.—*Confiteor; Ecce Agnus Dei; Domine, non sum dignus*—were at first used for Communion given out of Mass to those who could not be present; they were introduced into the Mass about the thirteenth century.

29. After the Post-Communion prayer the deacon formerly dismissed the people with the words: *Ite, missa est*—"Go, it is the dismissal." This was really the end of the Mass; the blessing and the last Gospel are later additions. The Mass now ends with the appropriate ejaculation *Deo gratias*—"Thanks be to God." The prayers recited by the celebrant and the people after a low mass were ordered by Leo XIII in 1884.**

30. The Rubrics, i.e., the directions printed in red in the Missal, demand only two *ringings of the sanctuary bell,* one at the Sanctus, the other at the Elevation. The ringing at the Domine non sum dignus is tolerated. At solemn Masses no ringing is prescribed. In many places the church bell is rung at the Elevation.

31. Liturgical Vestments.*—During the first four centuries no *special vestments* were worn by the clergy at divine service; but the ordinary garb which they used was gradually altered and ornamented until our present vestments grew out of it: the *amice,* the *alb,* the *cincture,* the *maniple,* the *stole,* and the *chasuble.* Up to the end of the twelfth century no particular colors were prescribed by the Church. "In the Middle Ages there was no kind of uniformity in this matter. All manner of combinations were used, and there was everywhere the custom of wearing the handsomest vestments, of any color, for great feasts."

The Church now uses five colors, and each has its meaning: *White* signifies innocence and spiritual joy (Feasts of Our Lord, the Blessed Virgin, the Angels, Confessors, and Virgins); *Red*

---

* For illustrations of vestments, see Appendix, page 144.

**These prayers are not said at the end of the *Novus Ordo* Mass.   —*Editor,* 1990.

is the color of fire and of blood (Pentecost, feasts of Martyrs) ; *Green* denotes the hope of eternal life (Sundays after Epiphany and Pentecost) ; *Purple* or *Violet* is the color of humility and penance (Advent and Lent, except on feast days) ; *Black* signifies mourning (Good Friday and at all Requiems). *Gold* vestments may be used as a substitute for white, red, or green. *Rose-colored* vestments may be used at solemn Mass on the Third Sunday in Advent and the Fourth Sunday in Lent, because these Sundays are of a somewhat joyful character, as is seen from the Introit.

C. Holy Communion

1. Nature and Necessity of Communion

1. At the Last Supper Jesus gave His Sacred Body and His Precious Blood to His Apostles, saying: "Take ye and eat—Take ye and drink." The Body and Blood of Christ are, therefore, nourishment, food and drink. "My Flesh is meat indeed, and My Blood is drink indeed" (John 6,56). This food nourishes the soul by preserving and increasing its supernatural life. The partaking of this nourishment is called **Communion**—union of the faithful with Christ and with one another.

Holy Communion is the receiving of the real Body and Blood of Jesus Christ for the nourishment of our souls.

2. We are obliged to receive Holy Communion.—

a) By the *command of Christ Himself*: "Amen, amen, I say unto you: Except you eat the Flesh of the Son of Man and drink His Blood, you shall not have life in you" (John 6,54), and: "Do this in remembrance of Me" (Luke 22,19).

b) By the *command of the Church*: The Fourth Council of the Lateran (1215) decreed that "all the faithful, after they come to the years of discretion, shall receive the Sacrament of the Eucharist at least once a year, and that at Easter time."

3. Only those who have attained "the years of discretion" are *bound* to receive the Sacrament of the Eucharist. In the early Church Holy Communion formed part of the rite of initiation into the Church. The catechumens were usually adults who had been instructed for a long time in the mysteries of the Faith. After infant Baptism became the general custom, Holy Communion still remained part of the rite of initiation and was given to the infants immediately after Baptism and Confirmation under the species of wine. This is still done in the Eastern Churches. Since the sacraments work *ex opere operato*,* an infant really and truly receives the Body and Blood of Christ and derives due benefit from the Sacrament. In the course of time it became customary to put off the reception of Holy Communion until the child had reached the *age of discretion* and could "discern the Body of the Lord," that is, until he knew what he was receiving.

4. But what is the "age of discretion"?—It is clear that it is the *time in a child's life when it can choose between right and wrong, when it is capable of committing a mortal sin.* From this time begins the obligation of going to confession, and surely, too, the duty of receiving Holy Communion; for as soon as a child can commit a mortal sin, there is no reason why it should be refused the most powerful means of preserving its baptismal innocence.

5. In a decree dated August 8, 1910, Pope Pius X laid down the rules which are to be observed in regard to the **First Communion** of children. They may be summed up as follows:

a) The age of discretion is seven, more or less.

b) From this time begins the obligation of Confession and Communion.

c) A full knowledge of Christian doctrine is not necessary; it is sufficient that the child can distinguish the Eucharistic Bread from common bread.

d) The parents of the child and the confessor are the judges of the child's fitness to receive Holy Communion.

e) After their first Communion the utmost care must be taken that the children receive very often, and if possible even daily.

6. Not only children, but all the faithful should partake frequently of the Sacred Banquet.—The early Christians communicated every time they assisted at Mass. In the third and fourth centuries daily Communion was almost a universal custom. In the course of time the faithful became so neglectful of receiving Holy Communion that the Church had to make the law referred to above. The Council of Trent renewed this law and expressed the desire that all who assist at the Holy Sacrifice should also take part in the Sacrificial Banquet.

The Sacred Congregation of the Council by a decree, dated December 20, 1905, and approved by Pope Pius X, once for all decided the much-discussed question regarding the *dispositions necessary for frequent or daily Communion,* by laying down the following rules:

---

*The meaning is that a Sacrament works virtually "automatically"; it does what it signifies, provided no obstacle is placed in the way. Literally, the phrase means "from the work performed." —*Editor,* 1990.

a) Frequent and daily Communion is open to the faithful of whatever degree or condition, so that no one who is in the state of grace, and approaches the altar with a proper and devout disposition, should be kept away from Holy Communion.

b) The *proper disposition* consists in this, that he who approaches the Holy Table does not do so through custom or vanity, or for merely human motives, but because he wishes to please God and to apply the divine medicine as a remedy for his infirmities and defects.

c) It suffices to be free from mortal sin, and to have the sincere purpose of avoiding venial sin.

d) Assiduous preparation should precede and suitable thanksgiving follow Holy Communion, according to the ability, condition, and duties of each communicant.

7. In order to share in the graces of the Sacrament of the Altar, it is not necessary to receive it under both kinds; for under the appearance of bread we receive Christ whole and entire, therefore also His Blood.—

a) We have proved above that Christ is present whole and entire under each species. Hence we fulfill Our Lord's command to eat His Flesh and drink His Blood if we receive Him only under one kind.

b) Christ promised eternal life also to those who receive Him only under one kind: "If anyone eat of this Bread, he shall live forever" (John 6,52).

c) Christ instituted the Holy Eucharist in both kinds because He instituted it, not only as a sacrament, but also as a sacrifice, for which both kinds are required. Hence, priests who celebrate Mass *must* consecrate and receive under both kinds, but when they do not celebrate, they communicate under one kind only.

d) It is true that down to the Middle Ages the faithful throughout the whole Church usually received Holy Communion under both kinds; but the Church, from the beginning, also permitted Communion under one kind. Children, as we have seen, received under the form of wine alone; the sick, under the form of bread alone.

e) When the Manichaeans (in the fourth century), who looked upon wine as an invention of the devil, refused to communicate under both species, Pope Leo the Great, to counteract their error, made it obligatory on all to receive Communion under both kinds, and when, many centuries later, John Hus and Jerome of Prague asserted the *necessity* of Communion under both kinds, the Council of Constance (1414) decreed that henceforth Communion

DISTRIBUTING HOLY COMMUNION UNDER BOTH KINDS
IN THE EARLY CHURCH

should be given to the faithful only under the species of bread. To the Hussites who returned to the Church permission was given in 1433 to receive under both kinds. Thus we see that the reception of Communion under one or both kinds by the faithful is a matter of Church discipline. It could be changed by lawful authority at any time, just like the exclusive use of Latin in the liturgy.*

f) Fear of irreverence—because the Precious Blood could be easily spilled—and regard for the feelings of those who would not like to drink with others from the same cup, no doubt led to the gradual withdrawing of the chalice from the faithful.

---

*At the time Fr. Laux wrote, Latin was the exclusive language used in the Liturgy of the Roman or Latin Rite of the Roman Catholic Church. —*Editor,* 1990.

2. *Dispositions for Receiving Holy Communion*

1. Holy Communion being a Sacrament of the living, the soul must be in the state of grace to receive it worthily.

He who has committed a *mortal sin* must make a good confession before he may receive Holy Communion. An act of contrition would not be enough. Food cannot profit a body that is dead; neither can Holy Communion, the divine food of the soul, profit a soul that is dead to the grace of God. Hence St. Paul says: "Let a man prove himself, i.e., make sure of the state of his conscience, and so let him eat of that Bread and drink of that Chalice" (1 Cor. 11,28).

2. As regards the preparation of the body, we are commanded by the Church to observe the *Eucharistic fast*; that is, from midnight preceding our Communion we must abstain from

Rembrandt
CHRIST WITH THE DISCIPLES AT EMMAUS

everything *in the way of food or drink.** But if, while cleaning the teeth, one were unintentionally to swallow a drop of water; or were accidentally to inhale a flake of snow or a drop of rain; or to swallow blood coming from the lips or gums, the fast would not thereby be broken, because that would not be taking something *in the way of food or drink.*

3. Eucharistic Fast.—The custom of receiving the Holy Eucharist fasting goes back to the second century when Mass began

*See page 196 for this note. —Editor, 1990.

to be celebrated early in the morning. In the fourth century the *Eucharistic fast* had become universal. "Out of respect for the Blessed Sacrament," says St. Augustine, "no Christian in the whole world partakes of any other food before receiving the Body of the Lord" (Letter 54).*

Persons who are dangerously ill and receive the Holy Eucharist as *Viaticum* are dispensed from fasting. By virtue of an indult (a special favor) granted by Pope Pius X in 1906 those who have been sick for a whole month without hope of a speedy recovery, are allowed to receive Holy Communion once or twice a week after taking medicine or some liquid food, such as soup, tea, coffee, with which some solid substance may be mixed.*

4. Preparation for Communion.—In order to prepare ourselves in a way *becoming the dignity* of the Blessed Eucharist, we should purify ourselves from venial sins as far as possible, and awaken lively sentiments of faith, hope and love, contrition and desire. But we must remember that these sentiments are not *feelings*: we may have true devotion in our hearts without feeling it. God regards the heart and the will, not the feelings.

5. Whoever dares to communicate unworthily is guilty of the blackest ingratitude and commits a sacrilege.

"Whosoever shall eat this Bread, or drink the Chalice of the Lord unworthily, shall be guilty of the Body and of the Blood of the Lord; he eateth and drinketh judgment to himself, not discerning the Body of the Lord" (1 Cor. 11,27-29).

Sumunt boni, sumunt mali:	Good and bad, they come to greet Him:
Sorte tamen inaequali,	Unto life the former eat Him,
Vitae vel interitus.	And the latter unto death;
Mors est malis, vita bonis:	These find death and those find heaven.
Vide paris sumptionis,	See, from the same life-seed given,
Quam sit dispar exitus.	How the harvest differeth.

—From the *Lauda Sion*.

6. After receiving Holy Communion we should spend some time in devout prayer, adoring Our Savior, thanking Him, offering ourselves to Him, and asking His graces for ourselves and others.

No time is more precious than that immediately following Holy Communion It is then that Our Savior is most lavish of His graces, and gratitude is always pleasing to Him. It is then that the devout soul forgets all earthly cares and preoccupations and is lost in contemplation and admiration of the infinite goodness and love of her heavenly guest and friend.

*See page 196, the note for page 87, for this note. —*Editor,* 1990.

With the spouse in the Canticle of Canticles she cries: "I have found Him whom my soul loveth; I will hold Him and will not let Him go"; and with the Psalmist: "What shall I render to the Lord for all the things that He hath rendered to me?" Like the holy Patriarch Jacob she too says to the Lord: "I will not let Thee go except Thou bless me" (Gen. 32,26).

3. Effects of Holy Communion

The wonderful effects produced in the soul by Holy Communion can be summed up as follows:

1. *It preserves and increases the supernatural life of the soul.*

As food maintains our natural life, so this Heavenly Food maintains and increases our supernatural life of grace. God is Life, and Our Lord received this Life from His Father and comes to share it with us. "I am come that they may have life, and may have it more abundantly" (John 10,10). He shares this life with us in many ways, but most of all by means of the *Bread of Life* (John 6,57-58).

2. *It unites the soul more closely with Christ.*

Holy Communion makes us *abide* in Christ, that is, united to His mind and will, as He is united with His Father (John 15,1-10). When we eat ordinary food we change it into our substance, but when we eat this Bread of Life it changes us into itself. Every Holy Communion transforms us more into Christ, by increasing our love for Him and therefore our likeness to Him. "I live, now not I, but Christ liveth in me" (Gal. 2,20).

3. *By uniting all the faithful with Christ, Holy Communion unites them with each other in charity.*

St. Paul proclaims this brotherly love promoted by Holy Communion when he writes: "For we, being many, are one bread, all that partake of one bread" (1 Cor. 10,7). Hence St. Augustine calls the Holy Eucharist "the Sacrament of affection, the sign of unity, the bond of charity."

4. *It remits venial sin, and preserves us from mortal sin.*

Just as bodily food repairs what we lose by daily wear and tear, so likewise is this Divine Food a remedy for the spiritual infirmities of each day. But we must remember that it remits those venial sins only for which we no longer retain an affection.

5. *It is a pledge of future glory.*

We receive the risen Body of Christ, and it confers on us a

title to a glorious resurrection and to the Beatific Vision in heaven which Our Lord will share with us. "He that eateth My flesh hath everlasting life, and I will raise him up at the last day" (John 6,55). Hence St. Ignatius of Antioch calls the Holy Eucharist the "medicine of immortality and the antidote that we die not."

Se nascens dedit socium,	At birth our Brother He became;
Convescens in edulium,	At meat Himself as food He gives;
Se moriens in pretium,	To ransom us He died in shame;
Se regnans dat in praemium.	As our reward in bliss He lives.

—From the Hymn *Verbum supernum.*

SUGGESTIONS FOR STUDY AND REVIEW

1. An excellent manual to assist the student in the study of the Mass has been recently published by Benziger Brothers: *Holy Mass*, An Explanation of the Doctrinal Meaning of the Mass and Its Ceremonies, by Rev. Winfrid Herbst, S.D.S. We recommend its use at this stage of the study of the Sacraments.

   Other helps for the study of the Mass are, besides the *Missal*:

   William Busch, *The Mass-Drama.*

   Virgil Michel, O.S.B., *My Sacrifice and Yours.*

   Paul C. Bussard, *If I Be Lifted Up.* An Essay on the Sacrifice of the Mass. (All three published by the Liturgical Press, Collegeville, Minn.)

   J. A. Dunney, *The Mass* (Macmillan, N. Y.).

2. Write a composition on the *Lauda, Sion, Salvatorem*—Sion, Lift Thy Voice and Sing—St. Thomas' Sequence for Mass of Corpus Christi. This famous hymn has been called the "supreme example of theological poetry." The original Latin text with an English translation follows:

1. Lauda, Sion, Salvatorem,	Sion, lift thy voice and sing:
Lauda ducem et pastorem	Praise thy Savior and thy King;
In hymnis et canticis.	Praise with hymns thy Shepherd true:
Quantum potes, tantum aude:	Dare thy most to praise Him well;
Quia maior omni laude,	For He doth all praise excel;
Nec laudare sufficis.	None can ever reach His due.
2. Laudis thema specialis,	Special theme of praise is thine,
Panis vivus et vitalis	That true living Bread divine,
Hodie proponitur;	That life-giving flesh adored,
Quem in sacrae mensa coenae	Which the brethren twelve received,
Turbae fratrum duodenae	As most faithfully believed,
Datum non ambigitur.	At the Supper of the Lord.
3. Sit laus plena, sit sonora,	Let the chant be loud and high;
Sit iucunda, sit decora	Sweet and tranquil be the joy

Mentis iubilatio.
Dies enim solemnis agitur,
In qua mensae prima recolitur
Huius institutio.

Felt to-day in every breast;
On this festival divine
Which recounts the origin
Of the glorious Eucharist.

4. In hac mensa novi Regis
Novum Pascha novae legis
Phase vetus terminat.
Vetustatem novitas,
Umbram fugat veritas,
Noctem lux eliminat.

At this table of the King,
Our new Paschal offering
Brings to end the olden rite;
Here, for empty shadows fled,
Is reality instead;
Here, instead of darkness, light.

5. Quod in coena Christus gessit,
Faciendum hoc expressit
In sui memoriam.
Docti sacris institutis,
Panem, vinum in salutis
Consecramus hostiam.

His own act, at supper seated,
Christ ordained to be repeated,
In His memory divine;
Wherefore now, with adoration,
We the Host of our salvation
Consecrate from bread and wine.

6. Dogma datur Christianis,
Quod in carnem transit panis
Et vinum in sanguinem.
Quod non capis, quod non
vides,
Animosa firmat fides
Praeter rerum ordinem.

Hear what holy Church maintaineth,
That the bread its substance changeth
Into Flesh, the wine to Blood.
Doth it pass thy comprehending?
Faith, the law of sight transcending,
Leaps to things not understood.

7. Sub diversis speciebus,
Signis tantum, et non rebus,
Latent res eximiae:
Caro cibus, sanguis potus;
Manet tamen Christus totus
Sub utraque specie.

Here in outward signs are hidden
Priceless things, to sense forbidden;
Signs, not things, are all we see:—
Flesh from bread, and Blood from
wine;
Yet is Christ, in either sign,
All entire confessed to be.

8. A sumente non concisus,
Non confractus, non divisus:
Integer accipitur.
Sumit unus, sumunt mille;
Quantum isti, tantum ille:
Nec sumptus consumitur.

They too who of Him partake
Sever not, nor rend, nor break,
But entire their Lord receive.
Whether one or thousands eat,
All receive the selfsame meat,
Nor the less for others leave.

9. Sumunt boni, sumunt mali:
Sorte tamen inaequali,
Vitae vel interitus.
Mors est malis, vita bonis:
Vide, paris sumptionis
Quam sit dispar exitus.

Both the wicked and the good
Eat of this celestial Food;
But with ends how opposite!
Here 'tis life; and there 'tis death;
The same, yet issuing to each
In a difference infinite.

10. Fracto demum Sacramento,
Ne vacilles, sed memento,
Tantum esse sub fragmento,
Quantum toto tegitur.
Nulla rei fit scissura,
Signi tantum fit fractura,
Qua nec status nec statura
Signati minuitur.

Nor a single doubt retain,
When they break the Host in twain,
But that in each part remains
What was in the whole before;
Since the simple sign alone
Suffers change in state or form,
The Signified remaining One
And the Same forevermore.

11. Ecce panis Angelorum,
Factus cibus viatorum,
Vere panis filiorum,
Non mittendus canibus.
In figuris praesignatur,
Cum Isaac immolatur;
Agnus Paschae deputatur,
Datur manna patribus.

Lo! upon the Altar lies,
Hidden deep from human eyes,
Angels' Bread from Paradise
Made the food of mortal man:
Children's meat to dogs denied;
In old types foresignified;
In the manna from the skies,
In Isaac, and the Paschal Lamb.

12. Bone Pastor, panis vere,
Jesu, nostri miserere,
Tu nos pasce, nos tuere,
Tu nos bona fac videre,
In terra viventium.
Tu, qui cuncta scis et vales,
Qui nos pascis hic mortales,
Tuos ibi commensales,
Cohaeredes et sodales,
Fac sanctorum civium. Amen.

Jesu! Shepherd of the sheep!
Thy true flock in safety keep.
Living Bread! Thy life supply;
Strengthen us, or else we die;
Fill us with celestial grace:
Thou, who feedest us below!
Source of all we have or know!
Grant that with Thy Saints above,
Sitting at the Feast of Love,
We may see Thee face to face. Amen.

You may use the following outline for your composition:

I. INTRODUCTION: Summons to the Faithful to raise their voices in hymns of praise to their Eucharistic Lord. The theme of their song specified (Stanzas 1-3).

II. EXPOSITION:

　1. *Historical Part* (St. 4 & 5).
　　a) Relation of the Old Testament to the New (St. 4).
　　b) The New Testament (St. 5).
　2. *Dogmatic Part* (St. 6-11).
　　a) Transubstantiation (St. 6).
　　b) Christ present under both species (St. 7).
　　c) Every communicant receives the whole Christ, and Christ remains wholly present. Think of the miracle of the Multiplication of the Loaves in the desert which was typical of this greater miracle (St. 8).
　　d) Different effects of Holy Communion according to the worthiness of the communicant (St. 9).
　　e) Christ is also wholly present in every particle of the Host (St. 10).

    f) The Food from the home of the Angels has become the Soul Food of the earthly pilgrims (St. 11).

III. CONCLUSION: Petitions to the Good Shepherd (St. 12).

Queries: 1. Give the literal and the metaphorical meaning of the word *Sion.*

    2. Quote the words of Our Lord referred to in St. 5.

    3. What are the various meanings of the word *host*? What is its meaning in St. 5?

    4. Of what words of St. Paul does St. 9 remind you? (1 Cor. 11,29).

    5. What incident in Our Lord's life is referred to in St. 11?

3. Enter into your Religion Note Book the best passages, in prose and verse, which you meet with in your reading on the Holy Eucharist and the Holy Sacrifice of the Mass. Here are a few examples:

The Basis of the Mass-Structure.—"The Mass is an interchange of gifts; we give to God and God gives to us. This double motive is the basis of the entire Mass-structure. It determines the division into two parts of both the Mass of the Catechumens and the Mass of the Faithful. In the Mass of the Catechumens we first give to God, in the prayer-part, and then God gives to us, in the instruction-part. Likewise in the Mass of the Faithful, the sacrifice-oblation is our gift to God, the while the sacrifice-banquet is God's gift to us. In both cases the interchange is effected through our intimate union with Christ who is both God and man, according to the ever-recurring phrase: "per Christum Dominum nostrum: through Christ our Lord."—BUSCH, *The Mass-Drama,* p. 11.

Who Should Communicate Frequently.—"Two classes of people must receive Holy Communion frequently: the *perfect* that they may become still more perfect; the *imperfect* that they may attain perfection; the *strong* that they may not become weak, and the *weak* that they may become strong. Those who are *overburdened with work* must communicate often, because they need invigorating nourishment; those *who have little to do* should communicate often, because they have the time and the opportunity to do so."—ST. FRANCIS DE SALES, *Introduction to a Devout Life,* II, 21.

Divine Audience.—Though Chancellor of England, with many engrossing occupations, Bl. Thomas More heard Mass every day. Once, as he was at Mass, a message was brought to him from the King, requiring his attendance on a matter of importance. "A little patience," replied the Chancellor; "I have not yet completed my homage to a higher Sovereign, and I must await the end of the Divine Audience."

Effects of Holy Communion.—"O Sacred Banquet, wherein *Christ is received,* the *memory of His Passion is renewed,* the *mind is filled with grace,* and the *pledge of future glory* given unto us."—ST. THOMAS AQUINAS. (The Fourth Book of the *Imitation of Christ* is rich in quotable passages on Holy Communion.)

4. In your Religion Note Book, under the heading: *"The Holy Eucharist in Art,"* paste reproductions of the great masterpieces of painting and

sculpture whose subject is the Blessed Sacrament or the Mass, such as the *Disputà* of Raphael; also reproductions of the works of modern artists.

5. Do you know who is the "Dramatist of the Eucharist"? Consult the *Catholic Encyclopedia* on "Calderon de La Barca" and his "Autos Sacramentales," sacred allegorical dramas on the Eucharist.

6. Name some of the commonest symbols of the Holy Eucharist.

7. Write a paragraph on each of the following: "Eucharistic Congresses," "Forty Hours' Devotion," "Holy Hour," "Altar, or Tabernacle Societies," "Communion of Reparation," "Perpetual Adoration," "Eucharistic Fast," "Visits to the Blessed Sacrament," "Pange Lingua," "Viaticum."

8. When praying the Mass with the priest you will perhaps have noticed that in a few prayers the singular number instead of the plural is used; also that, whereas most of the prayers are addressed to God, a few are addressed directly to Christ or to the Blessed Trinity. The explanation is this: From the ninth to the sixteenth century a number of additions were made to the Mass. These additions were not of Roman origin. They are for the greater part prayers of private devotion, formerly said by the priest outside Mass. Little by little they slipped into the Masses, and thence into the Missal. In other cases the additions owe their origin to the tendency, common in the Middle Ages, to explain a gesture by a formula or prayer. "In the place where the gesture had been sufficient, as for the Fraction, the Communion, the Kissing of the Altar, etc., formulas were added; here an *Aufer a nobis,* there the *Oramus Te,* elsewhere the *Quod ore sumpsimus,* etc. If we did not know by other evidence that these additions were not of Roman origin, we could guess it from the style of the prayers (singular instead of plural); and from other features, such as prayers addressed directly to God the Son, to the Trinity, etc." (Dom Fernand Cabrol, *The Mass of the Western Rites,* pp. 180-181.)

Supplementary Reading
"It Is The Mass That Matters."

In an article entitled, "What Happened at the Reformation?" written by the eminent English Protestant Essayist Augustine Birrell for the April issue of the *Nineteenth Century* for 1896 we read the following words on the Mass:

"Nobody nowadays, save a handful of vulgar fanatics, speaks irreverently of the Mass. If the Incarnation be indeed the one divine event to which the whole creation moves, the miracle of the altar may well seem its restful shadow cast over a dry and dusty land for the help of man, who is apt to be discouraged if perpetually told that everything really important and interesting happened once for all, long ago, in a chill historic past. . . . It is doubtful whether any poor sinful child of Adam (not being a paid agent of the Protestant Alliance) ever witnessed, however ignorantly, and it may be with only the languid curiosity of a traveller, the Communion Service according to the Roman Catholic ritual without emotion. It is the Mass that matters; it is the Mass that makes the difference: so hard to define, so subtle is it, yet so perceptible, between a Catholic country and a Protestant one."

CHAPTER V

Penance

1. Nature and Necessity of the Sacrament of Penance

The word *penance*—Lat. *poenitentia*—means sorrow, regret, change of mind or heart.

1. As a theological term penance is, first, the name of a virtue, which inclines the sinner to repent of his sins because they are an offense against God. In this sense the word was used by St. John the Baptist when he said: "Do penance, for the kingdom of God is at hand."

Then penance came to mean the outward acts by which sorrow for sin is shown. The Scripture says: "David did penance."

Lastly, penance is the name given to one of the sacraments of the New Law. Christ instituted the Sacrament of Penance for the remission of sins committed after Baptism. God alone can forgive sins; in this sacrament, however, He has made the priests His representatives, and they forgive sins in His name. But the sinner must do what God demands of him: he must be sorry for his sins, confess them, and be ready to make satisfaction for them.

Penance is, therefore, a sacrament in which the priest, in the place of God, forgives sins, if the sinner is heartily sorry for them, confesses them sincerely, and is willing to make satisfaction for them.

2. The remote matter of the Sacrament of Penance is the sins of the penitent. The **proximate matter** is the acts of the penitent: contrition, confession, and satisfaction.

The form of the sacrament is the words of the priest: *Ego te absolvo a peccatis tuis in nomine Patris et Filii et Spiritus Sancti* —I absolve thee from thy sins in the name of the Father, etc.

3. Christ gave His apostles a special power to forgive sins committed after Baptism.

a) Christ *promised* this power to the Apostles. To Peter He said: "I will give to thee the keys of the Kingdom of Heaven" (Matt. 16,19). Heaven was closed through sin; Peter is to open it by forgiving sin. Later Christ promised the same power to all the Apostles: "Amen I say to you, whatsoever you shall bind upon earth, shall be bound also in Heaven, and whatsoever you shall loose upon earth, shall be loosed also in Heaven" (Matt. 18,18).

b) After His resurrection Christ *gave* His Apostles the power he had promised them. Appearing to them in the Upper Chamber in Jerusalem, He said: "As the Father hath sent Me I also send you." He then breathed on them and continued: "Receive ye the Holy Ghost, whose sins you shall forgive, they are forgiven them, and whose sins you shall retain, they are retained" (John 20,21-23).

Luther and the other so-called reformers maintained that by these words Our Lord gave the Apostles merely the power of declaring to the faithful that their sins were forgiven them by God, provided they were sorry for them and aroused within themselves sentiments of faith and confidence. But why then did Christ give His Apostles also the power of *retaining*, that is, of not forgiving, the sins of the faithful? Christ evidently spoke of true forgiveness of sins. He uses the same words that He employed elsewhere to signify real forgiveness of sins. "Thy sins are forgiven thee," He said to the paralytic (Matt. 9,2), and on the same occasion He declared: "The Son of man hath power on earth to forgive sins." He sent His disciples as the Father had sent Him. that is, with the same power. Therefore, as Christ had power to forgive sins, so did He confer this power on His disciples.

By giving His Apostles the power of remitting sins, Christ instituted the Sacrament of Penance; for the three elements of a sacrament are here present: 1. The outward sign—the acts of the penitent and absolution. 2. The inward grace—the remission of sin, and 3. The institution by Christ.

4. The Sacrament of Penance is a Means of Grace.—But Christ intended His graces for all men; hence the power of forgiving sins must continue till the end of time. It was handed on by the Apostles to their successors, the bishops and priests of the Catholic Church.

The highest powers of the priest are the power to offer sacrifice and the power to forgive sins; both are expressly conferred upon him at his ordination. Of the power to forgive sins St. John Chrysostom says: "Can there be any greater power than this? God gave it neither to the angels nor to the archangels, for not to them did He say: 'Whatsoever you shall bind on earth shall be bound also in Heaven, and whatsoever you shall loose on earth shall be loosed also in Heaven.'"

5. For the valid administration of the Sacrament of Penance not only the *character of the priesthood* but also *jurisdiction,* that is, judicial power, is required. Christ appointed the Apostles and their successors judges over sins, leaving them free to forgive the sins of the faithful or not to forgive them. But a judge can exercise his power only over those who are subject to his jurisdiction. Hence the Council of Trent declared "that absolution given by a priest to one over whom he has not ordinary or delegated jurisdiction is null and void."

Ordinary jurisdiction is that connected with an office involving the ordinary care of souls. Thus the bishop has jurisdiction over his diocese and the parish priest over his parish.

Delegated jurisdiction is that of one not holding such an office, but empowered by the Pope or the bishop to administer the Sacrament of Penance.

Formerly the faithful had to confess to their parish priest; now they can confess to any priest anywhere in the world who is empowered by his bishop to hear confessions. But priests, as a rule, are empowered to hear confessions only in their own diocese; if they wish to hear confessions in another diocese, they must be empowered to do so by the bishop of that diocese.*

The Pope and the bishops, for good reasons, reserve to themselves the absolution from certain very grave sins, such as apostasy from the Church, marrying before a non-Catholic minister of religion, taking part in a duel, joining forbidden societies, maltreating persons consecrated to God.* Before a priest can absolve from these so-called *reserved cases*, he must obtain the necessary *special faculties* from the bishop or the Pope. *In danger of death*, however, every priest can absolve from every sin.

6. All sins committed after Baptism can be forgiven in the Sacrament of Penance.—This follows from the words of Christ: "Whose sins you shall forgive, they are forgiven." No exception is even hinted at.

The Church has always taught that every sin can be remitted in the Sacrament of Penance. In the second century the *Montanists* were condemned for denying that the Church possessed the power to absolve from the three so-called canonical sins: idolatry, adultery and murder. In the third century *Novatus* and his followers were excommunicated because they asserted that those who had denied the faith during the persecutions could never be received back into the Church.

*See page 196 for the notes to this page. —*Editor*, 1990.

An objection answered.—But does not Our Lord say that "whoever blasphemeth against the Holy Spirit never hath forgiveness, but is guilty of an everlasting sin?" (Mark 3,29). A *sin against the Holy Ghost,* therefore, can not be forgiven.

We answer: The blasphemy of the Scribes, to which Our Lord alludes, consisted in this: they obstinately and maliciously attributed to Satan works which only God could perform. Such a sin, says Our Lord, "hath no forgiveness"; not that God does not give the sinner sufficient grace to repent, or that the Church in His name has not the power to absolve from all sins; but Christ foresees that such a sin will never as a matter of fact be repented of and therefore never forgiven. *Obstinate resistance to the grace of God calling the sinner to repentance is the sin against the Holy Ghost* which can never be forgiven, because not even God can forgive sins without repentance on the part of the sinner.

7. The Sacrament of Penance is a necessary means of salvation for those who have fallen into mortal sin *after Baptism.* If it is impossible to receive the sacrament, perfect contrition only is required; but this contrition, which proceeds from perfect love of God, includes the will to do all that is necessary for salvation, consequently, to receive the Sacrament of Penance, if possible.

The desire to receive the Sacrament of Penance may be, like the desire to receive Baptism, *explicit* or *implicit.* Hence Catholics do not deny that God is ready to forgive the sins of non-Catholics who are in good faith and who turn to Him in loving sorrow. But the Protestant doctrine that confession of mortal sin is not an absolute duty imposed by the law of Christ, or that absolution is a benefit which the penitent is not absolutely bound to seek, is opposed to Catholic faith and practice from the very beginning of Christianity.

8. The Sacrament of Penance produces an abundance of graces in the souls of those who receive it worthily:

a) It remits the sins committed after Baptism;

b) It remits the eternal punishment, and at least a part of the temporal punishment due to sin;

c) It restores or increases the supernatural life of the soul;

d) It gives us strength not to fall back into sin.

9. In order to receive the Sacrament of Penance worthily we must do what the Prodigal Son in the Parable did:

a) As soon as he felt the grace of God working in his soul, he "returned to himself," thought over his misdeeds, and acknowledged them—*examination of conscience.*

b) He saw how ungrateful he had been to the best of fathers and was sincerely grieved at heart—*contrition.*

c) He made up his mind to return to his father's house and begin a new life—*purpose of amendment.*

d) He went back to his father, confessed his sins to him and implored forgiveness. The father fell upon his neck and kissed him—*confession and absolution.*

e) He protested that he was not worthy to be called his father's son, and wanted to be made one of his hired servants—*satisfaction.*

Thus we see that there are three essential parts to the Sacrament of Penance: *Contrition, Confession* and *Satisfaction.* Contrition necessarily includes the *Purpose of Amendment,* and Confession presupposes *Examination of Conscience.*

2. CONTRITION AND PURPOSE OF AMENDMENT

1. Peter deliberately denied his Lord and Master and thereby committed a grave sin. Jesus turned and looked on him, and this glance of love and mercy pierced his heart with the sharpness of a dagger. He went out and wept bitterly. Tears are a sign of pain. But Peter's pain was not a bodily pain, but a pain of the soul caused by the thought of his great sin. He detested his sin and was determined henceforth never to deny his Lord again. He had true *contrition* for his sin.

"Contrition is pain or grief of mind and detestation of sin committed, with the firm purpose of sinning no more" (Council of Trent).

Contrition is the most necessary part of our preparation for the reception of the Sacrament of Penance. Without contrition no sin is ever forgiven. Hence the act of contrition must be made *before* confession or at least before absolution is given.

2. Contrition Is an Act of the Will.—The penitent turns away from sin, detests it, regrets that he committed it, and is resolved to make satisfaction for it and to avoid it in future. Such an act of the will presupposes the *knowledge* that sin is an evil. Hence if we wish to become truly contrite we must think of the malice of sin and its dreadful consequences. An act of the intellect must precede the act of the will.

3. Our contrition, and therefore also our purpose of amendment, must be interior, universal, supreme, and supernatural.—

a) Our contrition is *interior* if we detest sin in our hearts as the greatest of all evils and sincerely wish we had never committed it. "Rend your hearts and not your garments," says the prophet (Joel 2,13). Sorrow that is expressed merely by the lips, or that exists only in the imagination, is no true sorrow at all.

Führich

THE RETURN OF THE PRODIGAL SON

b) Our contrition is *universal* if it covers all our mortal sins without exception. If we have only *venial sins* to confess, we must be truly sorry for at least one of them, otherwise our confession will be null and void. To guard against this it is well to be heartily sorry again for some more serious sin of our past life and to mention that sin in our confession.

c) Our contrition is *supreme* if we are resolved not to commit a mortal sin for the love or fear of anything whatsoever.

d) Our contrition is *supernatural* if it is produced by the grace of God and founded on motives which faith makes known to us, e.g., if we are sorry for our sins because by them we have offended God, lost Heaven, and deserved Hell. If we were sorry for our sins only because they brought disgrace or temporal loss of some kind upon us, our sorrow would be merely *natural* sorrow and of no avail for our salvation.

Supernatural contrition may be imperfect or perfect.—If we are sorry for our sins because we fear that God will punish us for them, our contrition is *imperfect* (attrition). It is imperfect because it is not born of the highest motive of love. "He that feareth is not perfected in love" (1 John 4,18). If, on the other hand, we are sorry because we have offended God, who is infinitely good and who is our greatest benefactor and most loving Father, our contrition is *perfect*. "Perfect love casteth out fear" (1 John 4,18).

The difference between imperfect and perfect contrition is beautifully expressed in the first and last verses of the hymn of St. Francis Xavier, *O Deus ego amo te*:

I love Thee, God;	Not for reward;
Yet not for hope of gain	But as Thou lovedst me,
Nor that I fear the pain	I love and shall love Thee,
Of Thy just rod.	My God, my Lord.

Perfect contrition at once blots out all mortal sins, even before we confess them,—just as the ten lepers were cured on their way to the priests. "He that loveth Me, shall be loved by My Father, and I will love him" (John 14,21).

Hence if we ever have the misfortune to fall into deliberate sin, we should make an act of perfect contrition immediately. Of course we are still bound to go to confession, in order to fulfill the ordinary law, and we should do so reasonably soon. When others are in danger of death, and no priest is present, we should help them to make acts of perfect contrition. "Perfect contrition is the key of Heaven."

We should always strive after perfect contrition for our sins. But who can say with certainty that his contrition is perfect? Therefore imperfect contrition must suffice for the reception of the Sacrament of Penance. "Imperfect contrition," says the Council of Trent, "though it cannot of itself, without the Sacrament of Penance, justify the sinner, yet disposes him to receive divine grace in the Sacrament of Penance."

4. Our contrition must be accompanied with a firm purpose of amendment.—We must resolve:

a) To avoid all sin, at least all mortal sins;

b) To shun the proximate occasion of sin and to use the means which are necessary for our amendment;

c) To perform our penance and to repair, as far as possible, any injury caused by our sin.

If we have only venial sins, we must firmly resolve to avoid them or at least to lessen their number.

By a *proximate occasion* of sin we mean anything that is likely to lead us into sin, such as bad companions, bad amusements, bad reading. "He that loveth danger shall perish in it" (Ecclus. 3,27).

If we are not resolved to avoid mortal sin or its proximate occasion we have no true contrition; we make a bad confession, and the absolution is of no use to us.

3. CONFESSION

a) *Necessity of Confession*

1. In order to obtain forgiveness of our sins we must confess them.—Christ said: "Whose sins you shall forgive, they are forgiven them, and whose sins you shall retain, they are retained." But how can the priest know whether he is to forgive our sins or to retain them, unless we lay open our conscience to him, unless we accuse ourselves of our sins? And unless we accuse ourselves of our sins, how can he impose a proper penance?

2. Confession has always been in use in the Church of God, and has been considered necessary for the forgiveness of sins.—

When St. Paul was at Ephesus, "many of them that believed came confessing and declaring their deeds" (Acts 19,18). St. John says: "If we confess our sins, He is faithful and just, so as to forgive us our sins" (1 John 1,9).

In the early Church public confession and public penance were demanded for very grave sins, such as idolatry, adultery, and murder. Absolution and readmittance to Holy Communion came at the end of the long and severe penance, and was given publicly by the bishop on Holy Thursday. Private absolution was given only on deathbeds. Pope Leo the Great (d. 461) changed public confession to private confession, although the system of public penance still went on.

Thus in the very earliest times all the essentials of the sacrament were present, but the satisfaction, or penance was emphasized more than now. We still call it the sacrament of *Penance* and not, as one might expect, the sacrament of *Absolution*.

The schismatic Churches of the East, although they separated from the Western Church in the fifth century, agree with her in the doctrine on confession,—a sufficient proof that the obligation of confessing our sins was not first imposed by Pope Innocent III in 1215, as some Protestants assert. Pope Innocent merely enforced the obligation of confessing *at least once a year.*

b) *Qualities of a Good Confession*

1. A good confession should be entire, sincere, and clear.—

a) Our confession must be *entire*, that is, we must confess all the mortal sins we remember, as well as their number, and those circumstances which change the nature of the sin.

We are not bound to confess venial sins; but it is profitable to do so. If we doubt whether a sin is mortal or venial, we are not strictly obliged to confess it.

The entirety of our confession is best guaranteed by a thorough **Examination of Conscience.** By this we mean a genuine attempt to find out in what we have offended God by sins of thought, word, deed, or omission since our last worthy confession. We should be *careful* in examining our conscience, but not *worried* or *scrupulous.* Scrupulosity is a disease of the soul which can be cured only by absolute obedience to the confessor.

If we purposely conceal a mortal sin in confession, we make a bad confession and commit a new mortal sin. Those who are tempted to conceal any sin through false shame, should remember that the confessor is bound by the *seal of confession* never to reveal the least thing heard in confession or to make any use whatever of such knowledge. Even persons who should happen to overhear something that is told in confession, are strictly bound to keep the secret to themselves. Since the priest is obliged under pain of mortal sin by the seal of confession, the penitent, too, should keep silence about what is said in confession.

If *without our fault* we omitted something we were obliged to confess, we have only to mention it in our next confession; but if we were seriously to blame for omitting it, we must mention not only the matter we omitted, but also the number of confessions in which we omitted it, and we must repeat all those confessions.

b) Our confession is *sincere* if we tell our sins as to God, without coloring or excuse. A lie in confession is doubly sinful, but it makes the confession invalid only if it concerns an important matter. In making known the circumstances of our sins we should never mention other people's names.

c) Our confession is *clear* if we distinctly name and specify our sins. The confessor cannot be our judge, physician and friend unless he knows the state of our conscience. Sins of impurity should be told clearly, but as briefly and modestly as possible.

2. A General Confession is one in which we repeat all or several confessions of our past life. A general confession is *necessary* whenever we have made one or more bad confessions. It is *advisable*

a) Before we enter upon a new state of life.

b) During a retreat, a jubilee, or a mission.

c) As a preparation for death.

4. SATISFACTION

1. Satisfaction (also called penance) is the performance of certain penitential works imposed by the confessor on the penitent.

The confessor imposes a penance partly as a *remedy* against relapse and a means of amendment, but chiefly as a *punishment* for sin.

2. When God remits sin, He always remits the *eternal* punishment due to sin, but He does not always remit the entire *temporal* punishment, that is, the punishment which we have to undergo either here on earth or in Purgatory. This is evident from Holy Scripture: "Nathan said to David: The Lord hath taken away thy sin; nevertheless, because thou hast given occasion to the enemies of the Lord to blaspheme, the child that is born of thee shall surely die" (2 Kings 12,13-14).

At Baptism God remits both the eternal and all the temporal punishment due to sin; but the Church always imposed penances on those who sinned grievously after Baptism. It is in accordance with the justice of God that a Christian who sins mortally should be more severely punished than one who is not baptized. Besides, it is Christ's will that as we are to share in His glory, we must first share in His sufferings for our sins.

The so-called Reformers of the sixteenth century maintained that Christ by taking away our sins also took away all punishment due to them. But Calvin himself had to admit that his teaching was opposed to the teaching of the Fathers of the Church on this point.

3. If we do not perform our penance, our confession is not bad, provided before receiving absolution we really intended to perform it; but we commit a sin and lose many graces. To omit a light penance imposed for venial sins only, would be a venial sin; to omit a serious penance imposed for a mortal sin would be a mortal sin.

4. The little sacramental penance given us by the confessor represents the heavy penances that we deserve and that would perhaps have been imposed upon us in the early times of Christianity; we should therefore perform it with special care and devotion, and, if possible, before we leave the church. It has a special value because it is part of the Sacrament of Penance. We should add to it of our own free will by self-denial and good works. The Church, like a good mother, helps us to shorten our sufferings in Purgatory by opening to us her treasure house of *indulgences*.

5. INDULGENCES

After the worthy reception of the Sacrament of Penance some punishment may still be due for our sins. We can discharge this debt in various ways: by performing works of mercy, by assisting at Mass, by receiving Holy Communion, and especially by gaining indulgences.

1. *An indulgence is a remission, in whole or in part, of the temporal punishment due to sin granted by the Church outside the Sacrament of Penance after sin itself has been forgiven.*

In order to understand the teaching and practice of the Church in regard to indulgences it will be necessary to glance at their **origin and development.** "Many err," says St. Jerome, "because of their ignorance of history." This is especially true of indulgences.

a) The power of binding and loosing given by Christ to His Church includes the power of excluding the sinner from receiving Holy Communion and of readmitting him to it, of imposing penances and of mitigating them or remitting them altogether.

b) In the early ages the Church imposed very severe penances on those guilty of grave offenses, and absolved them only after they had performed their penances. She wanted to remit not only the sins of the penitent but also *all* the punishment, eternal and temporal, due to them. For this reason the Sacrament of Penance was called in those days "a second baptism."

c) In the second and third centuries it happened that Christians who were in prison awaiting martyrdom sent "letters of peace" (*libelli pacis*) to the bishop in favor of some brother under penance for apostasy, and the bishop, if satisfied with the sinner's contrition, restored him to the peace of the Church.

d) In the fourth century and later we hear of Councils mitigating penances that seemed too long and severe. Thus the Council of Ancyra (314) reduced life-penances in certain cases to ten years.

These mitigations were not indulgences in the full sense of the word, for there was not question of a remission of punishment due to sin granted *outside the Sacrament of Penance*, but of prescriptions concerning the imposition of penances *in the Sacrament of Penance*.

e) The so-called *Redemptions*, that is, the substitution of other good works, especially prayers and alms, for the severe canonical penances, correspond more nearly to the later indulgences. In the early Middle Ages every priest who heard confessions used a *Penitential*, or *Penance Book*, which contained precise directions in regard to the penances to be imposed for the various sins. "Whosoever shall have partaken of food or drink near the temples of the false gods," we read in the Penitential ascribed to St. Columban, "if he did so merely for the sake of the good cheer, shall promise never to do so again, and fast forty days on bread and water. If he did not restrain his gluttony even after he had been warned by his parish priest that he was committing a sacrilege, he shall fast three times forty days (three quarantines). But if his act was one of formal demon or image worship, he shall fast for three years."

Under the influence of the Teutonic *wergild* law, according to which a person could procure exemption from corporal punishment for crime by paying a certain sum of money, the custom arose of procuring exemption from canonical penalties by giving money for charity or by performing other good works. Some Penance Books contained a regular tariff of public and private penances. Thus the recitation of fifty Psalms on twelve successive days was regarded as the equivalent of one year's canonical penance; the feeding of a poor person, the equivalent of a day's fasting on bread and water, etc. We may notice here the origin of the terminology still in use, when indulgences are granted for forty days, three years, seven years, etc.*

*The new *Enchiridion on Indulgences* issued in 1968 specifies that indulgences are now designated only as *partial* and *plenary* (complete), with no designation of a specific amount of time attached for partial indulgences. —*Editor, 1990.*

These *redemptions* were not *indulgences*; because they were not *remissions* but only *commutations* of the canonical penances.

In the course of time *redemptions* became more and more frequent. The penitent was at liberty either to perform the prescribed canonical penance or to have it changed by his confessor into a lighter one. From this practice to the granting of indulgences in the strict sense of the word was but a short step. *Practically* there is no difference between a redemption and an indulgence; in the case of a redemption a lesser penance is substituted for a greater one; in the case of an indulgence the performance of some good work is made the condition for a full or partial remission of the penance.

The famous plenary indulgence given by Pope Urban II at the Council of Clermont (1095) to the first Crusaders was in the form of a redemption: "To every one who marches to Jerusalem, not to seek glory and gold, but to fight for the freedom of the Church, this journey shall be accounted as equivalent to his whole penance—*iter illud pro omni poenitentia reputetur.*" In the following year the Pope published this *redemption* in the form of a real *plenary indulgence*: "To those who have undertaken the journey to Jerusalem for the salvation of their souls and the liberty of the Church we have, through the mercy of God and the intercession of the universal Church, *remitted the whole penance for their sins which they have rightly and fully confessed,* because they have risked their property and their lives for the love of God and their neighbor."

f) After the *Crusades* indulgences were more and more freely given. They were granted for pilgrimages to Jerusalem, Rome, and Compostella (Spain); on the occasion of the consecration of churches and the canonization of saints; for contributions towards the building of churches, hospitals, and bridges; they were attached to objects of devotion, such as the crucifix and the rosary, and the recitation of certain prayers; in time there was scarcely a devotion or good work of any kind for which they could not be obtained.

g) The idea that *almsgiving* is a powerful means of obtaining remission of the temporal punishment due to sin is *thoroughly Scriptural.* "Redeem thy sins with alms, and thy iniquities with works of mercy" (Dan. 4,24: see also Tob. 4,11, and Ecclus.

3,33). Still the custom of making almsgiving a condition for gaining an indulgence led in time to very grave abuses. Indulgences became a regular system of raising money for pious purposes. The Council of Trent passed strict laws against these abuses, but at the same time declared that Christ gave to His Church the power to grant indulgences, that their use was salutary for the faithful, and that the practice of granting them was to be continued.

2. When the Church grants an indulgence, she herself pays our debt of punishment to God.—She does this by drawing on the merits of Christ and the satisfaction of the Saints, especially of the Blessed Virgin. These merits and satisfactions are a boundless source of spiritual riches—the *spiritual treasury of the Church*—which the Church administers for the welfare of the faithful. Hence by an indulgence the temporal punishment due to our sins is not merely *canceled*, but real *satisfaction* is offered to God for it; God accepts from the hand of the Church the satisfaction made by Christ and the saints as if it had been made by us, on the principle that one member of the Church can perform penance instead of another—a consequence of the doctrine of the *Communion of Saints*.

3. Since the Church has no direct power over the departed, **indulgences can be applied to the souls in Purgatory** only "by way of intercession"; in other words, with the express sanction of the Church we offer certain indulgences to God for some particular soul or for all the souls in Purgatory, and leave it to the divine mercy and wisdom to remit the whole or a portion of the pains still due to their sins. We can never say with certainty that a particular soul to whom we apply a plenary indulgence is thereby freed from Purgatory. All that we know is that indulgences do profit the souls in Purgatory; the contrary opinion has been condemned by the Church.

4. There are two kinds of indulgences.—(a) *plenary,* through which all temporal punishment is remitted; (b) *partial,* through which a part only of this punishment is remitted. In granting partial indulgences the Church still uses, as we saw above, the terminology of the *Penance Books* and the *Redemptions*.

5. To gain an indulgence we must (a) comply with the conditions laid down, (b) be in the state of grace, at least before performing the last of the works prescribed, and (c) have at least a general intention of gaining the indulgence. We cannot gain an indulgence for another living person.

6. One in venial sin can gain a partial indulgence. To gain a plenary indulgence we must be free from venial sin and all affection for it. For the gaining of plenary indulgences Confession, Communion and prayers for the intentions of the Pope are as a rule required. The intentions of the Pope always include the exaltation of the Church, the spread of the faith, the uprooting of heresies, the conversion of sinners, and peace and harmony among Christian nations.

Those who are accustomed to confess twice a month are exempted from the prescribed Confession; daily communicants have the same privilege. This exemption does not, however, hold for jubilee indulgences, granted by the Pope every twenty-five years.

7. An indulgence attached to an object of devotion ceases only when the object is sold or destroyed. When a visit to a church must be made on a certain day in order to gain an indulgence, the visit may be made at any time from noon of the preceding day to midnight of the day itself.

8. Indulgences when properly used are a powerful means of sanctifying the soul: they promote the spirit of penance, the reception of the sacraments, and the performance of good works. They also furnish us an easy method of assisting the souls in Purgatory.

9. The *penance* given to us in Confession, the penalty of *excommunication* with which certain offenses are visited, and the *public reparation* still sometimes required for public sins—these are the only survivals of the penitential system of the early ages of the Church. "The Church now substitutes indulgences for penances almost universally, because indulgences depend entirely on our inward disposition for their effect, and internal sorrow is much more important than external penances."

10. To sum up.—An indulgence is not a remission of sin, past, present, or to come, but only a remission of some portion of the temporal punishment due to sin, after the sin itself has been forgiven. When the phrase "indulgence for the remission of all sins" occurs in the grant of an indulgence—and it does occur occasionally—it is clear from the context that the word sin is used in the wider sense for punishment.

The expression: "Indulgence (absolution, or remission) from guilt and punishment" is also met with, but only in the so-called "indulgence or confession letters." The person to whom such a letter was issued received thereby the right to choose any approved priest for his confessor, and this confessor was empowered by the Holy Father *to absolve him sacramentally* even from cases ordinarily reserved to the bishop or the Pope, and also to grant him a plenary indulgence once during his life and again at the hour of death; hence the phrase: "from guilt *and* punishment"; the guilt was remitted through the Sacrament of Penance, the punishment, by the plenary indulgence.

SUGGESTIONS FOR STUDY AND REVIEW

1. Write a short paper on the *Institution of the Sacrament of Penance.*
   I. Promise of the power to forgive sins. Matt. 16,18; 18,18.
   II. Fulfillment of the promise. John 20,21-23:
   1) The evening of the first Easter Sunday. The disciples in the Upper Room in Jerusalem.
   2) Jesus appears to them. "Peace be to you."
   3) He shows them His Sacred Wounds.
   4) He breathes upon them. "Receive ye the Holy Ghost." Gives them the power to forgive or to retain the sins of men.
2. What constitutes the Sacrament of Penance
   1) On the part of the penitent?
   2) On the part of the Priest?
3. Is the Sacrament of Penance *absolutely* necessary for salvation?
4. What are the effects of the worthy reception of the Sacrament of Penance?
   What does God *forgive*? What does He *give*?
5. Show from the Parable of the Prodigal Son what are the *essential parts* of the Sacrament of Penance.
6. How is the Sacrament of Penance administered?
   1) *Place of administration:* Ordinarily in a confessional.
   2) *Minister:* A Bishop or a Priest with ordinary or delegated jurisdiction. The Priest wears a surplice and a purple stole, or (usually) a stole alone. The stole signifies authority; the purple color, penance.
   3) *The Penitent:* After having invoked the Holy Ghost and carefully examined his conscience, enters the confessional, kneels down, and asks the blessing of the confessor: "Bless me, Father, for I have sinned."
   4) *Priest:* Makes the Sign of the Cross over the penitent, saying: "The Lord be in thy heart and on thy lips so that thou mayest worthily confess thy sins."
   5) *Penitent:* Says: "I confess to Almighty God and to you, Father, that I have sinned." He then states how long ago his last confession was, and whether he then received absolution and performed his penance. He then accuses himself of his sins as clearly and briefly as possible. He is *bound* to confess all his mortal sins

together with the circumstances that aggravated them or changed their nature; it is well also for him to confess his venial sins, and to mention some sin of his past life for which he is especially sorry.

6) *Priest:* If necessary he asks some questions, gives a short instruction, and imposes a *penance,* i.e., certain prayers to be said or good works to be done after confession.

7) *Penitent:* Says the Act of Contrition.

8) *Priest:* While the penitent says the Act of Contrition, the Priest recites the *Misereatur:* "May Almighty God have mercy upon thee, and forgive thee thy sins, and bring thee unto life everlasting. Amen." And the *Indulgentiam:* "May the Almighty and merciful Lord grant thee pardon, absolution and remission of thy sins. Amen." He then pronounces

   a) *The absolution from censures,* i.e., ecclesiastical penalties which the penitent may have incurred: "May our Lord Jesus Christ absolve thee; and I, by His authority, absolve thee from every bond of excommunication and interdict, inasmuch as in my power lieth and thou standest in need of."

   b) *The absolution from sins:* "Finally, I absolve thee from thy sins, in the name of the Father, and of the Son, and of the Holy Ghost. Amen."

   c) *A prayer for the penitent:* "May the Passion of our Lord Jesus Christ, the merits of the Blessed Virgin Mary and of all the Saints, whatsoever thou shalt have done of good and borne of evil, be unto thee for remission of sins, increase of grace, and reward of life everlasting. Amen."

   He then dismisses the penitent with the following words: "Go in peace, and God bless you," or "Praised be Jesus Christ."

9) *Penitent:* Retires to his place in church, thanks God for the graces of the Sacrament, performs his penance, and renews his purpose of amendment. If he has to make *reparation* or *restitution,* he will do so as soon as possible.

7. Why should we go to confession frequently even though we may have to confess only venial sins or mortal sins already forgiven? What effect has frequent confession had on your own spiritual life? Has it promoted self-knowledge? Has it increased conscientiousness? (We must remember that the Sacrament of Penance has been given to us not only for the forgiveness of sins but also for the amendment of our life. Its purpose is also to promote progress in virtue and by its graces to help us in our striving after Christian perfection.)

8. Reflect on the best means to amend our lives. Here are some of them:

   1) We must not limit our examination of conscience to the detection of our sins, but also of the *state of our souls.* We should ask ourselves, Which is my "ruling passion," that is, the evil inclination which is the source of most of my sins and failings and defects? Is it selfishness, vanity, sloth, sensuality, dishonesty, anger? Then we should ask, What am I going to do about it? What means am

I going to use to overcome my evil inclinations? Have I tried to overcome selfishness by acts of charity, etc.?

2) We must examine our conscience not only before going to confession, but every day, preferably in the evening before retiring.

3) We must endeavor always to live in the presence of God, and have the thought of Christ present in our mind, especially when we are attacked by temptation, or when we are necessarily exposed to the danger of sinning.

4) We must meditate frequently on the Last Things, on the Love of God, on the Passion and Death of Christ, on the virtues of the Mother of God and the Saints.

5) From time to time we should make a good retreat, not only during the school years, but also in after life. Opportunities are offered for men and women.

6) We should form the habit of reading spiritual books.

9. Show that Confession is not degrading and unmanly, nor an incentive to sin by making forgiveness easy.

10. Explain briefly: *Jurisdiction, Reserved Cases, Special Faculties, Scrupulosity, Sin against the Holy Ghost, Perfect Contrition, Imperfect Contrition, Proximate Occasion of Sin, Seal of Confession, General Confession, Auricular Confession, Annual Confession.*

11. *Reading:* John L. Stoddard, *Rebuilding a Lost Faith,* pp. 165-174, "The Sacrament of Penance."

APPENDIX : INDULGENCES

1. Explain briefly, in your own words, the Catholic Doctrine on Indulgences:

1) What an Indulgence is not.

2) What is an Indulgence?

3) Quote the Scripture text authorizing the granting of Indulgences. Matt. 18,18-19.

4) Give an instance of an Indulgence granted by an Apostle. 2 Cor. 2,10.

5) What is the "Spiritual Treasury of the Church"? Can one member of the Church perform penance instead of another? On what doctrine is this power founded?

6) What does the Church do when she grants an Indulgence? Does she merely *cancel* the temporal punishment due to sin?

7) What is necessary to gain an Indulgence?

8) Who can grant an Indulgence?

9) For whom can we gain an Indulgence? How far do Indulgences benefit the Souls in Purgatory?

10) How many kinds of Indulgences are there?

11) What is meant by the "Pope's intentions"?

12) What is meant by a "Jubilee Indulgence"? A *Toties Quoties* Indulgence?

13) Why are Indulgences open to abuse? Can an Indulgence be bought?

14) What were the so-called· "Indulgence or Confession Letters"?

15) What does the expression: "Indulgence for the remission of all sins" mean?

16) What is meant by "An Indulgence of seven years and seven quarantines"?

17) Mention some advantages of Indulgences.

2. Read carefully the following statement of the Council of Trent on Indulgences:

"Whereas the power of conferring Indulgences was granted by Christ to the Church, and she has even in the most ancient days used the said power delivered unto her by God, the sacred holy Synod teaches and enjoins that the use of Indulgences, for the Christian people most salutary and approved of by the authority of sacred Councils, is to be retained in the Church; and it condemns with anathema those who either assert that they are useless, or who deny that there is in the Church the power to grant them" (SESS. XXV).

What two things are we bound to believe according to this decree?

3. Prepare a floor-talk on the *Communion of Saints,* using this outline:

I. *Explanation of terms: Communion* means fellowship, close union with others, mutual sharing in spiritual riches. *Saints,* not only those members of the Church who are in heaven, but all children of God, all who are in a state of grace.

II. *What is meant by the ninth article of the Creed: I believe in the Catholic Church, the Communion of Saints?* Between the members of the Church—in Heaven, in Purgatory, and on earth—there exists, by reason of their intimate union with one another under Christ their Head, a mutual communication in spiritual riches. The Church is the *Mystical Body of Christ.* Christ is the Head; the faithful, whether still striving after eternal happiness in Heaven, or suffering to cleanse the remains of sin in Purgatory, or already enjoying the Beatific Vision in Heaven, are the living members of this Body. Therefore, there must necessarily exist an intimate union with one another and with Christ their common Head.

III. *The Spiritual Goods:* (a) the infinite merits of Jesus Christ; (b) the super-abundant merits of the Blessed Virgin and the Saints; (c) Indulgences, Prayers, good works of the faithful; (d) the Sacraments and the Holy Sacrifice; (e) Public Prayers and External Rites. (The Spiritual Treasury of the Church.)

IV. *These Goods are exchanged:* (a) between the Saints in heaven and the faithful on earth; (b) between the faithful on earth and the Souls in Purgatory; (c) by the faithful amongst themselves.

V. *Excluded from the exchange are:* Infidels, Heretics, Schismatics, Apostates, Excommunicates.

VI. *Those in mortal sin are not wholly excluded,* because they can be helped to recover the grace of God by the public prayers of the Church and the petitions and good works of those in a state of grace.

N.B. The following texts bear on the Communion of Saints: Acts 2,28;12,5; 2 Thess. 3,1; Phil. 1,2-11; 1 Cor. 2,10; 2 Cor. 2,10; Titus 3,10; Gal. 1,9.

4. Readings:

a) *Question Box,* pp. 293-299, "On Indulgences."

b) Stoddard, *Rebuilding a Lost Faith,* pp. 157-164, "Indulgences."

CHAPTER VI

Extreme Unction*

1. Extreme Unction is a sacrament instituted by Christ for the benefit of those who are suffering from a sickness which is liable to end with death.

It is called extreme unction because it is usually the last of the anointings administered by the Church.

2. That the Sacrament of Extreme Unction was instituted by Christ is clearly seen from the words of the Apostle St. James: "Is any one sick among you? Let him call in the priests of the Church, and let them pray over him, anointing him with oil *in the name of the Lord*. And the prayer of faith will save the sick man, and the Lord shall raise him up, and *if he have committed sins, he shall be forgiven*" (James 5,14-15).

The Apostle tells us that the anointing with oil and the prayer of the priest produce grace, viz., remission of sin. But sin could not be forgiven by the anointing with oil and by the prayer of the priest unless Christ had willed it so. Hence Christ Himself must have given this power to the anointing and the prayer, that is, He must have instituted the Sacrament of Extreme Unction. The divine institution is also indicated by the words: "In the name of the Lord": the priests anoint the sick in the name, that is, by the authority of the Lord.

The early Fathers seldom speak of Extreme Unction, because there was no public solemnity connected with its administration. Origen calls it a sacrament, and St. John Chrysostom says that priests forgive sins by Baptism and by anointing the sick.

3. The remote matter of the sacrament of Extreme Unction is *olive oil* blessed by the bishop. The **proximate matter** is the anointing of the sick person by the priest. The **form** consists of the words accompanying the anointing: "By this holy unction and His most tender mercy, may the Lord pardon thee whatever sins thou hast committed by thy sight, by thy hearing, etc."**

The senses are anointed separately, because through them sin

*Currently, this Sacrament is often referred to as "Anointing of the Sick." —*Editor*, 1990.
**This is the traditional form for this Sacrament. —*Editor*, 1990.

obtained entrance into the soul. In case of necessity one anoint-ing, preferably on the forehead, suffices.

4. Any Catholic who has been baptized and has attained the use of reason may and should receive this sacrament when dangerously ill.—It should be received, if possible, *before consciousness is lost,* in fact, just as soon as the sickness begins to be dangerous, for only then have we reason to hope that its full effects will be realized.

5. The effects of Extreme Unction are the following:

a) It blots out all sins, even mortal sins, provided the sick person is sorry for them and is no longer able to confess them;

b) It increases (or confers) sanctifying grace;

c) It completes the purification of the soul by destroying the *remains of sin* already forgiven. By remains of sin we mean the fear of death, the temporal punishment due to sin, and the inclination of the heart to evil. These are the consequences of sin, and generally *remain* even after the sins have been forgiven.

d) It confers a *special grace* upon the dying Christian, which strengthens him to bear suffering and temptation with fortitude, especially during the last agony;

e) It often brings relief to the body, and even causes complete recovery, if this be for the good of the soul.

6. People sometimes dread to be anointed because they believe this to be a sure sign of death, cutting off all hope of recovery. Such dread is both foolish and dangerous. Those in charge of the sick commit a sin if through their fault the sick do not receive the last sacraments in due time. They must also see that the sick-room is properly prepared. The following things ought to be at hand:

a) A table covered with a clean white cloth; on it a crucifix and two blessed candles;

b) A plate with six little balls of cotton and some bread or salt;

c) A clean towel;

d) A bottle with holy water and a glass of drinking water.

7. Extreme Unction may be received once in every case of dangerous sickness; but it may be received again in the same sickness if the danger passes and then returns, as often happens when persons suffer from heart disease, typhoid fever, or with consumption. Soldiers before battle and criminals before execution cannot receive Extreme Unction.

THE HAPPIEST DEATH

8. The Church's solicitude for her dying children does not end with the administration of Extreme Unction.—Our soul is not only cleansed from sin by the last Sacraments, but an *Apostolic Benediction* is bestowed upon us, and through it a *plenary indulgence.*

The imparting of the papal blessing with the indulgence attached thereto is no longer a privilege given to a few but a general right enjoyed by all priests who happen to attend the sick and dying. To gain the indulgence it is necessary that the sick person invoke the name of Jesus, either orally, if he can, or at least mentally.

In order to make sure of the inestimable blessing of a happy death, we should form the habit of praying for it every day. The following beautiful prayer was composed by Cardinal Newman:

"Oh, my Lord and Saviour, support me in that hour in the strong arms of Thy Sacraments, and by the fresh fragrance of Thy consolations. Let the absolving words be said over me, and the holy oil sign and seal me, and Thy own Body be my food, and Thy Blood my sprinkling; and let my sweet Mother, Mary, breathe on me, and my Angel whisper peace to me, and my glorious Saints . . . smile upon me; that in them all, and through them all, I may receive the gift of perseverance, and die, as I desire to live, in Thy faith, in Thy Church, in Thy service, and in Thy Love. Amen."

SUGGESTIONS FOR STUDY AND REVIEW

1. Manner of Administering the Sacrament of Extreme Unction:

On arriving at the place where the sick person lies, the Priest, with the holy Oil of the Sick, entering the room, says:
Peace be unto this house.
Resp. And unto all who dwell therein.
Then, after placing the Oil on a table, and putting on a surplice and purple stole, he offers the sick person a crucifix piously to kiss; after which he sprinkles both the room and the bystanders with Holy Water in the form of a Cross, saying:
Thou shalt sprinkle me, O Lord, with hyssop, and I shall be cleansed: Thou shalt wash me, and I shall be made whiter than snow.
Have mercy upon me, O God, according to Thy great mercy.
Glory be to the Father, etc.
Our help is in the name of the Lord. *R.* Who hath made heaven and earth.
V. The Lord be with you.
R. And with thy spirit.

Let us pray

May there enter, O Lord Jesus Christ, into this house, at the entrance of our lowliness, everlasting happiness, heaven-sent prosperity, peaceful gladness, fruitful charity, abiding health: may the devils fear to approach this place, may the Angels of peace be present therein, and may all wicked strife depart from this house. Magnify, O Lord, upon us Thy holy name, and bless our ministry: hallow the entrance of our lowliness, Thou who art holy and compassionate, and abidest with the Father and the Holy Ghost, world without end. Amen.

Let us pray and beseech our Lord Jesus Christ, that blessing He may bless this abode, and all who dwell therein, and give unto them a good Angel for their keeper, and make them serve Him, so as to behold wondrous things out of His law. May He ward off from them all adverse powers: may he deliver them from all fear and from all disquiet, and vouchsafe to keep in health them that dwell in this house. Who, with the Father and the Holy Ghost, liveth and reigneth God, world without end. Amen.

Let us pray

Hear us, O Holy Lord, Father Almighty, Everlasting God, and vouchsafe to send Thy holy Angel from Heaven, to guard, cherish, protect, visit, and defend all those that dwell in this house. Through Christ our Lord. Amen.

Then the Confiteor, with the general absolution, is said. (Before the Priest begins to anoint the sick person, he admonishes those present to pray for him.) After the Indulgentiam the Priest says:

In the name of the Father, and of the Son, and of the Holy Ghost, may all the power of the devil be extinguished in thee, by the laying on of our hands, and by the invocation of all holy Angels, Archangels, Patriarchs, Prophets, Apostles, Martyrs, Confessors, Virgins, and of the whole company of the Saints. Amen.

Then, dipping his thumb in the holy Oil, he anoints the sick person, in the form of a Cross, on the eyes, ears, nostrils, lips, hands, and feet, using the following form, the last word of which is changed according to the part anointed:

Through this holy unction and of His most tender mercy, may the Lord pardon thee whatsoever sins thou hast committed by sight, hearing, smell, taste and speech, touch, thy footsteps. Amen.

After the anointing, the Priest says:

Lord, have mercy. Christ, have mercy. Lord, have mercy.

Our Father (*inaudibly*).

And lead us not into temptation.

R. But deliver us from evil.

V. Save Thy servant, O Lord.

R. O my God, who putteth *his* trust in Thee.

V. **Send** him help, O Lord, from Thy holy place.

R. And defend him out of Sion.

V. Be unto him, O Lord, a tower of strength.

R. From the face of the enemy.

V. Let not the enemy prevail against him.

R. Nor the son of iniquity draw nigh to hurt him.

V. O Lord, hear my prayer.

R. And let my cry come unto Thee.

V. The Lord be with you.

R. And with thy spirit.

Let us pray

Lord God, who hast spoken by Thy Apostle James, saying: Is any man sick among you? Let him call in the priests of the Church, and let them pray over him, anointing him with oil in the name of the Lord: and the prayer of faith shall save the sick man, and the Lord will raise him up; and if he be in sins, they shall be forgiven him: cure, we beseech Thee, O our Redeemer, by the grace of the Holy Ghost, the ailments of this sick *man*; heal *his* wounds, and forgive his sins; drive out from him all pains of body and mind, and mercifully restore to him full health, both inwardly and outwardly : that, having recovered by the help of Thy loving kindness, he may be enabled to return to his former duties. Who, with the Father, etc.

Let us pray

Look down, O Lord, we beseech Thee, upon Thy servant, N., languishing through bodily ailment, and refresh the soul which Thou hast created, that, being bettered by chastisements, he may feel himself saved by Thy healing. Through Christ our Lord. Amen.

Let us pray

O Holy Lord, Father Almighty, Eternal God, who, by shedding Thy gracious blessing upon our failing bodies, dost preserve, by Thy manifold goodness, the work of Thy hands : graciously draw near at the invocation of Thy name, that, having freed Thy servant from sickness, and bestowed health upon him, Thou mayest raise him up by Thy right hand, strengthen him by Thy might, defend him by Thy power, and restore him to Thy holy Church, with all the prosperity he desires. Through Christ our Lord. Amen.

---

2. From the words of St. James (5,14-15) deduce the teaching of the Church on the Sacrament of Extreme Unction :
1) The Outward Sign.
2) The Institution by Christ.
3) The Minister.
4) The Recipient.
5) The effects of the Sacrament on the soul and the body.

3. What Sacraments are usually given before Extreme Unction? Why? What special name is given to one of them?

4. How should the sick room be prepared for the administration of the Last Sacraments (Rites) of the Church?

5. What does the following invocation in the Litany of the Saints mean: "From sudden and *unprovided* death, O Lord, deliver us"?

6. What is meant by the Apostolic Benediction? Why is the Indulgence attached to it called an Indulgence *in articulo mortis*: at the moment of death?

7. How is the Apostolic Blessing given?

The introductory prayers and ceremonies are the same as for the administration of Extreme Unction. The Priest then briefly instructs the sick person on the benefits of this Last Blessing, and exhorts him to bear his sufferings patiently as an expiation for the sins of the past; to offer himself wholly to God, prepared to accept cheerfully whatever may be His holy will; to beg forgiveness of those whom he has at any time offended in word or deed, and to forgive all those who have injured him. Then he bids him pronounce the Holy Name of Jesus, to repeat the ejaculation, My Jesus, mercy! to have great confidence in God, and to be assured that he will attain, through the riches of His exceeding bounty, a remission of temporal punishment, and the reward of everlasting life. The Priest then says:

Our help is in the name of the Lord, etc.

Let us pray

O most gracious Father of mercies and God of all comfort, who wouldest not that any should perish who believeth and trusteth in Thee; according to the multitude of Thy tender mercies, look favorably upon Thy servant, N., whom the true faith and hope of Christ do commend unto Thee. Visit him in Thy saving power; and through the Passion and Death of Thine Only-begotten, graciously grant him pardon and remission of all his sins; that his soul at the hour of its departure may find Thee a most merciful Judge; and, cleansed from every stain in the Blood of the same, Thy Son, may be found worthy to pass to life everlasting. Through the same Christ our Lord. Amen.

After the Confiteor, the Misereatur, etc., the Priest says:

May our Lord Jesus Christ, Son of the Living God, who gave to His blessed Apostle Peter the power of binding and loosing, of His most tender mercy receive thy confession, and restore unto thee that first robe which thou didst receive in Baptism; and I, by the power committed to me by the Apostolic See, grant thee a Plenary Indulgence and remission of all thy sins. In the name of the Father, and of the Son, and of the Holy Ghost. Amen.

Through the most sacred mysteries of man's redemption may God Almighty remit unto thee the pains of the present and the future life, open to thee the gates of Paradise, and bring thee to everlasting joys. Amen.

May God Almighty bless thee: the Father, the Son, and the Holy Ghost. Amen.

8. What must we do to insure a happy death hour? Who is the Patron of a happy death? Do you belong to a Confraternity whose purpose is to obtain a happy death for its members? (*Bona Mors* Confraternity.)

Reading:

Edwin G. Kaiser, C.PP.S., *Our Spiritual Service to the Sick and Dying* (Benziger).

Richard E. Power, *God's Healing* (Liturgical Press, Collegeville, Minn).

CHAPTER VII

Holy Orders

1. The Priesthood Established.—In the earliest age of human history sacrifice was offered to God by man individually, as we see from the story of Cain and Abel. Later on it was offered by the head of the family or tribe. Finally as the tribes grew into nations and states the public worship of God and the offering of sacrifices was entrusted to a separate class of men— the *Priesthood.*

The priesthood instituted by God Himself for His Chosen People was hereditary and was restricted to the house of Aaron, the rest of the tribe of Levi being the assistants of the priests. At the head of the priesthood stood the High Priest, the first-born of the family of Aaron. He alone could enter the Holy of Holies on the Day of Atonement and offer sacrifice for the sins of the whole nation.

The priesthood of the Old Law, like the sacrifices of the Old Law, was fulfilled in Jesus Christ. He is our true High Priest, who on the Cross offered the only sacrifice worthy of God and thereby secured for us "everlasting redemption."

But since Christ desired His sacrifice on the Cross to be offered up on earth till the end of time, He had to make men sharers in His own high-priestly power—He had to institute a *Christian Priesthood.* This He did when at the Last Supper He gave His Apostles the power and the command to change bread and wine into His Body and Blood and thus to renew the Sacrifice of Calvary: "Do this in remembrance of Me."

2. The Priesthood Handed On.—The Apostles are dead. Did the priesthood cease with them? No more than the Church ceased with their death. The Apostles handed on to others the powers they had received from their Divine Master. They ordained assistants and successors for themselves.

The first ordination took place in Jerusalem; it was that of the seven *Deacons,* or ministers. "And they chose Stephen, a man full of faith and of the Holy Ghost, and Philip, and Prochorus, and Nicanor, and Timon, and Parmenas, and Nicolas, a proselyte

Marillier

THE ANOINTING OF AARON

of Antioch. These they set before the Apostles: and they praying, imposed hands upon them" (Acts 6,5-6).

On the eve of their departure on their first missionary journey Paul and Barnabas were consecrated bishops at Antioch: "Fasting and *praying and imposing their hands upon them,* they sent them away" (Acts 12,3). Paul and Barnabas, in their turn, ordained priests to take their place in the Christian communities which they had founded: "And when they had ordained priests in every church, and had prayed with fasting, they commended them to the Lord" (Acts 14,23).

The Sacrament of Holy Orders.—That *interior grace* was conferred by the imposition of the hands of the Apostles, is clear from the words of St. Paul to Timothy: "I admonish thee, that thou stir up the *grace of God* which is in thee by the *imposition* *of my hands"* (2 Tim. 1,6). But Christ alone could have joined this interior grace to the outward sign of the imposition of hands. Hence the imposition of hands with the accompanying prayer was a true sacramental act. The Apostles administered a sacrament—the *Sacrament of Holy Orders.*

3. *Holy Orders is a sacrament which makes those who receive it share in the priesthood of Christ, and gives them the power and grace to discharge their duties validly and worthily.*

It is called the sacrament of Order, because by it order and organization are established in the Church. "Order is the disposition of things superior and inferior, which are so arranged that each is in its proper position to the other. Since then in the ecclesiastical ministry there are many grades and various functions, all of which are definitely distributed and arranged, it is rightly and fitly called Order" (Catechism of the Council of Trent).

The Ministry of the Church Is Divided into Eight Degrees, or Orders:*

a) Four Minor Orders: Door-keepers, Lectors, Exorcists, and Acolytes;

b) Three Major or higher Orders: Subdeacons, Deacons, and Priests;

c) Bishops.

The four Minor Orders and the subdiaconate were instituted by the Church and are therefore not included in the Sacrament of Holy Orders. But since subdeacons are bound to observe celibacy and to say the Breviary, they have been numbered among the major orders since the twelfth century. Bishops have the full powers of the priesthood, whereas priests share only some of these powers. Deacons, as their name implies, are the assistants of the bishops and priests.

Bishops, priests, and deacons constitute what is known as the **Hierarchy of the Church.** This hierarchy is of divine origin. "If any one shall say that in the Catholic Church there is not a hierarchy instituted by divine ordination, which consists of bishops, priests, and deacons, let him be anathema" (Council of Trent).

The *tonsure,* which every candidate for Minor Orders must receive, is not an order, because by it no office or power is conferred; it is only an initiation into the *clerical state.* When a person receives the tonsure he is separated from the laity and in

*These are the traditional grades of Holy Orders. —*Editor,* 1990.

ORDINATION OF PRIESTS IN THE EARLY CHURCH

Catholic countries has "to wear the tonsure," that is, he has to shave the crown of his head in the form of a circle. (The words *clergy* and *clerical* come from the Greek word *Kleros,* which means *lot, inheritance, rank.*)

4. The Universal Priesthood.—Luther rejected the hierarchy and the sacrament of Holy Orders. He taught the *universal priesthood of all the faithful.* According to him the faithful have the right to choose their own ministers and to delegate their powers to them by the imposition of hands. It was only in this way that he could justify his rebellion against the existing ecclesiastical authority. He based his doctrine of the universal priesthood on the words of St. Peter: "You are a chosen race, a *royal priesthood,* a holy nation" (1 Pet. 2,9).

Now it is true that there is a universal priesthood, and that every baptized person shares in it. The fathers and doctors of the Church taught this long before Luther. But it is just as certain that this universal priesthood is not the only one in the Church. In virtue of this universal priesthood *all* are obliged, as St. Peter says, "to offer *spiritual sacrifices* well pleasing to God through Jesus Christ." Besides these spiritual sacrifices, or sacrifices in the wider sense, there is in the New Law a special sacrifice, the sacrifice of the Mass, and therefore also a special priesthood. In virtue of the universal priesthood the faithful join with Christ and with the priest at the altar in the offering of the Holy Sacrifice. All the faithful are indeed "an elect race, a royal priesthood," but they are not the representatives of Christ at the altar, they do not, in the Mass, change the bread and wine into the Body and Blood of Christ, they are not the "dispensers of the mysteries of God," not to them did Christ say: "Do this in remembrance of Me."

The same titles which St. Peter applies to the Christians God Himself in the Old Law applied to the Israelites (Ex. 19,6), and still He instituted amongst them a separate priesthood, and punished with death Core and his followers for arrogating to themselves the powers of the priesthood.

5. The Matter of the Sacrament of Holy Orders is the imposition of hands, to which is added in the Latin Church the touching of the corresponding sacred vessels or instruments used in the divine service by the respective order; thus for the order of the priesthood it is a chalice containing wine, and a paten with a host on it.*

The Form for the Order of Priesthood is: "Receive the power to offer sacrifice in the Church for the living and the dead, in the name of the Father, and of the Son, and of the Holy Ghost."*

6. The Effects of the Sacrament of Holy Orders are:

a) It increases sanctifying grace in him who receives it.

b) It gives sacramental grace which makes the ordained fit to exercise the duties of his sacred office.

c) It imprints an indelible character; and therefore it cannot be repeated.

7. The principal powers of the priest are to offer the Holy Sacrifice, to forgive sins, to administer the sacraments, and to preach the word of God. These powers are given to him when he receives the Sacrament of Holy Orders. But he cannot *lawfully* exercise these powers unless he has been *authorized* to do so by the Pope or the bishop. He can administer all the sacraments, except that of Penance, *validly* even without this authorization, and even if he was excommunicated, but he commits a sacrilege every time he does so.

8. Bishops Alone Are the Ministers of Holy Orders; they alone have power to consecrate other bishops, as well as priests and deacons. When delegated for the purpose by the Pope, a priest can confer tonsure, minor orders and the subdeaconship.

9. Only men are capable of receiving Holy Orders. The candidate must have been baptized and confirmed. In order to receive the major orders he must be unmarried, and must remain unmarried ever after. This law of *celibacy* is binding only in the Western Church. The Eastern Churches allow married men to take Holy Orders, but after ordination none may marry; and no one who is married can become a bishop.*

10. Vocation to the Priesthood.—It has been well said that "becoming a priest is not like becoming anything else"; the priest has to be called by God; he has to have a *vocation* to the priesthood. This vocation is manifested in various ways:

a) By the pious desires of the heart;

b) By innocence of life;

c) By sincere love of Christ;

d) By zeal for the glory of God and the salvation of souls;

e) By talent and liking for higher studies.

But vocation does not consist in the mere desire or aspiration

*See page 196 for the notes to this page. —*Editor*, 1990.

on the part of the candidate, nor in some sort of interior revelation made to him by God. All that is required on his part is that he should have a right intention and should be endowed with the qualities of nature and grace fitting him for the sacred office of the priesthood. But that does not give him a *right* to ordination until he has been *called by the bishop*. Hence the chief sign of a vocation to the priesthood is being chosen by the bishop.

11. Vocations to the priesthood are of such supreme importance to the Church that Christ made them the object of special prayers: "Pray ye the Lord of Harvest that He send forth laborers into His harvest" (Matt. 9,38). According to ancient custom the Sacrament of Holy Orders is administered on the Saturdays of the Ember weeks, while the whole Church fasts and prays.

SUGGESTIONS FOR STUDY AND REVIEW

1. Copy the following texts and use them in answering questions on the Sacrament of Holy Orders: Luke 22,19; Acts 6,6; Acts 13,3; Acts 14,23; 1 Tim. 5,22; 1 Tim. 4,14; 2 Tim. 1,6; Eph. 4,11-12; Phil. 1,1; Titus 1,5-7.

2. Summarize the teaching of the Church on the Sacrament of Holy Orders:
    1) Matter.
    2) Form.
    3) Effects.
    4) Institution by Christ.
    5) Minister.
    6) Recipient.

3. Which are the principal powers of the priest? What powers has a Bishop which a priest has not?

4. Name the Major and the Minor Orders. Which Orders constitute the Hierarchy of the Church?

5. Is there such a thing as a *universal Priesthood* of all the faithful? Explain the difference between this universal Priesthood and the special Priesthood instituted by Christ.

6. What does *clerical celibacy* mean? Was clerical celibacy commanded by Christ or is it a Church Law? Where do you find married priests?

7. What does vocation to the Priesthood mean? What are the signs of a vocation? If a young man has these signs, does that give him a *right* to be ordained?

8. At what seasons of the year especially should we pray for an increase of priestly vocations? Why?

9. Where are young men usually prepared for the Priesthood? Why should

all the faithful help to defray the expenses of educating poor boys for the Priesthood?

10. Why do Catholics call their priests "Father"? 1 Cor. 4,15.

11. Why should all Catholics pray for their priests?

12. Why should not the sad fact that there are some "bad" priests turn a Catholic away from the Church? Think of Judas. Remember, priests are men, not angels. Priests are subject to temptation as well as other people.

13. Write a brief essay on *The Priesthood.* (*a*) The word "priest"; (*b*) the priesthood before the coming of Christ among pagan nations and among the Jews; (*c*) why Christ instituted a Christian Priesthood; (*d*) the ordination of the Apostles; (*e*) the ordination of the first Deacons; (*f*) the ordination of St. Paul and St. Barnabas; (*g*) if you ever assisted at an ordination, describe it briefly.

14. *Reading:*

    a) *Imitation of Christ,* Bk. IV, ch. 5: "Of the Dignity of the Sacrament of the Altar, and of the Office of the Priest."

    b) John F. Sullivan, *The Visible Church,* pp. 59-69: "The Ceremonies of Holy Orders" (Kenedy).

CHAPTER VIII

Matrimony

There are three states in the Church to which a special sacredness attaches: the *sacerdotal state*, which is founded on the sacrament of Holy Orders; the *religious state,* which is composed of those who have bound themselves by the vows of poverty, chastity and obedience; and the *married state,* to which all Christians belong who have been united in marriage by the sacrament of *Matrimony*.

1. Marriage in pre-Christian Times

1. Marriage was instituted by God Himself in the Garden of Eden. The **divine charter of marriage** is preserved in Holy Writ:

"And the Lord God said: It is not good for man to be alone; let us make him a help like unto himself.

And the Lord built the rib which He took from Adam into a woman and brought her to Adam.

And Adam said: This now is bone of my bones and flesh of my flesh.

And God blessed them saying: Increase and multiply and fill the earth" (Gen. 1,27-28; 2,18-23).

2. From this account of the first marriage it is clear

a) That marriage is a holy state—it was instituted and blessed by God;

b) That marriage is a contract between *one* man and *one* woman, i.e., that one man is to have only one wife, and one woman only one husband; *monogamy* not *polygamy* was intended by God;

c) That the marriage contract cannot be dissolved by the contracting parties—God joined them; God alone can put them asunder;

d) That the prime object of marriage is to preserve and increase the human race;

e) That woman is the companion and helpmate of man in marriage, not his slave.

3. The first marriage was to be the model of all subsequent marriages. But like so many other things that God had ordained and that were "very good," it was debased by men. Sin came into the world, and with it a host of vices. Impurity in its most degrading forms, contempt of woman, and neglect of the child despoiled marriage of its original crown of *sanctity*. Then its *unity* was sacrificed. Polygamy became the rule amongst most of the nations of the East and was tolerated even amongst the Israelites. But the severest blow of all was that dealt to the *indissolubility* (inseparability) of marriage. The laws of the various nations, almost without exception, gave the husband the right to put away his wife for the most trivial reasons. Even the Law of Moses had to permit *divorce* and remarriage in certain cases on account of the "hardness of heart" of the Jews and in order to prevent greater evils. A greater than Moses was needed to restore marriage to its original sacredness.

2. Marriage in Christian Times

1. Christ began His work on earth by renewing the family. —In Mary, His blessed Mother, He placed before men the ideal

Fra Angelico

THE ESPOUSALS OF THE BLESSED VIRGIN

wife and mother. He Himself became a child, and thereby taught men to love the child and to reverence and cherish it as the heir of the kingdom of Heaven. With His Mother and His disciples He attended the marriage feast in Cana, and on this occasion worked His first public miracle. In His parables He used marriage as a symbol of the most sacred relations between God and the human soul. Almost in the same breath He *pronounced a blessing on the little children* their mothers brought to Him, and *denounced the evil of divorce.* Three evangelists record the incident:

"And Pharisees came up and asked Him, tempting Him, 'Is it lawful for a man to put away his wife?'

But He answered and said to them, 'What did Moses command you?'

And they said, 'Moses permitted us to write a bill of divorce and to put her away.'

CHRIST BLESSING THE BRIDE AND GROOM AT CANA

Jesus said to them, 'Because of your stubbornness of heart he wrote you this commandment. But from the beginning of creation "male and female He made them: therefore shall a man leave his father and mother, and the two shall become one flesh":

so that they are no longer two but one flesh. *What God, then, hath joined together let no man put asunder.'*

And on coming indoors the disciples questioned Him again on this matter; and He saith to them, 'Whosoever putteth away his wife and marrieth another, committeth adultery against her; and she, if she put away her husband and marry another, committeth adultery.'

And they were bringing little children unto Him in order that He might touch them; and the disciples rebuked them. But Jesus, seeing it, was moved to indignation, and said to them, 'Suffer the little children to come unto Me, hinder them not; for of such is the kingdom of God.'

And He took them into His arms, and laying His hands upon them He blessed them" (Mark 10,2-16). The significance of Christ's joining the blessing of children to His pronouncement against divorce is clear.

2. What God Hath Joined Together Let No Man Put Asunder.—By these words Christ withdrew absolutely the concession made to the Jews by the Mosaic Law in the matter of divorce. Henceforth no human power, civil or ecclesiastical, has the right to dissolve a marriage validly contracted.

3. But Christ did more than give back to marriage its original character—**He raised it to the dignity of a sacrament.** From the beginning God's blessing accompanied the marriage contract if the contracting parties were worthy of it; Christ gave power to the outward sign of the contract to produce sacramental grace.

Matrimony may, therefore, be defined as *"the sacrament by which a Christian man and woman bind themselves together forever as husband and wife, and receive grace to discharge the duties of their state faithfully until death."*

a) We know from Scripture that Matrimony is a sacrament, although we do not know when Christ instituted it. In his Epistle to the Ephesians (5,22-32), St. Paul tells us that the contract of marriage between a Christian man and woman bears a mystical meaning, that it is an emblem of the union between Christ and His Church. He emphasizes the fact that marriage amongst Christians is *not a merely natural relation, but has received a supernatural consecration:* it is founded on grace and on love ennobled by grace, just as the marriage of Christ with His Church is founded on divine grace and love. "Husbands love your wives, as Christ also loved the Church and gave Himself up for her sake, that He might sanctify her."

b) *The Church has always regarded Matrimony as a sacrament, and defended its sanctity against the attacks of heretics.* St. Augustine puts it on the same line with Baptism and Holy Orders. Popes Innocent I and Leo the Great are equally explicit in their teaching. The ceremonies and prayers used for many centuries for the celebration of Matrimony both in the Latin and the Greek Rite emphasize the sacramental character of the marriage contract. Against Luther and the other so-called reformers, who struck Matrimony from the list of sacraments and claimed that it was nothing but "an external and worldly thing," the Council of Trent declared: "If any one assert that Matrimony is not really and truly one of the seven sacraments of the New Law, instituted by Christ, but that it is of human invention; let him be anathema."

4. *The words or signs which express the consent of the contracting parties are the matter and the form of the Sacrament of Matrimony.* Both parties must freely express their consent.

The *minister* of the sacrament is not the priest, but the *contracting parties themselves.*

3. The Marriage Laws of the Church

1. Since Christian marriage bears a sacramental character, and since the contract of marriage and the sacrament of marriage form an inseparable unity, the Church as the dispenser of the *sacrament,* and she alone, has the right to determine the form and the conditions of the *contract.*

2. Summary of the Most Important Matrimonial Laws of the Church:

a) In order to be *validly married* the bridegroom and the bride must declare in the presence of the parish priest (or the bishop) and of two witnesses that they agree to be husband and wife, and then the priest blesses their union.

b) Catholics who attempt to contract marriage before a civil magistrate sin grievously, and their marriage is null and void. Those who attempt to contract marriage before a non-Catholic minister of religion, are excommunicated.* They cannot be reconciled to the Church without a dispensation from the bishop. They must then contract marriage according to the laws of the Church.

---

*This act no longer carries the penalty of excommunication, but it remains a mortal sin, and the "marriage" is null and void. —*Editor,* 1990.

c) An *engagement* to marry, in order to be *legally* binding, must be in writing and signed by the two parties in presence of the pastor of one of them, or the bishop, or two other witnesses. Every engagement, no matter under what form it be made, is, of course, binding *in conscience.**

d) There are two kinds of *impediments to marriage:* such as make marriage *unlawful;* such as make it *null and void.*

Marriage is unlawful when one of the parties is bound by the simple vow of chastity; when one of them is a Protestant; when the banns have not been published.* *Solemn* marriage, i.e., with the nuptial Mass and solemn nuptial blessing, is forbidden from the first Sunday of Advent to Christmas, and from Ash Wednesday to Easter.*

Marriage is null and void when there is *blood relationship to the third degree inclusive,* i.e., if the great-grand-parents of the parties who intend to marry were brother and sister; when there is *affinity* to the second degree inclusive, e.g., a man could not marry his deceased wife's cousin, because his wife's cousin became his cousin by affinity, which is a relationship whereby the husband becomes related to the wife's family, and the wife to the husband's; when there is spiritual relationship (see Baptism); when one of the parties is not baptized; when fear or force was inflicted from without on one or both parties; when the bridegroom has not completed his sixteenth and the bride her fourteenth year; or for other reasons.

e) All who know of any existing impediment are bound to reveal it before the celebration of the marriage to the bishop or the pastor.

f) If the civil law prescribes *certain formalities* prior to marriage, such as obtaining a license, it must be obeyed.

g) The Church regards the *marriages of non-baptized persons, and those of baptized non-Catholics as valid,* until their invalidity has been proved. No new marriage ceremony is required of Protestants or the unbaptized who become Catholics.

h) Catholics who renounce the Church and declare themselves Protestants cannot marry validly outside the Church.

i) The marriage of unbaptized persons may be dissolved under certain conditions, when one party is converted to the faith. This dissolution of marriage is called the *Pauline Privilege* (1 Cor. 7,12-15).

*See page 196 for the notes to this page. —*Editor,* 1990.

j) Those who procure a *civil divorce* and contract another marriage are excommunicated by the Church.* This second marriage is not valid. In the words of Christ such persons are living in adultery.

k) The Church can dispense from some of the impediments which make marriage null and void, when there are sufficient reasons, but not from all; on this subject the parties must confer with their pastor.

3. Mixed Marriages.—Strict conditions are laid down by the Church for those who apply for dispensation to contract *mixed marriage*. Both parties must sign contracts in the presence of two witnesses: First, the non-Catholic party must guarantee to the Catholic full liberty of conscience and free exercise of his religious duties; secondly, both must agree to bring up their children in the Catholic faith and according to Catholic rules of education; thirdly, the Catholic party must promise to do his or her very best to win the non-Catholic party over to the Catholic religion, especially by prayer, good example and frequentation of the Sacraments.

4. The Church Forbids Mixed Marriages

1. Because such marriages are a cause of disagreement between husband and wife in the most important of all matters, religion;

2. Because the Catholic husband or wife is exposed to great danger of losing the faith or of becoming careless about it;

3. Because it is usually difficult and often impossible to give the children a thorough Catholic education;

4. Because non-Catholics usually think it lawful for husband and wife to separate and marry again.

The prohibition of mixed marriages is nothing new in the Church. As early as A.D. 451 the Council of Chalcedon forbade marriages with heretics except on condition that the heretical party promised to embrace the Catholic faith.

Mixed marriages are not celebrated in the Church; the banns are not published; nuptial Mass is not celebrated; the nuptial blessing is not given; the priest assists at the marriage without surplice or stole; the ring given to the bride is not blessed.**

The Church sometimes permits married persons *to live apart.* Catholics who think they have a sufficient cause for separation must submit their case to the bishop. They are always bound to be reconciled when it is possible.

*This act no longer carries the penalty of excommunication, but it remains a mortal sin. —*Editor*, 1990.
**These prescriptions for mixed marriages are no longer in force. —*Editor*, 1990.

5. Preparing for a Happy Marriage.—The *matrimonial laws* of the Church cannot prevent unhappy marriages, if the persons who intend to enter upon the married state are not filled with a sense of their own responsibility, i.e., if they do not examine themselves very carefully in order to see whether they are really fit, *physically, mentally, and spiritually,* to take upon themselves the obligations of Matrimony. They should not be reckless nor hasty in becoming engaged; they should lead a pure life during the time of their engagement; they should be free from every infectious disease; they should be properly instructed on the duties of married people; they should go to Confession and Communion before their marriage; they should enter the married state with a pure and holy intention.

"We are children of the saints," said Tobias to his bride, *"and we must not be joined together like heathens that know not God"* (Tob. 8,5).

SUGGESTIONS FOR STUDY AND REVIEW

1. To which three states in the Church is a special sacredness attached!
2. Quote the words of Scripture which describe the institution of marriage. What do these words tell us about the nature of Matrimony?
3. How were the original sanctity, unity and inseparability of marriage marred and destroyed in the course of time?
4. Show how Christ restored Matrimony to its original dignity?
5. Read carefully Eph. 5,22-32. Show from St. Paul's words that Matrimony is a true Sacrament.
6. What has the Church always held in regard to Matrimony? Quote the words of the Council of Trent against Luther.
7. Who is the Minister of the Sacrament of Matrimony? What are the Matter and Form? Why is marriage sometimes called "the Lay Sacrament"?
8. Can any human power dissolve the bond of marriage?
9. Why has the Church alone the right to determine what is required for a true marriage? Has the State anything to say in regard to marriage?
10. What is meant by a Matrimonial Impediment? How are these Impediments classified? Name six impediments that make marriage null and void. Can the Church dispense from all these impediments?
11. What is the difference between an *annulment* and a *divorce*? What is a *separation*?
12. What is meant by the publication of the *banns* of Matrimony? What is the purpose of this publication? Would a marriage be null and void if the banns were not published?
13. What is the Pauline Privilege?

14. What penalties does a Catholic incur who attempts marriage before a civil magistrate? Before a non-Catholic minister of religion?

15. How must Catholics be married?

16. Are Catholics forbidden to marry in Advent and Lent?

17. Does the Church consider the following marriages valid or invalid:

   a) A marriage between non-baptized persons;

   b) A marriage between baptized non-Catholics;

   c) Between a baptized Protestant and an infidel or unbaptized Protestant?

18. What is meant by a Mixed Marriage? What promises must the non-Catholic party to a Mixed Marriage make before the Church will permit such a marriage? What promises must the Catholic party make?

19. Why is the Church opposed to Mixed Marriages? Describe the ceremony of a Mixed Marriage.

20. How should Catholics prepare for marriage?

21. *Readings:*

   a) Pope Pius XI, *Encyclical Letter on Christian Marriage.*

   b) Martin J. Scott, S.J., *Marriage.*

   c) A number of excellent pamphlets dealing with various phases of Matrimony have been published by the *Queen's Work* (St. Louis), the *America Press* (New York), the *Paulist Press* (N. Y.) and the *International Catholic Truth Society* (Brooklyn).

The Ritual for the Celebration of Matrimony

The Priest, vested in a surplice and white Stole (but vested as for Mass, yet without maniple, if the Nuptial Mass is to follow), attended by an acolyte holding a vessel of Holy Water, asks, in the vernacular, in the hearing of at least two witnesses, the man and the woman separately as follows, concerning their consent. And first he asks the Bridegroom, who must stand at the right hand of the Bride:

N., wilt thou take N., here present, for thy lawful wife, according to the rite of our holy Mother Church?

R. I will.

Then the Priest asks the Bride:

N., wilt thou take N., here present, for thy lawful husband, according to the rite of our holy Mother Church?

R. I will.

The consent of one is not sufficient; it should be expressed by both, and there should be some sensible sign thereof.

Where customary the man and woman pledge themselves to each other in the following words, the man reciting them first:

I, N. N., take thee, N. N., for my lawful wife (husband), to have and to hold, from this day forward, for better, for worse, for richer, for poorer, in sickness and in health, until death do us part.

Having obtained this mutual consent, the Priest bids the man and woman to join their right hands. The Priest then says:

I join you together in marriage, in the name of the Father, and of the Son, and of the Holy Ghost. Amen.

He then sprinkles them with Holy Water. This done, he blesses the ring, saying:

Our help is in the name of the Lord, etc.

Let us pray

Bless, O Lord, this ring, which we bless in Thy name, that she who shall wear it, keeping faith unchanged with her husband, may abide in peace and obedience to Thy will, and live in mutual love. Through Christ our Lord. Amen.

Then the Priest sprinkles the ring with Holy Water in the form of a Cross; and the Bridegroom, having received the ring from the hand of the Priest, places it on the third finger of the left hand of the Bride. In some places the Bridegroom says after the Priest:

With this ring I thee wed, and plight unto thee my troth.

This done, the Priest adds:

V. Confirm, O God, that which Thou hast wrought in us.

R. From Thy holy temple which is in Jerusalem. Etc.

Let us pray

Look down, we beseech Thee, O Lord, upon these Thy servants, and graciously protect this Thine ordinance, whereby Thou hast provided for the propagation of mankind; that those who are joined together by Thy authority may be preserved by Thy help. Through Christ our Lord. Amen.

After this, if the Nuptial Blessing is to be given, the Mass is said pro Sponso et Sponsa, at which the newly-married parties assist, kneeling at the Altar-rail or on kneeling benches, according to custom, the man on the right, and the woman on the left.

THE THIRD PLENARY COUNCIL OF BALTIMORE ON THE CELEBRATION OF MATRIMONY

"Let those who have the cure of souls take every occasion earnestly to exhort the faithful to the keeping of that pious and praiseworthy custom of the Church whereby Marriages are celebrated, not in the night-time, but during Mass, and accompanied by the Nuptial Blessing. . . . This custom is held to be not merely a commendable but quite a necessary one, now in these present days, when the foes of religion are leaving nothing untried in their efforts to deprive, if possible, Holy Matrimony of all sanctity, and of all likeness to a Sacrament, and to degrade it to the level of a mere civil contract."

CHAPTER IX

The Sacramentals of the Church

1. Apart from the sacraments, there are in the Church other sacred rites and liturgical acts by which grace is conferred. They are called **Sacramentals,** because they resemble the sacraments externally. The sacramentals are generally divided into three classes: **Consecrations, Blessings,** and **Exorcisms.**

a) The Church *consecrates* persons and objects to *make them sacred* for the service of God. Thus she consecrates abbots, virgins, candidates for Minor Orders, churches, bells, cemeteries.

b) The Church *blesses* persons and objects to call down upon them the special blessing of God. There are two kinds of blessings:

1. Blessings which do not only call down the blessing of God upon the objects blessed, but also make them sacred, though not in the same sense that consecrated objects are made sacred. Thus rosaries, medals, scapulars, and crucifixes are blessed and retain the blessing until they are sold or destroyed;

2. Blessings which only call down the graces and protection of God upon the persons and objects blessed. Benediction of the Blessed Sacrament, the blessing of the sick, the blessing of houses, bridges, ships, are examples of such blessings.

c) By *Exorcism* we mean a *summons* addressed to Satan in the name of Christ to depart from a creature of God over which he had exercised a harmful influence.

2. When the Church consecrates, blesses and exorcises, she is but carrying out the command of God and imitating the example of Jesus Christ.

a) In the Old Law the altar and all the vessels thereof were sprinkled and anointed, as the Lord had commanded (Lev. 8,11).

b) Jesus blessed the little children (Matt. 19,15), the loaves and fishes (Luke 9,16), the Apostles, before He took leave of them (24,50).

c) Our Lord gave His disciples the power of driving out demons, and from the earliest times the Church made use of this power.

d) By the sin of Adam the curse of God extended to all

THE CONSECRATING OF BELLS AT BUCKFAST ABBEY

creatures (Rom. 8,20-22); by the blessings of the Church God's blessings are poured out over all. "Every creature is sanctified," says St. Paul, "by the word of God and prayer" (1 Tim. 4,5).

The order of *Exorcist* is the third of the Minor Orders. This order is mentioned as early as the third century. Power is still given to the exorcist to drive out the devil, but neither the exorcist nor the priest can make use of this power without express permission of the bishop. Exorcisms are used to this day at the baptism of children and adults, and over various inanimate objects, such as water.

3. Only persons in Holy Orders can bless and consecrate. —The consecration of the Holy Oils, of churches, chalices and bells is reserved to the bishop. Some blessings, such as the Stations of the Way of the Cross, are reserved to certain religious orders.

4. The Sacramentals Differ Essentially from the Sacraments:

a) The Sacraments were instituted by Christ Himself; the sacramentals were instituted by the Church;

b) The sacraments, when they are duly administered and worthily received, produce grace *ex opere operato*,* the sacramentals only in virtue of the prayers of the Church, and according to the disposition of those who make use of them;

*As explained on page 84, a Sacrament works, in a sense, "automatically," provided no obstacle is placed in the way. Literally, this phrase means "from the work performed." —Editor, 1990.

c) The sacraments can be applied only to human beings, whereas the sacramentals are applicable to man and nature, animate and inanimate;

d) The sacraments are in general necessary, and their reception is commanded by God; the sacramentals are only recommended by the Church as useful and salutary.

5. It may be asked, how water, or medals, or candles, or scapulars, can possibly help us on the way to Heaven.

In themselves these objects have no such power, and it would be superstition to attribute such power to them. But they tend to excite good dispositions in those who use them aright; they excite increased fear and love of God, and hatred of sin, and because of these movements of the heart towards God, they remit venial sin. "They have a special efficacy, *because the Church has blessed them with prayer,* and so, when a person takes Holy Water, accompanying the outward act with the desire that God may cleanse his heart, the prayer of the whole Christian people is joined to his own. There is surely no superstition in believing that if the Church prays that the sight or use of blessed objects may excite good desires in her children, God will listen to these prayers and touch in a special way the hearts of those who use them aright."

The following formula of blessing, which can be used by any priest for all those things that have no special blessing in the Roman Ritual, shows very well what the Church aims at in her sacramentals:

"O God, by whose word all things are sanctified, pour forth Thy blessing upon this creature and grant that whosoever shall use it with thanksgiving, according to Thy law and will, may receive from Thee, through the invocation of Thy Holy Name, health of body and peace of soul. Through Christ our Lord. Amen."

SUGGESTIONS FOR STUDY AND REVIEW

1. What do we understand by Sacramentals?
2. How are Sacramentals classified? Give two examples of each class.
3. Is there any Scriptural authority for the use of Sacramentals?
4. What is meant by Exorcism? Who can exorcise? What exorcisms are most frequently used?
5. Who alone can bless and consecrate objects and persons? Are any blessings and consecrations reserved to the Bishop or to certain religious orders?

6. What is the difference between Sacraments and Sacramentals?
7. Whence do the Sacramentals derive their efficacy?
8. Why should we make a devout use of Sacramentals?
9. Which two Sacramentals are most frequently used by all the faithful? Name a consecrated object used at Mass.
10. Write a composition on the *Blessing of Candles, Ashes and Palms.* See your missal for the Feast of the Purification, Ash Wednesday, and Palm Sunday.
11. *Reading:* John F. Sullivan, *The Visible Church,* pp. 119-170, "The Sacramentals."

APPENDIX

APPENDIX

1. THE ORDINARY OF THE MASS WITH THE PROPER OF THE MASS OF THE SACRED HEART ACCORDING TO THE ROMAN MISSAL. 2. BRIEF INSTRUCTIONS ABOUT THE ALTAR, SACRED VESSELS AND VESTMENTS.

I. The Ordinary of the Mass*with the Proper of the Mass of the Sacred Heart According to the Roman Missal

Perhaps the best way to learn how to follow the Mass intelligently will be to read the complete text of some particular Mass and carefully listen to the teacher explaining it step by step (see pages 73 to 83 in this book). An appropriate Mass is that of the Sacred Heart. It is found even in the small Students' Missals and is said on most First Fridays of the year. The Feast of the Sacred Heart is celebrated on Friday after the Octave Day of Corpus Christi. In 1928 Pius XI raised this feast to the dignity of a double of the first class with Octave and in 1929 prescribed a new Proper in which the riches of the love of the Divine Heart are extolled. The English translation of both the Ordinary and the Proper is based on the best existing ones, such as Father Lasance's Missal, the Leaflet Missal and St. Andrew's Missal; intelligibility rather than literalness is aimed at.

I. MASS OF THE CATECHUMENS

The Mass is the Sacrifice of the New Law, the sacrifice of the entire Church as well as the sacrifice of each individual member of the Church. Hence it calls for *preparation,* a passing from our work-a-day lives with their sins and cares to the dispositions required for worthily offering the Great Sacrifice. This preparation is twofold: *negative:* we must free ourselves from sin and worldly cares: Prayers at the Foot of the Altar to Collect; *positive:* we must be spiritually illumined, and our minds and hearts directed to God: Epistle or Lesson to Credo.

Negative Preparation for the Sacrifice

1. To-day Mass begins with the prayers at the foot of the altar. With the acolytes (servers) the celebrant recites the 42nd Psalm. (*Note:* The letter *P.* designates the versicle recited by the priest, while the letter *R.* meaning "response" is the answer made by the server.) As David prays for protection against his persecutors, so the priest asks God to protect him against the enemies of his salvation and to help him to celebrate the Sacred Mysteries worthily:

*This is the traditional ("Tridentine") Mass. —*Editor,* 1990.

144

At the Foot of the Altar

In Nomine Patris, ✠ et Filii, et Spiritus Sancti. Amen.

In the name of the Father, ✠ and of the Son, and of the Holy Ghost. Amen.

P. Introibo ad altare Dei.

P. I will go to the altar of God.

R. Ad Deum, qui lætificat juventutem meam.

R. To God, Who is the joy of my youth. (That is the *source of my joy.*)

PSALM XLII

To be omitted in Passion-tide and in Masses for the Dead.

P. Judica me, Deus, et discerne causam meam de gente non sancta: ab homine iniquo et doloso erue me.

P. Give judgment for me, O God, and decide my cause against an unholy people! Rescue me from the godless and treacherous *(the wicked angels).*

R. Quia tu es, Deus, fortitudo mea: quaro me repulisti, et quare tristis incedo, dum affligit me inimicus?

R. For Thou art my strength! Why hast Thou forsaken me? And why must I go about in sadness, humiliated by my enemy?

P. Emitte lucem tuam, et veritatem tuam: ipsa me deduxerunt, et adduxerunt in montem sanctum tuum, et in tabernacula tua.

P. O send forth Thy light and Thy Truth, that they may lead me, and guide me to Thy holy mountain, and to Thy tabernacle! (i.e., *the altar with the tabernacle).*

R. Et introibo ad altare Dei: ad Deum, qui lætificat juventutem meam.

R. That I may go in to the altar of God—to God who is the joy of my youth.

P. Confitebor tibi in cithara, Deus, Deus meus: quare tristis es, anima mea, et quare conturbas me?

P. That I may praise Thee with the harp, O God, my God! My soul, why art thou sad and why troublest thou me?

R. Spera in Deo, quoniam adhuc confitebor illi: salutare vultus mei, et Deus meus.

R. Put thy trust in the Lord, for even yet I will praise Him "My Rescuer and my God!"

THE PREPARATORY PRAYERS AT THE FOOT OF
THE ALTAR.

THE "GLORIA IN EXCELSIS."

© BB   THE "EPISTLE."

THE "GOSPEL."

P. Gloria Patri, et Filio, et Spiritui Sancto.

R. Sicut erat in principio, et nunc, et semper: et in sæcula sæculorum. Amen.

P. Introibo ad altare Dei.

R. Ad Deum, qui lætificat juventutem meam.

P. Adjutorium nostrum in nomine Domini.

R. Qui fecit cœlum et terram.

The priest says the Confiteor, at the end of which he asks the people to pray for him.

R. Misereatur tui omnipotens Deus, et dimissis peccatis tuis, perducat te ad vitam æternam.

P. Amen.

Then the Server:

Confiteor Deo omnipotenti, beatæ Mariæ semper virgini, beato Michaeli arch-angelo, beato Joanni Baptistæ, sanctis apostolis Petro et Paulo, omnibus sanctis, et tibi, Pater, quia peccavi nimis cogitatione, verbo, et opere: mea culpa, mea culpa, mea maxima culpa. Ideo precor beatam Mariam semper virginem, beatum Michaelem archangelum, beatum Joannem Baptistam, sanctos apostolos Petrum et Paulum, omnes sanctos, et te, Pater, orare pro me ad Dominum Deum nostrum.

P. Glory be to the Father, and to the Son, and to the Holy Ghost.

R. As it was in the beginning, is now, and ever shall be, world without end. Amen.

P. I will go to the altar of God.

R. To God, Who is the joy of my youth.

P. Our help is in the name of the Lord.

R. Who made heaven and earth.

R. May almighty God have mercy upon thee, forgive thee thy sins and bring thee to life everlasting.

P. Amen.

I confess to almighty God, to blessed Mary ever virgin, to blessed Michael the archangel, to blessed John the Baptist, to the holy apostles Peter and Paul, to all the saints, and to you, Father, that I have sinned exceedingly in thought, word, and deed: through my fault, through my fault, through my most grievous fault. Therefore I beseech the blessed Mary ever virgin, blessed Michael the archangel, blessed John the Baptist, the holy apostles Peter and Paul, all the saints, and you, Father, to pray to the Lord our God for me.

P. Misereatur vestri omnipotens Deus, et dimissis peccatis vestris, perducat vos ad vitam æternam.

R. Amen.

P. Indulgéntiam, absolutionem, et remissionem peccatorum nostrorum, tribuat nobis omnipotens et misericors Dominus.

R. Amen.

P. May almighty God have mercy on you and, having forgiven you your sins, bring you to life everlasting.

R. Amen.

P. May the almighty and merciful God grant us pardon, absolution, and full remission of our sins.

R. Amen.

Again bowing down, the priest goes on:

P. Deus, tu conversus vivificabis nos.

R. Et plebs tua lætabitur in te.

P. Ostende nobis, Domine, misericordiam tuam.

R. Et salutare tuum da nobis.

P. Domine, exaudi orationem meam.

R. Et clamor meus ad te veniat.

P. Thou wilt turn to us, O God, and bring us to life.

R. And Thy people shall rejoice in Thee.

P. Show us, O Lord. Thy mercy.

R. And grant us Thy salvation.

P. O Lord, hear my prayer.

R. And let my cry come unto Thee.

After these humble prayers, which are to purify the soul from all venial sins and prepare it for the Great Mystery and its graces, the priest invites the faithful to pray with him:

P. Dominus vobiscum.

P. The Lord be with you (i.e., may He give you the right spirit of prayer.)

And he receives the answer:

R. Et cum spiritu tuo.

R. And with you also.

This devout scriptural greeting is repeated each time that the celebrant summons the faithful to join with him in prayer.

Thereupon the priest goes up the steps, praying:

Aufer a nobis, quæsumus, Domine, iniquitates nostras: ut ad Sancta Sanctorum puris mereamur mentibus introire. Per Christum Dominum nostrum. Amen.

Take from us our sins, O Lord, that we may enter the Holy of Holies with pure minds. Through Christ our Lord. Amen.

Kissing the altar, the symbol of Christ, in the center, where the relics rest, he says:

Oramus te, Domine, per merita sanctorum tuorum, quorum reliquiæ hic sunt, et omnium sanctorum: ut indulgere digneris omnia peccata mea. Amen.

We beseech Thee, O Lord, by the merits of Thy saints, whose relics are here, that Thou wouldst vouchsafe to forgive me all my sins. Amen.

At Solemn High Mass the celebrant puts incense into the thurible (censer), blesses it with the words: "Mayest thou be blessed by Him in Whose honor thou art burned. Amen," and then incenses the altar in order to prepare it also for the Sacrifice.

2. Purified from sin and aided by God's grace, the priest begins the Mass proper with an introductory chant which forms as it were the prelude to the whole Mass, determining the character of the Mass and helping us to understand the other variable texts. This chant is called,

The Introit

Cogitatiónes Cordis ejus in generatióne et generatiónem: ut éruat a morte ánimas eórum et alat eos in fame. *Ps. ibid. 1.* Exsultáte, justi, in Dómino, rectos decet collaudátio. V. Glória Patri. Cogitationes Cordis.

The thoughts of His Heart are to all generations, that He may deliver their souls from death and feed them in famine. —Rejoice in the Lord, O ye just; praise becometh the upright.—Glory be to the Father . . . —The thoughts of His Heart. . . .

Originally the Introit consisted of a whole psalm sung by the choir as the Bishop and his assistants advanced to the altar, hence the name Introit, entrance chant. To-day only the antiphon and one verse of the psalm are chanted.

The Introit is followed by three prayers: the *Kyrie,* the *Gloria,* and the *Collect.*

3. All who come to the Holy Sacrifice are burdened with some cross or other. From all hearts the cry rises to Heaven:

Kyrie eleison—Lord, have mercy on us! (Three times.)
Christe eleison—Christ, have mercy on us! (Three times.)
Kyrie eleison—Lord, have mercy on us! (Three times.)

In the early Church the deacon used to chant a long prayer in the form of a litany in which he presented to God the needs and petitions of the community. To each clause the faithful answered: *Kyrie eleison.*

4. Then the Church intones her hymn of joy and peace, the *Gloria,* and raises the minds and hearts of the faithful high above the petty cares and worries of daily existence:

The Gloria

Gloria in excelsis Deo. Et in terra pax hominibus bonæ voluntatis. Laudamus te. Benedicimus te. Adoramus te. Glorificamus te. Gratias agimus tibi propter magnam gloriam tuam. Domine Deus, rex cœlestis, Deus Pater omnipotens, Domine Fili unigenite Jesu Christe. Domine Deus, Agnus Dei, Filius Patris, Qui tollis peccata mundi, miserere nobis. Qui tollis peccata mundi, suscipe deprecationem nostram. Qui sedes ad dexteram Patris, miserere nobis. Quoniam tu solus sanctus. Tu solus Dominus. Tu solus altissimus Jesu Christe, cum Sancto Spiritu, in gloria Dei Patris. Amen.

Glory be to God on high, and on earth peace to men of good will. We praise Thee, we bless Thee, we adore Thee, we glorify Thee. We give Thee thanks for Thy great glory. O Lord God, King of Heaven, God the Father Almighty. O Lord Jesus Christ the only-begotten Son. O Lord God, Lamb of God, Son of the Father. Thou Who takest away the sins of the world, have mercy on us. Thou Who takest away the sins of the world, receive our prayer. Thou Who sittest at the right hand of the Father, have mercy on us. For Thou only art Holy, Thou only art Lord, Thou only art Most High, O Jesus Christ, with the Holy Ghost, in the glory of God the Father. Amen.

Because of its joyful character, it is quite natural that the *Gloria* should be omitted in Lent and Advent and in all Masses when black or purple vestments are worn.

5. After the sorrows and cares of life have been overcome and all hearts are united in holy joy, the Church places one petition on the lips of all the worshipers—the petition for the supernatural graces of the Feast (or day). This prayer is called,

The Collect

Deus qui nobis, in Corde Fílii tui, nostris vulneráto peccátis, infinítos dilectiónis thesáuros misericórditer largíri dignáris; concéde, quáesumus, ut illi devótum pietátis nostræ præstántes obséquium, dignæ quoque satisfactiónis exhibeámus offícium. Per eúmdem Dóminum.

O God, Who in the Heart of Thy Son, wounded for our sins, dost deign mercifully to lavish upon us the treasures of Thy love: grant, we beseech Thee, that with the devout homage of our piety we may also offer Him worthy service of reparation.

Sometimes one or more prayers are added to the Collect of the Mass that is being celebrated. To the first and to the last only—the same holds true of the Secrets and Postcommunions—the following solemn ending is added:

"Through Jesus Christ, Thy Son our Lord, Who liveth and reigneth with Thee in the unity of the Holy Ghost, God, world without end. Amen."

Positive Preparation for the Sacrifice

The Collect is followed by the *Readings*. Originally there were several in each Mass; to-day we have only two (except on certain days, such as the Ember Days), one taken from the Gospels, the other from the other books of the Bible. The latter is called the "Epistle" if it is taken from one of the twenty-one Letters of the Apostles, and "Lesson" if it is a selection from the Old Testament, the Acts of the Apostles or the Apocalypse.

6. *The Epistle.* Moses and the Prophets, the Wise Men of Israel and the Apostles of Christ are not dead. Every day in the Epistle or Lesson of the Mass they raise their voices in order to arouse our consciences and to summon us to walk in the paths of the Lord. The Epistle for the Feast of the Sacred Heart is taken from the Epistle of St. Paul to the Ephesians (3, 8-19). The infinite riches of the love of the Sacred Heart for all men are emphasized:

The Epistle

Fratres, mihi ómnium sanctórum mínimo data est grátia hæc, in géntibus evangelizáre investigábiles divítias Christi: et illumináre omnes, quæ sit dispensátio sacraménti abscónditi a sáeculis in Deo qui ómnia

Brethren, unto me, the least of all saints, hath been given this same grace, to preach to the Gentiles the unsearchable riches of Christ, and to make clear what is the dispensation touching the mystery which

creávit: ut innotéscat principá-
tibus et potestátibus in cœlésti-
bus per Ecclésiam multifórmis
sapiéntia Dei: secúndum præ-
finitiónem sæculórum quam fecit in Christo Jesu Dómino nostro, in quo habémus fidúciam et
accéssum in confidéntia per
fidem ejus. Hujus rei grátia
flecto génua mea ad Patrem
Dómini nostri Jesu Christi, ex
quo omnis patérnitas in cœlis et
in terra nominátur: ut det vobis
secúndum divítias glóriæ suæ,
virtúte corroborári per Spíri-
tum ejus in interiórem hómi-
nem: Christum habitáre per
fidem in córdibus vestris: in
caritáte radicáti et fundáti: ut
possítis comprehéndere, cum
ómnibus sanctis, quæ sit lati-
túdo, et longitúdo, et sublímitas
et profúndum: scire étiam su-
pereminéntem sciéntiæ caritátem Christi, ut impleámini in
omnem plenitúdinem Dei.

from ages hath been hidden in
God the Creator of all, in order
that now through the Church
be made known to the princi-
palities and powers in heavenly
places the manifold wisdom of
God. Such was the eternal purpose which He hath brought to
pass in Christ Jesus our Lord,
in Whom we have assurance,
and through faith in Him con-
fident access [to God]. For this
cause, then, I bend my knees to
the Father, from Whom all
fatherhood in heaven and on
earth is named, that He grant
you according to the riches of
His glory [i.e., *His glorious
grace*] to be strengthened
powerfully through His Spirit
in the inward man—that Christ
may dwell in your hearts
through faith, so that, rooted
and founded in charity, ye may
be able to comprehend with all
the saints what is the breadth
and length and height and
depth—to know the charity of
Christ that surpasseth knowledge, that ye may be filled unto
all the fullness of God.

7. The Epistle is ended. The words of the Apostle have found an echo
in the hearts of the faithful—feelings of joy and confidence and love. The
Gradual gives expression to these feelings:

The Gradual

Ps. 24. 8-9. Dulcis et rectus
Dóminus, propter hoc legem
dabit delinquéntibus in via. *V.*

The Lord is sweet and righteous: therefore He gives a
law to sinners in the way.—He

Díriget mansuétos in judício, docébit mites vias suas. Allelúia, allelúia. *Matth. ix, 29.* Tollite jugum meum super vos et díscite a me, quia mitis sum et húmilis Corde, et inveniétis réquiem animábus vestris. Allelúia.

will guide the mild in judgment: He will teach the meek His ways.

8. The Gradual passes over into the joyous ejaculation *Alleluia:*

Alleluia, alleluia. Take My yoke upon you and learn of Me, because I am meek and humble of heart: and you shall find rest to your souls. Alleluia.

In Votive Masses after Septuagesima the Alleluia is replaced by,

The Tract

Ps. 112. 8-10. Miséricors et miserátor Dóminus, longánimis et multum miséricors. *V.* Non in perpétuum irascétur neque in ætérnum comminábitur. *V.* Non secúndum peccáta nostra fecit nobis, neque secúndum iniquitátes nostras retríbuit nobis.

The Lord is merciful and compassionate, long - suffering and plenteous in mercy.—He will not always be angry: nor will He threaten forever.— He hath not dealt with us according to our sins: nor rewarded us according to our iniquities.

In Eastertide both Gradual and Tract are omitted. Their place is taken by the following chant:

Allelúia, allelúia. *Matth. xi. 29, 28.* Tóllite jugum meum super vos et díscite a me, quia mitis sum et húmilis Corde, et inveniétis réquiem animábus vestris. Allelúia. *V.* Veníte ad me, omnes qui laborátis et oneráti estis et ego refíciam vos. Allelúia.

Alleluia, alleluia. Take My yoke upon you and learn of Me, because I am meek and humble of Heart: and you shall find rest to your souls.—Come to Me, all you that labor and are burdened: and I will refresh you. Alleluia.

9. The Alleluia announces the coming of the Son of God Himself to teach His people by the words and deeds of His Gospel, the "crown of all

Holy Scriptures." The priest prepares himself for the reading of the Holy Gospel by going to the middle of the altar, looking up to the Cross, then bowing low, and praying,

The Munda Cor Meum

Munda cor meum, ac labia mea, omnipotens Deus, qui labia Isaiæ prophetæ calculo mundasti ignito: ita me tua grata miseratione dignare mundare, ut sanctum Evangelium tuum digne valeam nuntiare. Per Christum Dominum nostrum. Amen.

Cleanse my heart and my lips, O Almighty God, Who didst cleanse with a burning coal the lips of the Prophet Isaias; and vouchsafe in Thy loving kindness so to purify me that I may be enabled worthily to announce Thy Holy Gospel. Through Christ our Lord. Amen.

Jube, Domine, benedicere.

Vouchsafe, O Lord, to bless me.

Dominus sit in corde meo, et in labiis meis: ut digne et competenter annuntiem evangelium suum. Amen.

The Lord be in my heart and on my lips that worthily and in a seemly manner I may announce His Gospel. Amen."

At Solemn High Mass it is the Deacon who asks and receives this blessing. Lights are carried by the acolytes in sign of joy and to symbolize Christ, the light of souls. The Deacon incenses the Gospel Book, the incense signifying the "good odor of Christ."

10. Christ is again in the midst of His faithful followers. Again words of eternal life fall from His lips. We listen to His message *standing* to indicate our readiness to carry it out. The *Gospel* for the Feast of the Sacred Heart describes the scene on Calvary after the death of Jesus (John 19, 31-37):

The Gospel

In illo témpore: Judáei, quóniam Parascéve erat, ut non remanérent in cruce córpora sábbato, erat enim magnus dies ille sábbati, rogavérunt Pilátum ut frangeréntur eórum crura et tolleréntur. Venérunt ergo mí-

At that time the Jews (because it was the Parasceve) that the bodies might not remain upon the cross upon the sabbath day (for that was a great sabbath day), besought Pilate that their legs might be

lites, et primi quidem fregérunt crura et altérius qui crucifíxus est cum eo. Ad Jesum autem cum veníssent, ut vidérunt eum jam mórtuum, non fregérunt ejus crura: sed unus mílitum láncea latus ejus apéruit, et contínuo exívit sanguis et aqua. Et qui vidit testimónium perhíbuit: et verum est testimónium ejus. Et ille scit quia vera dicit, ut et vos credátis. Facta sunt enim hæc ut Scriptúra implerétur: Os non comminuétis ex eo. Et íterum ália Scriptúra dicit: Vidébunt in quem transfixérunt.

broken: and that they might be taken away. The soldiers therefore came and broke the legs of the first, and of the other that was crucified with Him. But after they were come to Jesus, when they saw that He was already dead, they did not break His legs. But one of the soldiers with a spear opened His side and immediately there came out blood and water. And he that saw it hath given testimony, and his testimony is true. And he knoweth that he saith true, that you also may believe. For these things were done that the Scripture might be fulfilled: You shall not break a bone of Him. And again another Scripture saith: They shall look on Him Whom they pierced.

When he has finished reading the Gospel, the celebrant kisses the book, saying: "By the words of the Gospel may our sins be blotted out." Formerly it was customary to answer "Amen" at the end of the Gospel; now the beautiful words "Praise to Thee, O Christ" are used.

11. The Gospel is most appropriately followed by the *Creed,* a public profession of faith in the Gospel truths, as an expression of gratitude for the inestimable grace of the true Faith:

The Nicene Creed

Credo in unum Deum, Patrem omnipotentem factorem cœli et terræ, visibilium omnium, et invisibilium. Et in unum Dominum Jesum Christum, Filium Dei unigenitum. Et ex Patre natum ante omnia sæcula. Deum de Deo, lumen de lumine, Deum verum de Deo

I believe in one God, the Father almighty, maker of heaven and earth, and of all things visible and invisible.

And in one Lord, Jesus Christ, the only-begotten Son of God. Born of the Father before all ages. God of God, light of light, true God of true God.

vero. Genitum, non factum, consubstantialem Patri: per quem omnia facta sunt. Qui propter nos homines, et propter nostram salutem descendit de cœlis. *Et incarnatus est de Spiritu Sancto ex Maria Virgine: Et homo factus est.* Crucifixus etiam pro nobis, sub Pontio Pilato passus, et sepultus est. Et resurrexit terta die, secundum Scripturas. Et ascendit in cœlum: sedet ad dexteram Patris. Et iterum venturus est cum gloria, judicare vivos et mortuos: cujus regni non erit finis. Et in Spiritum Sanctum, Dominum et vivificantem: qui ex Patre Filioque procedit. Qui cum Patre et Filio simul adoratur et conglorificatur: qui locutus est per prophetas. Et unam sanctam catholicam et apostolicam Ecclesiam. Confiteor unum baptisma in remissionem peccatorum. Et exspecto resurrectionem mortuorum. Et vitam venturi sæculi. Amen.

Begotten, not made; of one substance with the Father; by Whom all things were made. Who for us men, and for our salvation, came down from heaven. *And was made flesh by the Holy Ghost, of the virgin Mary: and was made man.* He was also crucified for us, suffered under Pontius Pilate, and was buried. And on the third day He arose again according to the Scriptures. And ascended into heaven. He sitteth at the right hand of the Father. And He shall come again with glory, to judge the living and the dead: and of His kingdom there shall be no end.

And in the Holy Ghost, the Lord and Giver of life, Who proceedeth from the Father and the Son. Who together with the Father and the Son is adored and glorified; Who spoke by the prophets.

And in one, holy, catholic and apostolic Church. I confess one baptism for the remission of sins. And I expect the resurrection of the dead. And the life of the world to come. Amen.

The Creed marks the conclusion of the Mass of the Catechumens. The faithful are freed from the sins and cares of daily life; they have opened their hearts to the word of God, and have solemnly professed their unity— one Lord, one faith: they are ready for the Sacrifice. This is the repetition of what the Lord did at the Last Supper: "He took bread into His holy and venerable hands . . . gave thanks, blessed it, and broke it, and gave it to His disciples. . . ." Hence the Eucharistic Sacrifice falls into three parts:

A. Preparation of the Gifts (*Offertory*).

B. Prayer of Thanksgiving and Blessing—Preface to Pater Noster (*Canon*).

C. Breaking of the Bread and the Sacrifice-Banquet (*Communion*).

II. THE MASS OF THE FAITHFUL, OR THE ACTUAL EUCHARISTIC

SACRIFICE*

A. *The Offertory*

In the early Church the Catechumens as well as all those who did not belong to the Christian community were dismissed after the sermon, which followed the Gospel. The faithful then said a series of prayers for the whole world, for the Church, the benefactors, their enemies, all non-Christians, the infants, their own welfare (cf. the prayers on Good Friday before the unveiling of the Cross). In our present-day liturgy only the summons "Oremus" (Let us pray) has been retained. After these intercessions all the faithful proceeded to the altar and laid down their gifts— bread, wine, oil, fruits of the field, etc. They wished not only to "assist at" the Sacrifice, but also to make an offering themselves and to receive in return the Body and Blood of Christ. Our collection of money at the Offertory and the practice of giving stipends for Masses still represent the old offering of bread and wine by the faithful. During the offering of the gifts, the choir sang a psalm expressive of the feelings of the offerers. When the custom of public offering was discontinued, the psalm was reduced to one verse, known as the Offertory Antiphon, or simply the Offertory.

1. *The Offertory* for the Feast of the Sacred Heart is very appropriately taken from Ps. 68, 21 :

The Offertory

Ps. 68. 21 Impropérium exspectávit Cor meum et misériam, et sustínui qui simul mecum contristarétur et non fuit; consolántem me quæsívi et non invéni.

My Heart hath expected reproach and misery, and I looked for one that would grieve together with Me, but there was none: and for one that would comfort Me, and I found none.

2. *The Offertory Prayers.*

To-day bread and wine are not brought to the altar by the faithful; they are prepared beforehand: the bread in the shape of a wafer (altar-bread) is on the paten, the wine in a cruet on the credence table; a second cruet contains water.

---

*The essential Sacrificial Action consists in the Consecration. See pages 54 and 74. —*Editor,* 1990.

(a) *Offering of the Bread.*

The priest takes the paten with the host, raises it, looks up to heaven and then down at the host, and says silently the following prayer:

Suscipe, sancte Pater, omnipotens æterne Deus, hanc immaculatam hostiam, quam ego indignus famulus tuus offero tibi Deo meo vivo et vero, pro innumerabilibus peccatis, et offensionibus, et negligentiis meis, et pro omnibus circumstantibus, sed et pro omnibus fidelibus Christianis vivis atque defunctis: ut mihi et illis proficiat ad salutem in vitam æternam. Amen.

Accept, O holy Father, almighty and eternal God, this spotless host, which I, Thine unworthy servant offer unto Thee, my living and true God, for my countless sins, trespasses and omissions; likewise for all here present, and for all faithful Christians, whether living or dead, that it may avail me and them as a means of salvation unto life everlasting. Amen.

(b) *Preparation of the Chalice.*

The priest goes to the Epistle side, takes the cruet of wine from the server and pours as much as is needed into the chalice. He then pours a little water into the chalice. The wine is the symbol of the Divinity, the water the symbol of the Humanity. As in Christ Divinity and Humanity were united, so the Holy Sacrifice is to unite us with God. For this reason the priest blesses the water, saying:

Deus, qui humanæ substantiæ dignitatem mirabiliter condidisti, et mirabilius reformasti: da nobis per hujus aquæ et vini mysterium, ejus divinitatis esse consortes, qui humanitatis nostræ fieri dignatus est particeps, Jesus Christus Filius tuus Dominus noster: Qui tecum vivit et regnat in unitate Spiritus Sancti Deus: per omnia sæcula sæculorum. Amen.

O God, Who in creating man didst exalt his nature very wonderfully, and yet more wonderfully didst establish it anew; by the mystery signified in the mingling of this water and wine, grant us to have part in the God-head of Him Who vouchsafed to share our manhood, Jesus Christ Thy Son, our Lord, Who liveth and reigneth with Thee in the unity of the Holy Ghost, God; world without end. Amen.

(c) Offering of the Chalice.

Returning to the middle of the altar, the priest lifts the chalice to about the level of the eyes, and offers it to God with the following prayer:

Offerimus tibi, Domine, calicem salutaris, tuam deprecantes clementiam: ut in conspectu divinæ majestatis tuæ, pro nostra et totius mundi salute cum odore suavitatis ascendat. Amen.

We offer up to Thee, O Lord, the chalice of salvation, beseeching Thee that of Thy mercy our sacrifice may ascend with an odor of sweetness in the sight of Thy Divine Majesty, to avail for our own and for the whole world's salvation. Amen.

All visible gifts are only symbols. Bread and wine are not only to be the matter for consecration, but also a figure of the whole spiritual family, the congregation of the faithful, which offers itself as a sacrifice to God in the visible sacrificial gifts. For this reason the priest, bowing down over the altar, pronounces the beautiful words with which the three young Hebrews in the Babylonian captivity offered themselves to God in place of the legal sacrifices (Dan. 3, 39-40):

In spiritu humilitatis, et in animo contrito suscipiamur a te, Domine: et sic fiat sacrificium nostrum in conspectu tuo hodie, ut placeat tibi, Domine Deus.

Humbled in mind, and contrite of heart, may we find favor with Thee, O Lord; and may the Sacrifice we this day offer up, be well-pleasing to Thee, Who art our Lord and our God.

(d) Prayer to the Holy Ghost.

Raising his eyes to heaven, the priest invokes the Holy Ghost upon the oblation. "The Holy Ghost is the Transformer. As in the beginning of time He changed the primeval chaos into this beautiful universe, as on the first Pentecost Day He transformed the hearts of the Apostles and in the Sacraments makes children of God out of sinful men, so He is to change the gifts lying upon the altar into the Body and Blood of Christ at the Consecration":

Veni, sanctificator omnipotens æterne Deus, et benedic

Come, Thou the Sanctifier, God Almighty and Everlasting;

THE "OFFERTORY."
(Oblation of the Host.)

THE "LAVABO."
(The Washing of the Hands.)

© BB   THE "SANCTUS."

THE "HANC IGITUR."

hoc sacrificium tuo sancto no-
mini præparatum.

bless this Sacrifice prepared for
the glory of Thy holy Name.

At Solemn High Mass the offerings as well as the altar are incensed.
Whilst putting incense into the thurible, the priest says:

Per intercessiónem beáti Mi-
chaélis archángeli stantis a dex-
tris altáris incénsi, et ómnium
electórum suórum, incénsum
istud dignétur Dóminus bene-
dícere, et in odórem suavitátis
accípere. Per Christum Dóminum nostrum. Amen.

By the intercession of blessed
Michael the Archangel, who
standeth at the right hand of
the altar of incense, and of all
His elect, may the Lord vouchsafe to bless this incense and to
receive it for an odor of sweetness. Through Christ our Lord.
Amen.

He incenses the bread and wine on the altar with the words:

Incénsum istud a te benedíc-
tum, ascéndat ad te Dómine, et
descéndat super nos misericór-
dia tua.

May this incense, blessed by
Thee, ascend before Thee, O
Lord, and may Thy mercy de-
scend upon us.

Then he proceeds to incense the altar, saying meanwhile:

Dirigátur, Dómine, orátio
mea, sicut incénsum, in cons-
péctu tuo; elevátio mánuum
meárum sacrifícium vespertí-
num. Pone, Dómine, custódiam
ori meo, et óstium circumstán-
tiæ lábiis meis: ut non declínet
cor meum in verba malítiæ, ad
excusándas excusatiónes in
peccátis.

Let my prayer be directed, O
Lord, as incense in Thy sight;
let this lifting up of my hands be
as an evening sacrifice. Set a
watch, O Lord, before my
mouth, and a door about my
lips, that my heart may not in-
cline to evil words, nor to find
excuse for my sins.

The celebrant returns the censer to the deacon with the words:

Accéndat in nobis Dóminus
ignem sui amóris, et flammam
ætérnæ caritátis. Amen.

May the Lord enkindle in us
the fire of His love and the
flame of everlasting charity.
Amen.

Finally, the celebrant himself, the clergy and the people are incensed,
in order to sanctify them also for the Great Sacrifice. Meanwhile the
celebrant turns to the acolytes and washes his hands. The washing of

hands is necessary after handling the censer; but the action expresses the spiritual purity everyone who offers the Sacrifice should possess.

(e) *The Lavabo.*

Whilst washing his hands, the priest recites a portion of the 25th Psalm. From the first words of this psalm the ceremony is called the *Lavabo*—"I will wash":

The Lavabo

Lavabo inter innocentes manus meas:

Et circumdabo altare tuum, Domine.

Ut audiam vocem laudis:

Et enarrem universa mirabilia tua.

Domine, dilexi decorem domus tuæ:

Et locum habitationis gloriæ tuæ.

Ne perdas cum impiis, Deus, animam meam:

Et cum viris sanguinum vitam meam.

In quorum manibus iniquitates sunt:

Dextera eorum repleta est muneribus.

Ego autem in innocentia mea ingressus sum:

Redime me, et miserere mei.

Pes meus stetit in directo:

In ecclesiis benedicam te, Domine.

Gloria, etc.

I will wash my hands in innocence,

And walk in procession round Thy Altar,

To hear the words of praising song,

And to chant of all Thy wondrous deeds.

O Lord, I love Thy beauteous house,

And the place where Thy glory dwelleth!

Destroy not my soul with the impious, O God,

Nor my life with men of blood:

On whose hands injustice cleaveth,

And whose right hand is full of bribes.

But in blamelessness I come to Thee;

Rescue me and pity me!

My foot is on the straight path;

In the assemblies I will praise Thee, O Lord!

Glory, etc.

(f) *Prayer for the Fruits of the Sacrifice.*

After the *Lavabo* the priest returns to the center of the altar, where with bent body, he commends again the Sacrifice to God and asks for all the offerers a share in its fruits:

Suscipe, s a n c t a Trinitas, hanc oblationem, quam tibi offerimus ob memoriam passionis, resurrectionis, et ascensionis Jesu Christi Domini nostri: et in honorem beatæ Mariæ semper virginis, et beati Joannis Baptistæ, et sanctorum apostolorum Petri et Pauli, et istorum, et omnium sanctorum: ut illis proficiat ad honorem, nobis autem ad salutem: et illi pro nobis intercedere dignentur in cœlis, quorum memoriam agimus in terris. Per eumdem Christum Dominum nostrum. Amen.

Receive, O Holy Trinity, this oblation offered up by us to Thee, in memory of the Passion, Resurrection, and Ascension of Our Lord Jesus Christ, and in honor of blessed Mary ever a Virgin, of blessed John the Baptist, of the holy Apostles Peter and Paul, of Thy Saints whose relics are here, and of all Thy Saints, that it be to them for an increase of honor and to us of salvation; and may they whose memory we celebrate on earth vouchsafe to intercede for us in heaven. Through the same Christ our Lord. Amen.

Turning to the people, he asks them also to pray for the fruits of the Sacrifice:

The Orate Fratres

Orate, fratres, ut meum ac vestrum sacrificium acceptabile fiat apud Deum Patrem omnipotentem.

Pray, Brethren, that this Sacrifice, which is both mine and yours, may be well-pleasing to God the Father Almighty.

The servers answer for the people:

R. Suscipiat Dominus sacrificium de manibus tuis, ad laudem et gloriam nominis sui, ad utilitatem quoque nostram, totiusque Ecclesiæ suæ sanctæ.

R. May the Lord receive this Sacrifice at thy hands, to the praise and glory of His Name, to our good likewise, and to that of all His holy Church.

(g) *The Secret Prayer.*

The Offertory concludes with the prayer over the oblations commonly called the Secret prayer. Originally it was the only prayer said in blessing and petition over the offerings. Like the Collect, the Secret usually makes some direct reference to the feast or mystery of the day.

The Secret Prayer

Réspice, quæsumus, Dómine, ad ineffábilem Cordis dilécti Fílii tui caritátem : ut quod offérimus sit tibi munus accéptum et nostrórum expiátio delictórum. Per eúmdem Dóminum.

O Lord, we beseech Thee, look upon the inconceivable love of the Heart of Thy dear Son, so that our offering may be to Thee an acceptable gift, to us the expiation of sin. Through the same Lord. . . .

B. *The Consecration*

The Sacrifice is prepared, offered to God, and sanctified. The faithful have offered their gifts and in these gifts they have offered themselves as a spiritual sacrifice. Detached from all things of earth, purified and sanctified, they now enter upon the most sacred part of the Mass, the *Canon* (i.e., the "changeless rule," because it is the same in every Mass). The first prayer of the Canon is called the Preface, because, in the Roman Rite, it is regarded as an introduction to the Canon proper.

1. *The Preface.*

In our present Missals there are fifteen Prefaces. In all Prefaces there are two leading ideas: thanksgiving to God for the Incarnation and other benefits, with special allusion to the occasion of the Mass, and then calling on the angelic host to join us in honoring the majesty of God. The Preface for the Mass of the Sacred Heart was prescribed by Pope Pius XI. After the usual greeting, the priest calls upon the people to lift up their minds and hearts to the contemplation of heavenly things and to give thanks to God:

The Preface

P. Per omnia sæcula sæculorum.

P. World without end.

R. Amen.

R. Amen.

P. Dominus vobiscum.

P. The Lord be with you.

R. Et cum spiritu tuo.

R. And with thy spirit.

P. Sursum corda.

P. Lift up your hearts.

R. Habemus ad Dominum.

R. We have them lifted unto the Lord.

P. Gratias agamus Domino Deo nostro.

P. Let us give thanks to the Lord our God.

R. Dignum et justum est.

R. It is meet and just (i.e., fitting and proper).

P. Vere dignum et justum

P. It is truly meet and just,

est, æquum et salutáre, nos tibi semper, et ubíque grátias ágere: Dómine sancte, Pater omnípotens, ætérne Deus: Qui Unigénitum tuum in cruce pendéntem láncea mílitis transfígi voluísti, ut apértum Cor, divínæ largitátis sacrárium, torréntes nobis fúnderet miseratiónis et grátiæ, et quod amóre nostri flagráre nunquam déstitit, piis esset réquies et pœniténtibus patéret salútis refúgium. Et ídeo cum Angelis et Archángelis, cum T h r o n i s et Dominatiónibus, cumque omni milítia cœléstis exércitus, hymnum glóriæ tuæ cánimus, sine fine dicéntes:

right and availing unto salvation that we should at all times and in all places give thanks unto Thee, O Holy Lord, Father Almighty, everlasting God. Who didst will that Thy Son when hanging on the Cross should be pierced with a soldier's lance, so that His Heart, the treasury of divine bounty, should be opened to pour out upon us the streams of divine mercy, and that, burning with never-failing love for us, it should become the resting-place of pious souls, the refuge of salvation to the penitent. And therefore with A n g e l s and Archangels, with Thrones and Dominations, and w i t h the whole army of the heavenly host, we sing a hymn to Thy glory and unceasingly repeat: Holy, Holy, Holy, Lord God of Hosts! Heaven and earth are filled with Thy glory. Hosanna [hail to Thee] in the highest! Blessed is He that cometh in the Name of the Lord! Hosanna in the highest!

The Sanctus

Sanctus, sanctus, sanctus Dominus Deus Sabaoth.

Pleni sunt cœli et terra gloria tua.

Hosanna in excelsis.

Benedictus qui venit in nomine Domini.

Hosanna in excelsis.

Holy, holy, holy, Lord God of hosts.

The heavens and the earth are full of Thy glory.

Hosanna in the highest.

Blessed is He Who cometh in the name of the Lord.

Hosanna in the highest.

Christ, the God of Hosts (Sabaoth), the King of the heavenly armies, is approaching. The Angels of Heaven are summoned to sing to their King the *Trisagion* or *Thrice Holy,* which the Prophet Isaias heard the Seraphim sing (Isaias, 6, 1 ff.). United with them, the congregation awaits the coming of the "Son of David," repeating the jubilant acclamation of Palm Sunday (Matt. 21, 9).

2. *The Canon.*

"Deep silence, whispered prayers, which are always the same. It is as though a breath of eternity lay upon the prayers which enfold the Act of Consecration: Prayer for Blessing, Remembrance of the Living, Invocation of the Saints, Prayer of Acceptance of the Sacrifice—the Consecration—Prayer for Acceptance, Remembrance of the Dead, Invocation of the Saints, Solemn Conclusion."

(a) *Prayers before the Consecration.*

The priest, first raising his eyes to Heaven, joins his hands and, bowing down over the altar, reverently kisses the stone upon which Christ's Body will be laid. He then uplifts his hands in the traditional attitude of prayer and begins silently:

The Te Igitur

Te igitur, clementissime Pater, per Jesum Christum, Filium tuum, Dominum nostrum, supplices rogamus ac petimus, uti accepta habeas, et benedicas hæc ✠ dona, hæc ✠ munera, hæc ✠ sancta sacrificia illibata, in primis quæ tibi offerimus pro Ecclesia tua sancta catholica: quam pacificare, custodire, adunare, et regere digneris toto orbe terrarum: una cum famulo tuo Papa nostro N., et Antistite nostro N., et omnibus orthodoxis, atque catholicæ et apostolicæ fidei cultoribus.

Wherefore, we humbly beg and beseech Thee, Most Merciful Father, t h r o u g h Jesus Christ, Thy Son, our Lord, to receive and to bless these gifts, these oblations, these holy and spotless sacrificial offerings. We offer them up to Thee, in the first place, for Thy Holy Catholic Church. Do Thou vouchsafe in all the earth to bestow upon her Thy peace, to keep her, to gather her together, and to guide her with Thy servant *N.,* our Pope, *N.,* our Bishop, all true believers and all who promote the Catholic and Apostolic Faith.

This general intercession for the Church and her privileged members is followed by special intercessions, the so-called *Memento* or *Commemoration of the Living:*

Commemoration of the Living

Memento Domine, famulorum famularumque tuarum, N. et N., et omnium circumstantium, quorum tibi fides cognita est, et nota devotio, pro quibus tibi offerimus, vel qui tibi offerunt hoc sacrificium laudis, pro se suisque omnibus: pro redemptione animarum suarum, pro spe salutis, et incolumitatis suæ: tibique reddunt vota sua æterno Deo, vivo et vero.

Be mindful, O Lord, of Thy servants and of Thine handmaidens, *N.N.* (*Here the priest makes supplication by name for those for whom he desires more especially to pray*) and of all here present, the faith of each one of whom is known to Thee, as likewise their devotion. For them we offer up to Thee this Sacrifice of Praise, as they too offer it to Thee for themselves and all who are theirs, for the salvation of their own souls, for the health and welfare they hope for, and pay their vows to Thee, God Everlasting, Living and True.

The *Saints of Heaven* too are invoked to unite with the faithful for the reception of the Savior:

The Communicantes

Communicantes, et memoriam venerantes, in primis gloriosæ semper Virginis Mariæ, Genitricis Dei et Domini nostri Jesu Christi: sed et beatorum apostolorum ac martyrum tuorum, Petri et Pauli, Andreæ, Jacobi, Joannis, Thomæ, Jacobi, Philippi, Bartholomæi, Matthæi, Simonis et Thaddæi, Lini, Cleti, Clementis, Xysti, Cornelii, Cypriani, Laurentii, Chrysogoni, Joannis et Pauli, Cosmæ et Damiani, et omnium sanctorum tuorum; quorum meritis, precibusque concedas, ut in omnibus

Having communion with the Saints, we venerate the memory, in the first place, of the glorious Mary ever a Virgin, Mother of Jesus Christ, our God and our Lord; but also of thy blessed Apostles and Martyrs, Peter and Paul, Andrew, James, John, Thomas, James, Philip, Bartholomew, Matthew, Simon, and Thaddaeus; of Linus, Cletus, Clement, Xystus, Cornelius, Cyprian, Laurence, Chrysogonus, John and Paul, Cosmas and Damian and all Thy Saints: for the sake of

protectionis tuæ muniamur auxilio. Per eumdem Christum Dominum nostrum. Amen.

whose merits and prayers do Thou grant us to be in all things safeguarded by Thy sure defense. Through the same Christ, our Lord. Amen.

In the Old Testament, when an Israelite brought his goat, ox, or sheep to the Temple, he laid his hand on it to show that he gave it to God in expiation for his sins. So too in the Mass, the priest spreads his hands over the Oblation, praying that Almighty God might graciously accept it as a Propitiatory Sacrifice:

The Hanc Igitur

Hanc igitur oblationem servitutis nostræ, sed et cunctæ familiæ tuæ, quæsumus, Domine, ut placatus accipias: diesque nostros in tua pace disponas, atque ab æterna damnatione nos eripi, et in electorum tuorum jubeas grege numerari. Per Christum Dominum nostrum. Amen.

Wherefore, we beseech Thee, O Lord, to be appeased by this Oblation which we, Thy servants, and with us Thy whole family (*the congregation*), offer up to Thee, and graciously to receive it. Do Thou establish our days in Thy peace, nor suffer that we be condemned, but rather command that we be numbered in the flock of Thine elect. Through Christ, our Lord. Amen.

(b) The Consecration Prayers.

Using expressions found in the Roman Law, the priest makes a final offering of the sacrificial gifts to God, that they "may be changed into the Body and Blood of Jesus Christ."

Quam oblationem tu, Deus, in omnibus, quæsumus benedictam ✠, adscriptam ✠, ratam ✠, rationabilem, acceptabilemque facere digneris: ut nobis corpus ✠ et sanguis ✠fiat dilectissimi Filii tui Domini nostri Jesu Christi.

Do Thou, O God, in all ways vouchsafe to bless this same Oblation, to take it for Thy very own, to approve it, to perfect it, and to render it well-pleasing to Thyself, so that, on our behalf, it may be changed into the Body and Blood of Jesus Christ, Thy most dear Son, Our Lord—

Time fades away. It is again the eve of the Passion. Christ is present in Person amongst His people. In the person of the priest He Himself pronounces the almighty words of Consecration.

Qui pridie quam pateretur, accepit panem in sanctas ac venerabiles manus suas, et elevatis oculis in cœlum ad te Deum Patrem suum omnipotentem, tibi gratias agens, benedixit ✠, fregit, deditque discipulis suis, dicens: Accipite, et manducate ex hoc omnes:

Who the day before He suffered, took bread into His holy and venerable hands and, having lifted up His eyes to Heaven to Thee, God, His Almighty Father, giving thanks to Thee, blessed it, broke it, and gave it to His disciples, saying: Take ye all and eat of this:

Hoc Est Enim Corpus Meum. For This Is My Body

The priest makes a genuflection, and then elevates the sacred host that all present may adore it. (His Holiness, Pope Pius X, on May 18, 1907, granted an indulgence of seven years and seven quarantines, to all the faithful, who, at the Elevation during Mass, or at public exposition of the Blessed Sacrament, look at the sacred host and devoutly say: "My Lord and my God.") At the elevation the sanctuary bell is rung. Having placed the sacred host upon the corporal the priest again makes a genuflection. Uncovering the chalice, he says:

Simili modo postquam cœnatum est, accipiens et hunc præclarum calicem in sanctas ac venerabiles manus suas: item tibi gratias agens bene✠dixit, deditque discipulis suis, dicens: Accipite, et bibite ex eo omnes:

Hic est enim Calix Sanguinis mei, novi et æterni testamenti: mysterium fidei, qui pro vobis et pro multis effundetur in remissionem peccatorum.

Hæc quotiescumque feceritis, in mei memoriam facietis.

In like manner, when the supper was done, taking also into His holy and venerable hands this goodly Chalice, again giving thanks to Thee, He blessed it, and gave it to His disciples, saying: Take ye all and drink of this:

For this is the chalice of My blood, of the new and everlasting testament—the mystery of faith — which for you and for many shall be shed unto the remission of sins.

As often as ye shall do these things, ye shall do them in memory of Me.

The "Consecration of the Host."
"This Is My Body."

The "Elevation of the Host."
"My Lord and My God."

The Consecration of the Wine.
"This Is the Chalice of My Blood."

© BB

The Elevation of the Chalice.
"My Jesus, Mercy."

The great miracle of Transubstantiation is wrought; there is no longer bread and wine, but the Body and Blood of Christ; there is no longer the matter of the sacrifice, which was offered a little before, but the true Victim of Calvary veiled under the sacred species. The Host is separated from the Chalice because the Death of the Lord is represented, in which His Blood was spilt and separated from the Body. Here He lies, surrounded and adored by Angels, the Victim of Calvary, the Lamb that was slain, showing His Wounds and Blood to the Heavenly Father (Schouppe). All who belong to the Mystical Body of Christ are assembled around the Cross of the Lord. Looking up at the Consecrated Host and Chalice, elevated on high, the kneeling multitude utters the cry of the Apostle: "My Lord and my God!"

"Do this in remembrance of Me," the Lord had said. Fulfilling this command, the priest continues:

Unde et memores, Domine, nos servi tui, sed et plebs tua sancta, ejusdem Christi Filii tui Domini nostri, tam beatæ passionis, necnon et ab inferis resurrectionis, sed et in cœlos gloriosæ ascensionis: offerimus præclaræ majestati tuæ de tuis donis ac datis, hostiam ✠ puram, hostiam ✠ sanctam, hostiam ✠ immaculatam panem sanctum ✠ vitæ æternæ, et calicem ✠ salutis perpetuæ.

Wherefore, O Lord, we Thy servants, and likewise Thy holy people, calling to mind not only the blessed passion of the same Christ Thy Son, but also His resurrection from the dead, and finally His glorious ascension into heaven, offer unto Thy Supreme Majesty, of Thy gifts bestowed upon us, the pure, the holy, the all-perfect Sacrifice of thanks for our redemption—the holy Bread of life eternal and the Chalice of unending salvation.

(c) Prayers After the Consecration.

These gifts—"the holy Bread of Life eternal and the Chalice of unending salvation"—the priest now offers to God the Father as the only sacrifice that can satisfy the infinite holiness and justice of God:

Supra quæ propitio ac sereno vultu respicere digneris, et accepta habere, sicuti accepta habere dignatus es munera pueri tui justi Abel, et sacrificium Patriarchæ nostri Abrahæ: et

Vouchsafe to look upon it with a gracious and tranquil countenance, and to accept it, even as Thou wast pleased to accept the offerings of righteous Abel, Thy servant, the sac-

quod tibi obtulit summus sacerdos tuus Melchisedech, sanctum sacrificium, immaculatam hostiam.

rifice of Abraham, our Patriarch, and that which Melchisedech, Thy High Priest, offered up to Thee, a holy sacrifice, a victim without blemish.

Then the priest bows down over the altar and prays:

Supplices te rogamus, omnipotens Deus, jube hæc perferri per manus sancti angeli tui in sublime altare tuum, in conspectu divinæ majestatis tuæ: ut quotquot, ex hac altaris participatione, sacrosanctum Filii tui corpus ✠ et ✠ sanguinem sumpserimus, omni benedictione cœlesti et gratia repleamur. Per eumdem Christum Dominum nostrum. Amen.

Most humbly we beseech Thee, Almighty God, to command that by the hands of Thy holy Angel this our Sacrifice be uplifted to Thine Altar on high into the very presence of Thy Divine Majesty, that as many of us as, by partaking thereof from this altar, shall have received the adorable Body and Blood of Thy Son, may from Heaven be filled with all graces and blessings. Through the same Christ our Lord. Amen.

The Angel of the congregation who carries all prayers and good works before the throne of God (cf. Apoc. 8, 4) will present this Sacrifice also and in return bring back God's blessings and graces for the living and the dead. The priest prays for the *faithful departed* first:

Commemoration of the Dead

Memento etiam, Domine, famulorum famularumque tuarum N. et N., qui nos præcesserunt cum signo fidei, et dormiunt in somno pacis.

Ipsis, Domine, et omnibus in Christo quiescentibus, locum refrigerii, lucis, et pacis, ut indulgeas, deprecamur. Per eumdem Christum, etc. Amen.

Be mindful also, O Lord, of Thy servants and of Thy handmaidens, *N.N.* who have gone before us with the sign of faith and who sleep the sleep of peace.

For them, O Lord, and for all who rest in Christ, do Thou, we beseech Thee, appoint a place of solace, of light, and of peace. Through the same Christ our Lord. Amen.

Then the priest prays for himself and for the whole congregation, raising his voice and striking his breast in acknowledgment of his sins:

Nobis quoque peccatoribus famulis tuis, de multitudine miserationum tuarum sperantibus, partem aliquam, et societatem donare digneris, cum tuis sanctis apostolis et martyribus: cum Joanne, Stephano, Mathia, Barnaba, Ignatio, Alexandro, Marcellino, Petro, Felicitate, Perpetua, Agatha, Lucia, Agnete, Cæcilia, Anastasia, et omnibus sanctis tuis: intra quorum nos consortium, non æstimator meriti, sed veniæ, quæsumus, largitor admitte. Per Christum Dominum nostrum.

On ourselves too, who are sinners, but yet Thy servants, and who put our trust in the multitude of Thy tender mercies, vouchsafe to bestow some lot and fellowship with Thy holy Apostles and Martyrs: with Stephen, John, Matthias, Barnabas, Ignatius, Alexander, Marcellinus, Peter, Felicitas, Perpetua, Agatha, Lucy, Agnes, Cecilia, Anastasia, and with all Thy Saints. Into their company do Thou, we beseech Thee, admit us, not weighing our merits, but freely pardoning us our sins. Through Christ our Lord.

Here in the early Church the produce of the earth, oil for the sick, etc. were blessed:

Per quem hæc omnia, Domine, semper bona creas, sancti✠ficas, vivi✠ficas, bene✠dicis, et præstas nobis.

By Whom, O Lord, Thou dost at all times create, hallow, fill with life and bestow upon us all these good things.

The Consecration Prayers close with a solemn Doxology suggested by Rom. 11, 36:

Per ip✠sum, et cum ip✠so, et in ip✠so, est tibi Deo Patri ✠ omnipotenti, in unitate Spiritus ✠ Sancti, omnis honor et gloria. Per omnia sæcula sæculorum. Amen.

"Through Him, and with Him, and in Him, is to Thee, Who art God, the Father Almighty, in the unity of the Holy Ghost, all honor and all glory. World without end. Amen.

As the priest says "all honor and all glory," he elevates the Host and Chalice together a little above the altar. Formerly when the priest celebrated with his face turned towards the congregation, this was the only elevation. The first elevation at the Consecration was introduced during the Middle Ages. The concluding words of the Doxology are said by the priest in a loud voice in order to make known to the faithful present that the Canon is ended.

C. *The Communion*

"The command of the Lord has been carried out, the memory of His Passion has been renewed, not in mere words or symbols, but in mysterious actuality. Christ Himself lies upon the altar as the Victim of salvation, veiled under the sacramental species. But one thing is still wanting: the conclusion of the Sacrifice, the *sacrificial* Banquet, which is to make all the offerers sharers of the Godhead and perfect their mystical union with one another and with Christ. For this sublime act the congregation prepares itself by reciting the prayer which the Lord Himself gave them to be their daily table and family prayer—the Our Father." It was St. Gregory the Great who put the *Pater Noster* in its present place; it was he too who inserted the name of St. Andrew in the *embolism* after the Pater Noster, because he was the patron of the monastery which Gregory had founded in Rome.

1. *The Pater Noster.*

With solemn words the priest asks all to join in the Lord's Prayer:

The Pater Noster

Præceptis salutaribus moniti, et divina institutione formati, audemus dicere:

Pater noster, qui es in cœlis: sanctificetur nomen tuum: adveniat regnum tuum: fiat voluntas tua, sicut in cœlo, et in terra. Panem nostrum quotidianum da nobis hodie: et dimitte nobis debita nostra, sicut et nos dimittimus debitoribus nostris. Et ne nos inducas in tentationem.

R. Sed libera nos a malo.

P. Amen.

Admonished by salutary precepts, and following divine directions. we presume to say:

Our Father, Who art in heaven, hallowed be Thy name; Thy kingdom come; Thy will be done on earth as it is in heaven; give us this day our daily bread; and forgive us our trespasses, as we forgive those who trespass against us; and lead us not into temptation.

R. But deliver us from evil.

P. Amen.

Fearing lest sin and human frailty hinder the glorious effects of the Holy Sacrifice, the Church has expanded the last petition of the Our Father into a beautiful *Prayer of Supplication:*

Libera nos, quæsumus, Domine, ab omnibus malis, præteritis, præsentibus, et futuris: et intercedente beata et gloriosa

Deliver us, O Lord, we beseech Thee, from all evils, past, present, and to come; and through the intercession of the

semper virgine Dei genitrice Maria, cum beatis apostolis tuis Petro et Paulo, atque Andrea, et omnibus sanctis, ✠ da propitius pacem in diebus nostris : ut ope misericordiæ tuæ adjuti, et a peccato simus semper liberi, et ab omni perturbatione securi. Per eumdem Dominum nostrum Jesum Christum Filium tuum, qui tecum vivit et regnat in unitate Spiritus Sancti Deus. Per omnia sæcula sæculorum.

R. Amen.

glorious and blessed Mary ever a virgin, Mother of God, together with Thy blessed Apostles, Peter and Paul and Andrew, and all the Saints, grant of Thy goodness peace in our days, that, aided by the riches of Thy mercy, we may be always free from sin and safe from all disturbance : Through the same Jesus Christ, Thy Son, our Lord, Who liveth and reigneth with Thee, in the unity of the Holy Ghost, God, for ever and ever. Amen.

2. The Breaking of the Bread.

During the concluding words of the last prayer the priest breaks the Host into three parts; the two larger ones he places on the paten for his own Communion, makes the sign of the coss thrice over the Chalice with the third particle, saying :

P. Pax ✠ Domini sit ✠ semper vobis ✠ cum.

The peace of the Lord be ever with you.

He then lets the particle fall into the Chalice. Whilst doing so, he says a prayer which reminds us of the ancient custom of receiving Holy Communion under both forms by the faithful :

Hæc commixtio et consecratio corporis et sanguinis Domini nostri Jesu Christi, fiat accipientibus nobis in vitam æternam. Amen.

May this commingling and consecrating of the Body and Blood of our Lord Jesus Christ be to us who shall receive It unto life everlasting. Amen.

3. Prayers before Communion.

All is in readiness for the Sacrificial Banquet. All the offerers are about to receive the Holy Bread and in and with Christ become one soul. For this reason the faithful in ancient times gave each other the *Kiss of Peace* before Holy Communion. The kiss of peace is still given to-day, but only at Solemn High Mass, and is exchanged only between the celebrant and the clergy. The prayers which precede Holy Communion still remind us of the ancient custom :

(a) *Agnus Dei—*

Agnus Dei, qui tollis peccata mundi: miserere nobis.

Lamb of God, Who takest away the sins of the world: have mercy on us.

Agnus Dei, qui tollis peccata mundi: miserere nobis.

Lamb of God, Who takest away the sins of the world: have mercy on us.

Agnus Dei, qui tollis peccata mundi: dona nobis pacem.

Lamb of God, Who takest away the sins of the world: grant us peace.

(b) *Prayer for Peace.*

With head bowed down, the priest addresses the Divine Victim, beseeching Him to give peace to the universal Church:

Domine Jesu Christe, qui dixisti apostolis tuis: Pacem relinquo vobis, pacem meam do vobis; ne respicias peccata mea, sed fidem Ecclesiæ tuæ: eamque s e c u n d u m voluntatem tuam, pacificare et coadunare digneris: Qui vivis et regnas Deus, per omnia sæcula sæculorum. Amen.

O Lord Jesus Christ, Who didst say to Thine Apostles: Peace I leave you, My peace I give unto you; look not upon my sins but upon the faith of Thy Church, and deign to keep it in peace and unity, according to Thy will. Who livest and reignest, God, world without end. Amen.

(c) *The Priest's Immediate Preparation for Communion.*

Domine Jesu Christe, Fili Dei vivi, qui ex voluntate Patris, co-operante Spiritu Sancto, per mortem tuam mundum vivificasti: libera me per hoc sacrosanctum corpus et sanguinem tuum, ab omnibus iniquitatibus meis, et universis malis: et fac me tuis semper inhærere mandatis, et a te nunquam separari permittas: Qui cum eodem Deo Patre et Spiritu Sancto vivis et

O Lord Jesus Christ, Son of the living God, Who, fulfilling the Father's will, with the co-operation of the Holy Ghost, by Thy death hast given life to the world: for the sake of this Thy Sacred Body and Blood, free me from all my wickedness and from every evil. Make me to cleave to Thy Commandments and suffer not that at any time I be separated from Thee, Who

regnas Deus in sæcula sæculorum. Amen.

Perceptio corporis tui, Domine
Jesu Christe, quod ego indignus
sumere præsumo, non mihi pro-
veniat in judicium et condem-
nationem: sed pro tua pietate
prosit mihi ad tutamentum
mentis et corporis, et ad mede-
lam percipiendam: qui vivis et
regnas cum Deo Patre in unitate Spiritus Sancti Deus, per
omnia sæcula sæculorum. Amen.

with the same God the Father
and the Holy Ghost, livest and
reignest, world without end.
Amen.

Let not the partaking of Thy
Body, O Lord Jesus Christ,
which I, all unworthy, presume
to receive, turn to my judgment
and condemnation; but do
Thou, in Thy loving kindness,
make it to avail me to my healing and safekeeping in body
and in soul. Who livest and
reignest with God the Father,
in the unity of the Holy Ghost,
world without end. Amen.

(d) *The Priest's Communion.*

After this final preparation the priest takes the Sacred Host into his
hand, saying:

Panem cœlestem accipiam, et
nomen Domini invocabo.

I will take the Bread of
Heaven and will call upon the
Name of the Lord.

Then, humbly and devoutly, striking his breast, he raises his voice, and
three times repeats the words of the Centurion of Capharnaum:

Domine, non sum dignus, ut
intres sub tectum meum: sed
tantum dic verbo, et sanabitur
anima mea.

Lord, I am not worthy that
Thou shouldst enter under my
roof; but only say the word,
and my soul shall be healed.

He now makes the sign of the Cross with the Sacred Host, and reverently receives the Body of the Lord, saying before doing so:

Corpus Domini nostri Jesu
Christi custodiat animam meam
in vitam æternam. Amen.

May the body of Our Lord
Jesus Christ keep my soul unto
life everlasting. Amen.

The "Commemoration of the Dead."

The "Priest's Communion."

© BB   The "Blessing."

The "Last Gospel."

Gathering up any particles that may have fallen on the corporal, the priest says:

Quid retribuam Domino pro omnibus quæ retribuit mihi? Calicem salutaris accipiam, et nomen Domini invocabo. Laudans invocabo Dominum, et ab inimicis meis salvus ero.

What shall I render unto the Lord for all the good things He has rendered unto me? I will take the chalice of salvation and will call upon the name of the Lord. With high praises will I call upon the Lord, and I shall be saved from mine enemies.

Before drinking from the Chalice, he says:

Sanguis Domini nostri Jesu Christi custodiat animam meam in vitam æternam. Amen.

May the Blood of our Lord Jesus Christ keep my soul unto life everlasting. Amen.

When the priest has communicated, he distributes the Bread of Life to the faithful, saying to each: "May the Body of our Lord Jesus Christ keep thy soul unto life everlasting. Amen."

Whilst purifying the Chalice (*the ablutions*), the priest says:

Quod ore sumpsimus, Domine, pura mente capiamus: et de munere temporali fiat nobis remedium sempiternum.

"What we have taken like bodily food, O Lord, may we treasure in a pure heart; and may what is given to us in time be our provision for eternity.

Corpus tuum, Domine, quod sumpsi, et sanguis, quem potavi, adhæreat, visceribus meis: et præsta, ut in me non remaneat scelerum macula, quem pura et sancta refecerunt sacramenta: Qui vivis et regnas sæcula sæculorum. Amen.

May Thy Body, O Lord which I have eaten, and Thy Blood of which I have drunk, penetrate the depths of my soul, and grant that no taint of sin be found in me whom these pure and holy Mysteries have renewed. Who livest and reignest world without end. Amen.

(e) The Communion Verse.

In the Early Church the whole congregation took part in the "Wedding Feast of the Lamb." Only the public sinners were excluded. Meanwhile the choir chanted a Psalm (or several Psalms according to the number of communicants) suited to the solemn occasion. In our Mass to-day only one verse of this Psalm has remained. It is called the *Communion,* or

Communion Verse. It is taken from any part of Holy Scripture. The verse for the Feast of the Sacred Heart is taken from St. John 19, 34:

The Communion Prayer

Unus mílitum láncea latus ejus apéruit, et contínuo exívit sanguis et aqua.

A soldier with a spear opened His side, and immediately came forth blood and water.

In votive Masses during Eastertide the following is read:

Si quis sitit véniat ad me et bibat. Allelúia, allelúia.

If any man thirst, let him come to Me and drink. Alleluia, alleluia.

(f) *The Post-Communion*

With an act of thanksgiving and petition, known as the Post-Communion, the Mass, in ancient times, came to a close. The Post-Communion corresponds to the Collect and Secret, and like them makes reference to the mystery of the day. For the Feast of the Sacred Heart it reads:

The Post-Communion

Práebeant nobis, Dómine Jesu, divínum tua sancta fervórem; quo dulcíssimi Cordis tui suavitáte percépta, discámus terréna despícere, et amáre cœléstia: Qui vivis.

May Thy Holy Mysteries kindle divine fervor in us, O Lord: so that, having experienced the sweetness of Thy most loving Heart, we may learn to despise the things of earth and to cleave to those of Heaven. Who livest and reignest. . . .

(g) *Conclusion.*

In ancient times the Deacon dismissed the faithful after the Post-Communion with the words:

P. Ite, missa est.

P. Go, you are dismissed.

To which they answered:

R. Deo gratias.

R. Thanks be to God.

On days of a penitential character the priest or deacon says (or sings):

Benedicamus Domino.

Let us praise the Lord!

On such days the faithful used to remain in church after Mass and sing the *Office* of the Day with the clergy. In Masses for the Dead a prayer for the departed is substituted:

Requiescant in pace.   May they rest in peace!

Bowing down over the altar, the priest says the following prayer to the Blessed Trinity:

Placeat tibi, Sancta Trinitas, obsequium servitutis meæ: et præsta, ut sacrificium quod oculis tuæ majestatis indignus obtuli, tibi sit acceptabile, mihique, et omnibus pro quibus illud obtuli, sit, te miserante, propitiabile. Per C h r i s t u m Dominum nostrum. Amen.

May the lowly homage of my service be pleasing to Thee, O Most Holy Trinity: and do Thou grant that the Sacrifice which I, all unworthy, have offered up in the sight of Thy Majesty may be acceptable to Thee and, because of Thy loving kindness, may avail to atone to Thee for myself and for all those for whom I have offered it up. Through Christ our Lord. Amen.

Then the priest kisses the altar and, with eyes and hands raised to Heaven, "as if drawing blessings from the very Heart of Jesus," he pours these benedictions on the people in the Name of the Most Holy Trinity:

The Blessing

Benedicat vos omnipotens Deus, Pater, et Filius, ✠ et Spiritus Sanctus.
R. Amen.

May God Almighty bless you: the Father, the Son, and the Holy Ghost. Amen.

After the Blessing, the priest reads the *Beginning of the Gospel* according to St. John:

The Last Gospel

In principio erat Verbum, et Verbum erat apud Deum, et Deus erat Verbum. Hoc erat in principio apud Deum. Omnia per ipsum facta sunt, et sine ipso factum est nihil quod factum est. In ipso vita erat, et vita erat lux hominum; et lux

In the beginning was the Word, and the Word was with God, and the Word was God. The same was in the beginning with God. All things were made by Him, and without Him was made nothing that was made. In Him was life, and the life

in tenebris lucet, et tenebræ eam non comprehenderunt. Fuit homo missus a Deo, cui nomen erat Joannes. Hic venit in testimonium, ut testimonium perhiberet de lumine, ut omnes crederent per illum. Non erat ille lux, sed ut testimonium perhiberet de lumine. Erat lux vera, quæ illuminat omnem hominem venientem in hunc mundum. In mundo erat, et mundus per ipsum factus est, et mundus eum non cognovit. In propria venit, et sui eum non receperunt. Quotquot autem receperunt eum, dedit eis potestatem filios Dei fieri, his qui credunt in nomine ejus, qui non ex sanguinibus, neque ex voluntate carnis, neque ex voluntate viri, sed ex Deo nati sunt.

was the light of men: and the light shineth in darkness, and the darkness did not comprehend it. There was a man sent from God, whose name was John. This man came for a witness to give testimony of the light, that all men might believe through him. He was not the light, but was to give testimony of the light. That was the true light which enlighteneth every man that cometh into this world. He was in the world, and the world was made by Him, and the world knew Him not. He came unto His own, and His own received Him not. But as many as received Him, to them He gave power to become the sons of God: to them that believe in His name: who are born, not of blood, nor of the will of the flesh, nor of the will of man, but of God.

Et Verbum caro factum est, et habitavit in nobis: et vidimus gloriam ejus, gloriam quasi unigeniti a Patre, plenum gratiæ et veritatis.

R. Deo gratias.

And the Word was made flesh, and dwelt among us, and we saw His glory, the glory as of the only-begotten of the Father, full of grace and truth.

R. Thanks be to God.

"In the beginning was the Word, and the Word was with God, and the Word was God. The same was in the beginning with God. All things were made by Him. . . . And the Word was made Flesh, and dwelt among us. . . ."

With this majestic profession of faith in the Divinity of Christ, which alone gives meaning, truth, and efficacy to the Mass, and the heartfelt *Deo gratias* of the faithful for the inestimable benefits they have received, the Mass according to the Roman Rite comes to a fitting close. The prayers recited by the celebrant and the people after a Low Mass were ordered by Leo XIII in 1884.

2. BRIEF INSTRUCTION ABOUT THE ALTAR, SACRED VESSELS AND VESTMENTS[1]

Furniture and Articles on Altar and in Sanctuary.

Observe well the picture of the altar and sanctuary. It is here the Holy Sacrifice of the Mass is offered up. This picture shows everything that is necessary for Mass, and gives the proper name of the furniture of the sanctuary.

1. Crucifix.
2. Canopy or Throne of the Altar.
3. Tabernacle covered by veil (wherever used the veil is of the color of the day or white).
4-9. Large Candlesticks (are lighted only for High Mass and Benediction).
10, 11. Small Candlesticks (are lighted only for Low Mass).
12, 13, 14. Altar Cards (the larger is in the center, containing prayers which the priest reads at the Offertory and Canon. The smaller one on the Epistle side has the prayers read by the priest when washing his hands after the Offertory. The other smaller one on the Gospel side has the Gospel of St. John, which is most frequently read at the end of Mass).
15. First Gradine or Candlebench for the smaller Candlestick.
16. Second Gradine or Candlebench for the larger Candlestick.
17. Mensa or Altar Table.
18. Altar Table Coverings (one wax and three linen cloths cover the altar table. The fourth or top one of linen frequently edged with lace hangs down over the side of the altar to the floor).
19. Antependium or Frontal (wherever customary a cloth of the color of the day hangs down in front of the altar).
20. Gospel Side of the Altar.
21. Epistle Side of the Altar.
22. Sanctuary Floor.
23. First Altar Step.
24. Second Altar Step.
25. Predella or Altar Platform (sometimes called the Footpace).

---

[1] From "The Missal and Holy Mass" by Rev. William J. Lallou, D.D., and Sister Josefita Maria, S.S.J., Ph.D.

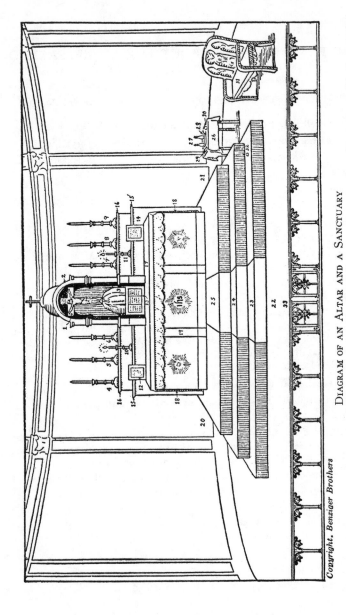

Copyright, Benziger Brothers

DIAGRAM OF AN ALTAR AND A SANCTUARY

The different articles shown in this picture of the Altar and Sanctuary are numbered to agree with the number of their names in the list on pages 183 and 185.

26. Credence Table.

27. Water and Wine Cruets.

28. Finger Basin.

29. Towel.

30. Communion Paten.

31. Sedilia or Priests' Bench.

32. Bell.

33. Communion Rail.

THE ALTAR

The Altar. The altar is the raised structure of wood or stone at which the Mass is celebrated. More correctly, the altar is the stone on which the Holy Sacrifice is offered, for even when the main portion of the altar structure is of wood the chalice and the Host must rest on a slab of stone. So we have two kinds of altars.

> (*a*) The Fixed or Immovable altar
> (*b*) The Movable altar.

The Fixed or Immovable Altar. The Fixed or Immovable Altar is one that is permanently fixed to the floor of the Church. (Figure No. 1.)

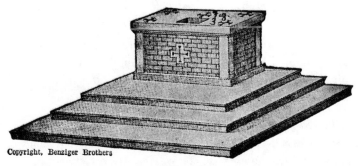

Copyright, Benziger Brothers

Fig. 1
A FIXED ALTAR.

The Movable Altar. The Movable Altar is a rectangular slab of stone inserted in the middle of the table of a wooden altar structure. (Figure No. 2.)

Copyright, Benziger Brothers

Fig. 2

THE TABLE OF A MOVABLE ALTAR WITH THE ALTAR STONE IN PLACE.

The Altar Must Be Solemnly Consecrated. The Altar, before it is used for the celebration of Mass, must be solemnly *consecrated* by the Bishop. The ceremony of consecration is a very long and involved one, in the course of which the altar table, or altar stone, is sprinkled with holy water, specially blessed for the occasion, and anointed many times with holy oils. Near the end of the ceremony relics of Martyrs are always enclosed in a little cavity cut for that purpose in the center of the altar. (See "Fig. 3" in table of movable altar, Figure 1.) In evidence of the Consecration, five crosses are also cut into the stone, one at each corner and one in the centre. The Fixed or Immovable altar is consecrated as a whole, while the movable altar has only a consecrated slab or stone.

The Tabernacle. In the middle of most altars we find a more or less elaborate box, like a little house. This is the *Tabernacle* for the reservation of the Blessed Sacrament and it should be enveloped in a veil of some rich material. This veil may be white in color or it may vary to accord with the color proper to the office of the day.

Altar Steps. The altar is raised above the floor and approached by steps, usually three but sometimes more, and sometimes only one, an uneven number of steps being always employed. (See Figure 1.)

The Sacred Vessels

THE CHALICE AND ITS APPURTENANCES

The Chalice. (fig. a.) This is a cup made of gold or silver, or if of silver, the interior must be of gold. It holds the wine for the Holy Sacrifice, and is a striking figure of the Sacred Heart of Jesus.

The Purificator. (fig. b) This is a linen cloth used for wiping the chalice, and the fingers and mouth of the celebrant after Communion. It is spread over the cup of the chalice at the beginning and end of Mass.

The Paten. (fig. c) This is a plate of gold or silver upon which the large bread for consecration rests until the Offertory. Of old it was necessarily larger than now, for it held all the breads to be consecrated.

The Pall. (fig. d) This is a square pocket-shaped piece of linen with a cardboard inserted in order to stiffen it. It is placed over the chalice to prevent dust or other matter falling into it.

The Chalice Veil. (fig. e) This is the cloth which covers the chalice until the Offertory, and again after the Communion. It also is made of the same material and color as the vestments.

The Burse and Corporal. (fig. f) The *Burse* is a square container for the corporal when the latter is not in use. It is made of the same material and color as the vestments. The *Corporal* is a square piece of linen. In size and appearance it resembles a small napkin. It is spread out on the altar, and the chalice is placed upon it. During the Mass the Sacred Host rests for a time on the Corporal.

The Sacred Vestments

By God's command the Jewish priests wore a distinctive garb when they ministered in the Temple. The Bible tells us they were vested in violet and purple, scarlet twice dyed, and fine linen. Gold and precious stones were also used to give the person of the priest that dignity demanded by his exalted office.

No special dress was at first prescribed for the Christian priesthood. During the early days the garments worn at the Holy Sacrifice were not dissimilar in form to the clothing of civilians.

The Chalice and Its Appurtenances

(a) *The Chalice*

(b) *Chalice and Purificator*

(c) *Chalice, Purificator and Paten with host*

(d) *Chalice, Purificator, Paten and Pall*

(e) *All now covered by Chalice Veil— note the different parts under the Veil*

(f) *The Burse and the Corporal*

(g) *The Chalice completely covered*

They were distinguished, however, from profane apparel in richness and beauty of decorations; and, of course, their use was restricted to divine worship.

Secular fashion changed, but the Church clung to the old style. Thus it was that garments once common to all, presently became the privileged dress of the clergy. Faith then saw in each particular vestment a symbol relating to the Passion of Our Lord, and a reminder of some Christian duty.

The Vestments Worn at Mass

The priest's vestments may be considered now: (a) According to their present use. (b) According to their historical origin. (c) According to their symbolism.

The Amice. (fig. h) The amice is a piece of fine linen in the form of an oblong. The priest places it for a moment on his head, and then allows it to rest upon his shoulders. As he does so he prays: "Place, O Lord, on my head the helmet of salvation, that so I may resist the assaults of the devil."

HISTORICAL ORIGIN: A covering for the head and neck worn like a hood. When indoors it was lowered and thrown over the shoulders.

SYMBOLIC REFERENCE: (a) The linen cloth that the soldiers put over Our Lord's head; when thus blindfolded, He was mockingly asked who struck Him. (b) The helmet of Salvation. (Cf. Ephes. 6:17.)

The Alb. (fig. i) A wide linen robe reaching to the feet and covering the whole body. The vesting prayer is: "Make me white, O Lord, and cleanse my heart; that being made white in the Blood of the Lamb I may deserve an eternal reward."

HISTORICAL ORIGIN: The alb, or tunic, was worn in ancient times by all who enjoyed any dignity.

SYMBOLIC REFERENCE: (a) The garment with which Herod clothed Our Lord. (b) Signifies the purity of conscience demanded of God's priest.

The Cincture. (fig. j) The cincture, or girdle, is a cord of linen fastened about the waist to confine the alb. The vesting prayer is: "Gird me, O Lord, with the cincture of purity, and quench in my heart the fire of concupiscence, that the virtue of continence and chastity may abide in me."

HISTORICAL ORIGIN: Walking and active exertion made it necessary for one to gird up a long garment like the alb. Hence the cincture was an essential article of dress.

SYMBOLIC REFERENCE: (a) The cord that bound Our Lord to the pillar when He was being scourged. (b) Symbolizes modesty, and also readiness for hard work in God's service.

The Maniple. (fig. k) A strip of silken cloth worn on the left arm of the priest. The vesting prayer is: "May I deserve, O Lord, to bear the maniple of weeping and sorrow in order that I may joyfully reap the reward of my labors."

HISTORICAL ORIGIN: Originally a strip of linen worn over the arm. During the long services, and in the intense heat of southern countries its use was frequently necessary to wipe the perspiration from the face and brow.

SYMBOLIC REFERENCE: (a) The rope whereby Our Lord was led, and the chains which bound His sacred hands. (b) An emblem of the tears of penance, the fatigue of the priestly office and its joyful reward in heaven.

The Stole (fig. l). A long band of silk of the same width as the maniple, but three times its length. It is worn around the neck and crossed on the breast. The vesting prayer is: "Restore to me, O Lord, the state of immortality which I lost through the sin of my first parents and, although unworthy to approach Thy Sacred Mysteries, may I deserve nevertheless eternal joy."

HISTORICAL ORIGIN: A kind of neck-piece or kerchief; a part of the dress of the upper classes. It gradually became the distinctive mark of spiritual authority in the higher clerics, viz., the priest and deacon.

SYMBOLIC REFERENCE: (a) The cords with which Jesus was tied. Worn as it is over the shoulders, it reminds us, too, of the cross Our Lord carried. (b) A reminder of the yoke of Christ. The priest's burden is a heavy one, which Christ nevertheless makes sweet.

The Chasuble. (fig. m) The chasuble is the outer and chief vestment of the priest. It is essentially *the* Mass vestment and is now exclusively reserved to the priest. The vestment is familiar

HOW THE PRIEST VESTS TO SAY MASS

(h) *Priest in Amice*

(i) *Priest in Alb*

(j) *Priest adjusting the Cincture*

(k) *Priest putting Maniple on left arm*

(l) *Priest with the Stole*

(m) *Priest in Chasuble is now completely Vested*

to all by reason of the cross usually embroidered on it. The vesting prayer is: "O Lord, who hast said, 'My yoke is sweet and My burden light,' grant that I may so carry it as to merit Thy grace."

HISTORICAL ORIGIN: Imagine a large circular cloth with a hole cut in the center for the head. This will help one to visualize the ancient chasuble, which was an immense cloak, without opening in front, and without sleeves. It was put on over the head and completely enveloped the body. When it was necessary to use the hands, the garment had to be folded up on each side over the arms. Because of its inconvenience (for two assistants were needed to manipulate it), the vestment was gradually cut and altered until it now has its present shape. It is usually ornamented with a large cross on the back, and sometimes on the front of the garment (fig. n). We occasionally see chasubles made in the *Gothic* or *Medieval* style (fig. o). These are more ample and drape over the shoulders down to the wrists. The cross on such chasubles has the shape of the letter "Y," the top arms of which extend over the shoulders towards the front.

Fig. n
A CHASUBLE IN THE USUAL FORM.

Fig. o
A SEMI-GOTHIC CHASUBLE.

SYMBOLIC REFERENCE: (a) The purple cloak worn by Our Lord when He stood before Pilate. (b) An emblem of love. When the ordaining bishop gives it to the new priest, he says: "Receive the priestly garment, for the Lord is powerful to increase in you love and perfection."

VESTMENTS OF THE DEACON, SUBDEACON AT SOLEMN MASS

The Deacon. This word means servitor. One of the principal duties of this sacred minister is to assist the priest during the holy mysteries. He is always at his side, and, by the place of honor which he occupies, he reminds us of the Beloved Disciple leaning on the Heart of Jesus during the last supper, and standing under the cross on Calvary.

The deacon chants the Gospel, and dismisses the people at the end of Mass by intoning: *"Ite, missa est."*

His vestments are the amice, girdle, stole and *dalmatic* (fig. p) ; except the latter, all have already been explained.

The Dalmatic. It was originally worn at Dalmatia, whence it was brought to Rome. It is a long and ample garment, with very large but short sleeves, descending only to the elbow. From the second century among the Romans it was the vestment of the emperors; the Church adopted it for the Sovereign Pontiff and the bishops. The deacons received it from Pope Sylvester, but the privilege of wearing it was confined to the deacons of the Church at Rome, and for them only granted on festival-days as a sign of joy; consequently, it was laid aside during Advent, Lent, and fast-days, periods of sadness and mourning in the Church.

The dalmatic is of the same color as the chasuble of the priest.

The deacon does not wear the stole in the same manner as the priest; he places it on the left shoulder, and brings the extremities under the right arm. The stole being formerly a robe, the deacon necessarily had to roll it up under the right arm in order more easily to serve the priest at the altar.

The Subdeacon. This minister is charged with the preparation of the sacred vessels, the bread and wine of the sacrifice, giving the water to the celebrant when he washes his hands, and reading the epistle. His vestments are the amice, alb, girdle, maniple, and *tunic.* The tunic was formerly distinguished from the dalmatic by its form and material; now it is in all respects like it (fig. p), hence it is unnecessary to speak of it.

From the "Offertory" until the "Pater Noster" at Solemn Mass he wears the *humeral veil* (fig. r), like a shawl over his shoulders, in the folds of which he holds the paten. This veil is an oblong piece of silk of color of the vestments of the day. It has strings to tie it in front.

Fig. p
DALMATIC AND TUNIC.

Fig. q
THE COPE.

Fig. r
THE HUMERAL VEIL.

THE VESTMENTS WORN AT BENEDICTION AND OTHER TIMES

The Cope (fig. q). This is a familiar vestment. It is a large semi-circular cloak, reaching to the feet and having a small cape in the back. It is clasped in front at the breast. The cope is worn by the officiating priest at Benediction of the Blessed Sacrament and in processions. It is likewise used at the "Asperbes" before High Mass, at funeral services, and in solemn blessings connected with Mass,—like the blessing of the ashes on Ash-Wednesday and of the palms on Palm Sunday.

The Surplice. The surplice is a loose-fitting garment of white linen, or of linen and lace, reaching almost to the knees and having wide sleeves. It is worn by the priest over his cassock, when he is assisting at services in the sanctuary, or acting as celebrant at certain functions, such as the administration of the Sacraments,

Vespers or Benediction of the Blessed Sacrament. The surplice is also worn by altar-boys acting as servers of Mass or attending sacred functions in the Church.

The Humeral Veil. The vestment has already been described (fig. r). It is also worn by the celebrant at Benediction when giving the blessing with the Blessed Sacrament and whenever carrying the Blessed Sacrament on other occasions.

NOTES TO THE 1990 EDITION

Page 37: These words are just a paraphrase or an approximation of the correct words for the act of Consecration, much as the paraphrase in the four Scriptural references to them, for none of the actual Consecration formulae of the various rites of the Roman Catholic Church uses merely the words, "This is My Blood," but rather a complete clause, something like, "This is the chalice of My Blood, which shall..."

Page 71: This refers to the traditional Latin Mass, often called the Tridentine Mass. Actually, in 1570, Pope St. Pius V, in the bull *Quo Primum*, decreed that the Missal then in use in the diocese of Rome would thereafter be used throughout the Latin Rite of the Roman Catholic Church (except where a particular liturgical tradition was 200 years old or more). This missal, called the "Roman Missal," with only a few, very slight changes, was in general use (officially) until 1969, when Pope Paul VI issued the *Novus Ordo Missae* by the Apostolic Constitution *Missale Romanum*.

Page 80, note 1: This was the case until 1962, when the name of St. Joseph was added to the traditional Roman Canon of the Mass.

Page 80, note 2: There is a tradition in the Roman Catholic Church that the words of Consecration used in the Traditional Mass of the Latin Rite are the exact words used by Our Lord after the Last Supper.

Page 87: The current law, promulgated by Pope Paul VI, calls for fasting from food and drink for one hour before Communion. Water and genuine medicine do not break the fast and can therefore be taken at any time. The sick, as well as those who care for them, are not required to fast before Communion. (Canon 919, 1983 *Code of Canon Law*).

Page 97, note 1: Currently, a priest who has faculties from his own bishop may hear confessions anywhere in the world, unless the bishop of a diocese denies it in a particular case.

Page 97, note 2: Under the 1983 *Code of Canon Law,* not all of these are reserved cases; e.g., marrying before a non-Catholic minister of religion, while still a mortal sin, is no longer a *reserved* sin.

Page 126, note 1: Even though the Church still uses this symbolic action, the touching of the chalice and paten are not required for validity, according to norms established by Pope Pius XII.

Page 126, note 2: This is the traditional form for the Sacrament of Holy Orders.

Page 126, note 3: Currently, celibacy is required for priests of the Eastern Rites in the United States and Canada; elsewhere in the world, they may marry before, but not after ordination. Bishops may not be married.

Page 134, note 1: Nevertheless, an engagement is not yet a marriage, and an engagement can be, and sometimes should be, broken for a good reason.

Page 134, note 2: Canon 1067 of the 1983 *Code of Canon Law* states that there must be "the marriage banns or other appropriate means for carrying out the necessary inquiries which are to precede marriage."

Page 134, note 3: The 1983 *Code of Canon Law* does not contain this prohibition, though couples are discouraged from marrying during these times.

Index

Accidents, the, 44
Administration of the Sacraments, 7
Adoration, Eucharistic, 46 ff.
Adoro Te, 47, 48
Agape, the, 70
Agnus Dei, the, 80
Alleluia, the, 76
Almsgiving and Temporal Punishment, 107
Altar, the, 183 f., 185 ff.
Ambo, the, 76
Ambrose, St., on Baptism of Desire, 18
Ambrosian Rite, the 71
Apostolic Benediction, the, 116; Rite of. 119
Apostolic Constitutions, the, 70; Mass according to, 71 ff.
Appearances, the, 44
Armenian Monophysites, 3
Aspersion, Baptism by, 12
Assisting at Mass, 68 f.
Atonement, the Day of, 51
Augustine, St., on Matter and Form, 2; on Indelible Character, 6; on Baptism by Judas, 8; on Institution of Baptism, 15; on Martyrs, 18; on Confirmation, 26; on the Holy Eucharist, 43; on the Mass, 56, 64; on Centurion's Prayer, 82; on Eucharistic Fast, 87; on Matrimony, 133

Balsam, 28
Baptism, 12 ff.; Ceremonies of, 18 f.; Rite of, 21 ff.
Baptismal Vows, 19
Baptists, the, 16
Bell, the, at Mass, 82
Benediction, of the Blessed Sacrament, 48; Apostolic, 116, 119
Berengarius, 43
Blessed Virgin, the, and Coming of Holy Ghost, 30; the Ideal Wife and Mother, 130
Blood, Baptism of, 18
Blow on the Cheek at Confirmation, the, 27
Breaking of the Bread, 80

Canon of the Mass, the, 71, 80 f.
Catacombs, the, 43 f.
Catechumens, 18, 19, 43; Mass of, 71
Celibacy, 125 f.

Ceremonies, Sacramental, 3
Character, Indelible, 6
Chrism, Holy, 28
Collect, the 76
Colors, the Liturgical, 82
Columban, St., 106
Communion of the People, 82; *see also* Holy Communion.
Communion under Both Kinds, 86
Confession, 102 ff.
Confession Letters, 109.
Confirmation, 26 ff.; Rite of, 32 ff.
Consecration, the Words of, 74 f., 80
Contrition, 99 ff.
Coptic Monophysites, 3.
Corpus Christi, Feast of, 48 f.
Covenant of Baptism, 18
Creed, the, 78
Cyprian, St., on Baptism by Heretics, 7; on Baptism of Infants, 17; on Confirmation, 26
Cyril of Jerusalem, St., on Transubstantiation, 45

Dead, Sacraments of, 5
Desire, Baptism of, 18
Devotion to the Holy Eucharist, 47 f.
Didache, the, 15, 60
Discipline of the Secret, the, 43
Discretion, Age of, 84
Division of the Sacraments, 5 f.
Divorce, 130, 135
Docetes, the, 42
Domine, Non Sum Dignus, the, 81
Dominus Vobiscum, the, 76
Donatists, the, 8

Effects of the Sacraments, 6 ff.
Elevation, the, 80
Embolism, the, 80
Ends of Mass, the Four, 62
Engagements, 134
Examination of conscience, 103
Ex opere operato, 6
Exorcism, 139 f.
Exposition of the Blessed Sacrament, 48
Extreme Unction, 114 ff.; Rite of, 117 ff.

Faithful, the Mass of, 72; Priesthood of, 16, 62 f., 125
Fast, the Eucharistic, 87 f.

Figures of the Holy Eucharist, 35 f.
First Christians, the, 70
First Communion, 84
Fish, the Symbol of, 43
Forty Hours' Exposition, the, 48
Fraction of the Host, the, 80
Francis de Sales, St., and Baptismal Font, 25; and Frequent Communion, 93
Free Choice, Sacraments of, 5
Frequent Communion, 85 f., 93
Frescoes in the Catacombs, 44 f.
Fruits of the Mass, 62 f.
Furniture, Altar, 183 f.

Gallican Rite, the, 70
General Confession, 104
Gifts of the Holy Ghost, 30
Gloria in Excelsis, the, 76
Golden Sequence, the, 31
Gospel, the, 77 f.
Grace, Sacramental, 7
Gradual, the, 76
Greek Church, 3
Gregory, St., on Baptism, 15

Hierarchy, the, 123
High Mass, 70, 74
Holy Communion, 30, 83 ff.
Holy Eucharist, the, Introduction, 35; as a Sacrament, 35 ff.; as a Sacrifice, 49 ff.
Holy Ghost, the, Sin against, 98
Holy Hour, the, 48
Holy Orders, 121 ff.

Ignatius of Antioch, St., on the Real Presence, 42
Immersion, Baptism by, 12
Immolation, 49
Impediments, Matrimonial, 134
Importance of the Sacraments, 6
Incense, 75
Indulgences, 105 ff., 108
Infant Baptism, 16 ff.
Infusion, Baptism by, 12
Innocent I, Pope, on Kiss of Peace, 43; on Matrimony, 133
Innocent III, Pope, and Confession, 103
Institution of the Sacraments, 2 f.
Introit, the, 75
Inward Grace, 2, 6 f.
Irenaeus, St., on Infant Baptism, 17; on the Mass, 60 f.
Ite, Missa Est, the, 82

Jerome, St., on the Priesthood of the Laity, 105
John Chrysostom, St., on Confirmation, 6; on Holy Eucharist, 43 f.; on Mass, 69; on Centurion's Prayer, 81; on Sacrament of Penance, 96; on Extreme Unction, 114

Julian the Apostate, 10
Juliana, Bl. and the Feast of Corpus Christi, 48
Jurisdiction, 97 f.
Justin Martyr, St., on the Holy Eucharist, 42; on the Mass, 60, 70 f.

Kiss of Peace, the, 36, 81 f.
Kyrie Eleison, the, 76

Language of the Mass, 73 f.
Lauda Sion, 36, 46 f., 48, 88, 90 ff.
Lavabo, the, 79
Leo the Great, Pope on Matrimony, 133
Letters of Peace, 105
Limbo of Children, 17
Liturgies, the Ancient, 61
Liturgy, the Sacred, 69; Notes on, 74 ff.
Living, Sacraments of, 5
Low Mass, 70, 74
Low or White Sunday, 20
Luther, 45, 96, 133
Lutherans, 3 f., 62

Manichaeans, the, 85
Manna, 36
Marriage Laws of the Church, the, 133 ff.
Martyrdom, 18
Mass, the, Institution of, 56 ff.; Rite of, 69 ff.; Essentials of, 69 f.; of the Catechumens, 71; of the Faithful, 72 f.; Kinds of, 74; Language of, 73 f.; Notes on Liturgy of, 74 ff.; Ordinary of, 144
Matrimony, 129 ff.; Rite of, 137 f.
Matter and Form, 1 f.
Means of Grace, the, 1
Missal, the, 70
Mixed Marriages, 135
Monogamy, 129
Monophysites, 3
Montanists, the, 97
Mozarabic Rite, the, 71

Newman, Cardinal, Prayer of, for a Happy Death, 116
Novatus, 97
Number of Sacraments, 3 ff.

Oblation, 50
Offertory, the, 74, 79
Oil, 28
Orate, Fratres, the, 79
Ordinary of the Mass, 144
Origin, on Infant Baptism, 17; on Centurion's Prayer, 81

Pange Lingua, 48
Paschal Lamb, the, 51
Pater Noster, the, 80
Pauline Privilege, the, 134

Penance, 95 ff.; Rite of, 110
Penitential Books, 106 f.
Peter Canisius, St., Defines the Mass, 54
Pius X, Pope, on Holy Communion, 84 f., 88
Polygamy, 129
Pomps of Satan, 18
Pontifical Mass, 74
Preaching, 77
Preface, the, 79
Preparation for Holy Communion, 88 f.
Priest, Vesting of the, 191
Priesthood, the, 121 ff.
Priesthood of the Faithful, 16, 62, 125
Processions of the Blessed Sacrament, 48
Prophecy, Gift of, 30
Purgatory, Souls in, and Indulgences, 108
Purpose of Amendment, Firm, 99

Real Presence, the, 38 ff.
Reception of the Sacraments, 7 f.
Redemptions, 106 f.
Remains of Sin, 115
Reserved Cases, 97
Rites of the Mass, 70 f.
Roman Rite, the, 71; Mass according to, 71 ff.
Rubrics, the, 82

Sacrament, definition, 1
Sacramentals, the, 139 ff.
Sacraments in General, 1 ff.
Sacred Vessels, 183 f., 187 f.
Sacrifice, 49 ff.
Sacrifice of the Cross, the, 53 f.
Sacrifice of the Mass, the, 54 ff.
Sacrifices of the Old Law, 51
Sacrilege, 8
Sacris Solemniis, 48
Sanctifying Grace, 7

Sanctuary Furniture, 183; Lamp, 48
Sanctus, the, 80
Satisfaction, 104 f.
Scapegoat, the, 52
Secret, the, 79
Sequence, the, 77
Solemn Mass, 74
Species, the, 44
Spiritual Life of Man, the Sacraments and, 4 f.
Sponsors, at Baptism, 19; at Confirmation, 30
Stipend Offerers, the, 64
Stipends, 66 f.
Syrian Monophysites, 3

Tertullian, on Confirmation, 26
Thanksgiving after Holy Communion, 88
Thomas Aquinas, St., on Baptism, 15; hymns of, 38, 46, 47, 89 f.; on Effects of Holy Communion, 93
Thomas More, Bl., and Holy Mass, 93
Tongues, Gift of, 30
Tract, the, 76
Transubstantiation, 44 ff.
Treasury, Spiritual, of the Church, 108
Types of the Holy Eucharist, 35 f.

Veni, Sancte Spiritus, 31
Verbum Supernum, 48, 90
Vessels, Sacred, 183 f., 187 f.
Vestments, the Liturgical, 82 f., 183 f., 187 f.
Vesting of the Priest, 191
Viaticum, Holy, 35, 87 f.
Victim, 50
Vocation to the Priesthood, 127

White Garment, the, 20
White Sunday, 20

A COMPLETE SERIES

A COURSE IN RELIGION for Catholic High Schools and Academies. Fr. John Laux, M.A. 4-vol. set. PB. Impr. A set of 4 books, originally published in 1928, designed to give high school students a fantastic knowledge of their Faith. Also great for college and for adults to read on their own. Fr. Laux purposely wrote his books this way. One of the most gifted writers we have encountered: He is brief, clear, understandable and *interesting!* Moreover, he writes in a virtually undated and undatable manner, concentrating overall on the timeless truths of the Faith. Therefore, these books are *not* anachronisms! It is a *very rare* Catholic who would not learn a vast amount from any or all of these books!

1084 CHIEF TRUTHS OF THE FAITH—A Course in Religion, Book I. Fr. John Laux, M.A. 176 pp. PB. Impr. 54 Illus. Indexed. Suggestions for Study. The Sources of Faith; the Holy Scriptures; the Nature of God; the Mystery of the Holy Trinity; the Creation; the Redemption; Sanctification and Grace; and the Four Last Things. Best brief outline of our Faith we know. **8.00**

1085 MASS AND THE SACRAMENTS—A Course in Religion, Book II. Fr. John Laux, M.A. 199 pp. PB. Impr. 72 Illus. Indexed. Suggestions for Study. Covers the Seven Sacraments, the Holy Sacrifice of the Mass, sacramentals and indulgences, with an appendix containing the Ordinary of the Tridentine Mass in Latin and in English with rubrics and explanatory notes, plus illustrations of the traditional altar, priest's vestments and sacred vessels. **8.00**

1086 CATHOLIC MORALITY—A Course in Religion, Book III. Fr. John Laux, M.A. 164 pp. PB. Impr. 40 Illus. Indexed. Suggestions for study. A brief but complete book on traditional Catholic morality. Covers every basic aspect—the purpose of life, free will, the Natural Law, positive divine law, human positive laws, elements of a moral act, virtues, Christian perfection, Evangelical Counsels, nature of sin, kinds of sin, duties toward God, ourselves, our neighbor, the family, the state, the Church, etc. **8.00**

1087 CATHOLIC APOLOGETICS—A Course in Religion, Book IV. Fr. John Laux, M.A. 134 pp. PB. Impr. 38 Illus. Indexed. Suggestions for Study. This is one of the best apologetics books we have ever seen. Covers the nature of our knowledge and sources of our knowledge, justification for our belief, proofs for the existence of God, immortality of the soul, Revelation and evidence of Revelation, genuineness of the Gospels, claims of Jesus, reasonableness of our belief in the Church, nature of the Church, primacy of the Pope, his infallibility, etc. **8.00**

1083 INTRODUCTION TO THE BIBLE. Fr. John Laux, M.A. 326 pp. PB. Impr. 57 Illus. Indexed. Maps. Suggestions for Study. The nature, history, authorship and content of the Holy Bible, with selections from and commentaries on most of the various books. Covers Old and New Testaments. An excellent and unparalleled introduction to the Bible. Written originally as a textbook for students, but also intended by the author—as with all his books—for adult readership. **13.00**

0231 CHURCH HISTORY: A Complete History of the Catholic Church to the Present Day. Fr. John J. Laux, M.A. 659 pp. PB. 141 Illus. Index. Impr. Discussion questions for each chapter. If you ever wanted to know Church history and did not know where to start, this is the book. It was written by a master teacher for both students and adults. Anyone who becomes familiar with this book will have an excellent background in Church history. We know no other book that gives such a wealth of information in such an absorbing manner. **20.00**

At your bookdealer or direct from the Publisher.

Prices guaranteed through 12/31/91.

If you have enjoyed this book, consider making your next selection from among the following . . .

The Facts About Luther. Msgr. Patrick O'Hare....................13.50
Little Catechism of the Curé of Ars. St. John Vianney.............. 5.50
The Curé of Ars—Patron Saint of Parish Priests. Fr. B. O'Brien...... 4.50
Saint Teresa of Ávila. William Thomas Walsh....................18.00
Isabella of Spain: The Last Crusader. William Thomas Walsh........16.50
Characters of the Inquisition. William Thomas Walsh..............12.00
Blood-Drenched Altars—Cath. Comment. on Hist. Mexico. Kelley....16.50
The Four Last Things—Death, Judgment, Hell, Heaven. Fr. von Cochem 5.00
Confession of a Roman Catholic. Paul Whitcomb.................. 1.25
The Catholic Church Has the Answer. Paul Whitcomb.............. 1.25
The Sinner's Guide. Ven. Louis of Granada......................11.00
True Devotion to Mary. St. Louis De Montfort.................... 6.00
Life of St. Anthony Mary Claret. Fanchón Royer..................12.00
Autobiography of St. Anthony Mary Claret......................10.00
I Wait for You. Sr. Josefa Menendez............................ .75
Words of Love. Menendez, Betrone, Mary of the Trinity............ 4.50
Little Lives of the Great Saints. John O'Kane Murray..............16.00
Prayer—The Key to Salvation. Fr. Michael Müller................. 7.00
Sermons on Prayer. St. Francis de Sales........................ 3.50
Sermons on Our Lady. St. Francis de Sales...................... 9.00
Sermons for Lent. St. Francis de Sales.........................10.00
Passion of Jesus and Its Hidden Meaning. Fr. Groenings, S.J.........12.00
The Victories of the Martyrs. St. Alphonsus Liguori............... 7.50
Canons and Decrees of the Council of Trent. Transl. Schroeder......12.00
Sermons of St. Alphonsus Liguori for Every Sunday...............13.50
A Catechism of Modernism. Fr. J. B. Lemius.................... 4.00
Alexandrina—The Agony and the Glory. Johnston................. 3.50
Blessed Margaret of Castello. Fr. William Bonniwell............... 5.00
The Ways of Mental Prayer. Dom Vitalis Lehodey.................11.00
Fr. Paul of Moll. van Speybrouck............................. 9.00
St. Francis of Paola. Simi and Segreti.......................... 6.00
Communion Under Both Kinds. Michael Davies.................. 1.50
Abortion: Yes or No? Dr. John L. Grady, M.D................... 1.50
The Story of the Church. Johnson, Hannan, Dominica............16.50
Religious Liberty. Michael Davies............................. 1.50
Hell Quizzes. Radio Replies Press............................. 1.00
Indulgence Quizzes. Radio Replies Press........................ 1.00
Purgatory Quizzes. Radio Replies Press......................... 1.00
Virgin and Statue Worship Quizzes. Radio Replies Press............ 1.00
The Holy Eucharist. St. Alphonsus............................. 7.50
Meditation Prayer on Mary Immaculate. Padre Pio................ 1.00
Little Book of the Work of Infinite Love. de la Touche............. 1.50
Textual Concordance of The Holy Scriptures. Williams..............35.00
Douay-Rheims Bible. Leatherbound............................35.00
The Way of Divine Love. Sister Josefa Menendez.................16.50
The Way of Divine Love. (pocket, unabr.). Menendez............. 7.50
Mystical City of God—Abridged. Ven. Mary of Agreda.............18.50

Prices guaranteed through December 31, 1992.

Raised from the Dead. Fr. Hebert........................13.50
Love and Service of God, Infinite Love. Mother Louise Margaret.10.00
Life and Work of Mother Louise Margaret. Fr. O'Connell.......10.00
Autobiography of St. Margaret Mary........................ 4.00
Thoughts and Sayings of St. Margaret Mary................. 3.00
The Voice of the Saints. Comp. by Francis Johnston............ 5.00
The 12 Steps to Holiness and Salvation. St. Alphonsus.......... 6.00
The Rosary and the Crisis of Faith. Cirrincione & Nelson....... 1.25
Sin and Its Consequences. Cardinal Manning................. 5.00
Fourfold Sovereignty of God. Cardinal Manning............... 5.00
Catholic Apologetics Today. Fr. Most...................... 8.00
Dialogue of St. Catherine of Siena. Transl. Algar Thorold....... 9.00
Catholic Answer to Jehovah's Witnesses. D'Angelo............. 8.00
Twelve Promises of the Sacred Heart. (100 cards)............. 5.00
St. Aloysius Gonzaga. Fr. Meschler.......................10.00
The Love of Mary. D. Roberto............................ 7.00
Begone Satan. Fr. Vogl................................. 2.00
The Prophets and Our Times. Fr. R. G. Culleton..............10.00
St. Therese, The Little Flower. John Beevers................. 4.50
St. Joseph of Copertino. Fr. Angelo Pastrovicchi.............. 4.50
Mary, The Second Eve. Cardinal Newman................... 2.50
Devotion to Infant Jesus of Prague. Booklet.................. .75
The Faith of Our Fathers. Cardinal Gibbons.................13.00
The Wonder of Guadalupe. Francis Johnston................. 6.00
Apologetics. Msgr. Paul Glenn........................... 9.00
Baltimore Catechism No. 1................................ 3.00
Baltimore Catechism No. 2................................ 4.00
Baltimore Catechism No. 3................................ 7.00
An Explanation of the Baltimore Catechism. Fr. Kinkead........13.00
Bethlehem. Fr. Faber...................................13.50
Bible History. Schuster.................................10.00
Blessed Eucharist. Fr. Mueller...........................13.00
Catholic Catechism. Fr. Faerber.......................... 5.00
The Devil. Fr. Delaporte................................ 5.00
Dogmatic Theology for the Laity. Fr. Premm................15.00
Evidence of Satan in the Modern World. Cristiani............. 8.50
Fifteen Promises of Mary. (100 cards)...................... 5.00
Life of Anne Catherine Emmerich. 2 vols. Schmoger...........37.50
Life of the Blessed Virgin Mary. Emmerich.................13.50
Manual of Practical Devotion to St. Joseph. Patrignani.........12.50
Prayer to St. Michael. (100 leaflets)....................... 5.00
Prayerbook of Favorite Litanies. Fr. Hebert.................. 8.50
Preparation for Death. (Abridged). St. Alphonsus............. 7.00
Purgatory Explained. Schouppe...........................12.50
Purgatory Explained. (pocket, unabr.). Schouppe.............. 5.00
Fundamentals of Catholic Dogma. Ludwig Ott................16.50
Spiritual Conferences. Tauler............................10.00
Trustful Surrender to Divine Providence. Bl. Claude........... 4.00
Wife, Mother and Mystic. Bessieres....................... 7.00
The Agony of Jesus. Padre Pio........................... 1.00

Prices guaranteed through December 31, 1992.

Is It a Saint's Name? Fr. William Dunne...................... 1.50
St. Pius V—His Life, Times, Miracles. Anderson.............. 4.00
Who Is Teresa Neumann? Fr. Charles Carty.................. 1.25
Martyrs of the Coliseum. Fr. O'Reilly.......................15.00
Way of the Cross. St. Alphonsus Liguori..................... .75
Way of the Cross. Franciscan version......................... .75
How Christ Said the First Mass. Fr. Meagher................15.00
Too Busy for God? Think Again! D'Angelo................... 4.00
St. Bernadette Soubirous. Trochu............................15.00
Passion and Death of Jesus Christ. Liguori................... 7.50
Treatise on the Love of God. 2 Vols. St. Francis de Sales.......16.50
Confession Quizzes. Radio Replies Press..................... 1.00
St. Philip Neri. Fr. V. J. Matthews......................... 4.50
St. Louise de Marillac. Sr. Vincent Regnault.................. 4.50
The Old World and America. Rev. Philip Furlong.............13.50
Prophecy for Today. Edward Connor......................... 4.50
The Book of Infinite Love. Mother de la Touche............... 4.50
Chats with Converts. Fr. M. D. Forrest...................... 8.00
The Church Teaches. Church Documents....................13.50
Conversation with Christ. Peter T. Rohrbach.................. 8.00
Purgatory and Heaven. J. P. Arendzen....................... 3.50
What Is Liberalism? Sarda y Salvany........................ 5.00
Spiritual Legacy of Sr. Mary of the Trinity. van den Broek...... 9.00
The Creator and the Creature. Fr. Frederick Faber.............13.00
Radio Replies. 3 Vols. Frs. Rumble and Carty.................36.00
Convert's Catechism of Catholic Doctrine. Fr. Geiermann....... 3.00
Incarnation, Birth, Infancy of Jesus Christ. St. Alphonsus....... 7.50
Light and Peace. Fr. R. P. Quadrupani....................... 5.00
Dogmatic Canons & Decrees of Trent, Vat. I. Documents....... 8.00
The Evolution Hoax Exposed. A. N. Field.................... 5.00
The Primitive Church. Fr. D. I. Lanslots..................... 8.50
The Priesthood. Bishop Stockums............................10.00
The Priest, the Man of God. St. Joseph Cafasso...............10.00
Blessed Sacrament. Fr. Frederick Faber......................15.00
Christ Denied. Fr. Paul Wickens............................ 2.00
New Regulations on Indulgences. Fr. Winfrid Herbst........... 2.50
A Tour of the Summa. Msgr. Paul Glenn.....................15.00
Spiritual Conferences. Fr. Frederick Faber....................12.50
Latin Grammar. Scanlon and Scanlon........................12.50
A Brief Life of Christ. Fr. Rumble.......................... 1.50
Marriage Quizzes. Radio Replies Press....................... 1.00
True Church Quizzes. Radio Replies Press.................... 1.00
St. Lydwine of Schiedam. J. K. Huysmans.................... 7.00
Mary, Mother of the Church. Church Documents.............. 3.00
The Sacred Heart and the Priesthood. de la Touche............. 7.00
Revelations of St. Bridget. St. Bridget of Sweden.............. 2.50
Magnificent Prayers. St. Bridget of Sweden................... 1.50
The Happiness of Heaven. Fr. J. Boudreau................... 7.00
St. Catherine Labouré of the Miraculous Medal. Dirvin.........11.00
The Glories of Mary. (pocket, unabr.). St. Alphonsus Liguori.... 8.00

Prices guaranteed through December 31, 1992.

The Two Divine Promises. Fr. Hoppe........................ 1.25
Eucharistic Miracles. Joan Carroll Cruz..................... 13.00
The Incorruptibles. Joan Carroll Cruz....................... 12.00
Birth Prevention Quizzes. Radio Replies Press................ 1.00
Pope St. Pius X. F. A. Forbes............................. 6.00
St. Alphonsus Liguori. Frs. Miller and Aubin................ 13.50
Self-Abandonment to Divine Providence. Fr. de Caussade, S.J.... 15.00
The Song of Songs—A Mystical Exposition. Fr. Arintero, O.P.... 18.00
Prophecy for Today. Edward Connor........................ 4.50
Saint Michael and the Angels. Approved Sources.............. 5.50
Dolorous Passion of Our Lord. Anne C. Emmerich............ 13.50
Modern Saints—Their Lives & Faces. Ann Ball............... 15.00
Our Lady of Fatima's Peace Plan from Heaven. Booklet......... .75
Divine Favors Granted to St. Joseph. Pere Binet.............. 4.00
St. Joseph Cafasso—Priest of the Gallows. St. John Bosco....... 3.00
Catechism of the Council of Trent. McHugh/Callan............ 20.00
The Foot of the Cross. Fr. Faber........................... 13.50
The Rosary in Action. John Johnson........................ 8.00
Padre Pio—The Stigmatist. Fr. Charles Carty................. 12.50
Why Squander Illness? Frs. Rumble & Carty................. 2.00
The Sacred Heart and the Priesthood. de la Touche............ 7.00
Fatima—The Great Sign. Francis Johnston................... 7.00
Heliotropium—Conformity of Human Will to Divine. Drexelius... 11.00
Charity for the Suffering Souls. Fr. John Nageleisen........... 13.50
Devotion to the Sacred Heart of Jesus. Verheylezoon........... 12.50
Who Is Padre Pio? Radio Replies Press...................... 1.00
Child's Bible History. Knecht.............................. 4.00
The Stigmata and Modern Science. Fr. Charles Carty........... 1.00
The Life of Christ. 4 Vols. H.B. Anne C. Emmerich........... 55.00
St. Anthony—The Wonder Worker of Padua. Stoddard.......... 3.50
The Precious Blood. Fr. Faber............................. 11.00
The Holy Shroud & Four Visions. Fr. O'Connell.............. 1.50
Clean Love in Courtship. Fr. Lawrence Lovasik............... 2.00
The Prophecies of St. Malachy. Peter Bander................. 4.00
St. Martin de Porres. Giuliana Cavallini..................... 10.00
The Secret of the Rosary. St. Louis De Montfort.............. 3.00
The History of Antichrist. Rev. P. Huchede.................. 2.50
The Douay-Rheims New Testament. Paperbound............... 12.00
St. Catherine of Siena. Alice Curtayne...................... 11.00
Where We Got the Bible. Fr. Henry Graham................. 5.00
Hidden Treasure—Holy Mass. St. Leonard................... 4.00
Imitation of the Sacred Heart of Jesus. Fr. Arnoudt........... 13.50
The Life & Glories of St. Joseph. Edward Thompson........... 12.50
Père Lamy. Biver... 10.00
Humility of Heart. Fr. Cajetan da Bergamo.................. 6.00
The Curé D'Ars. Abbé Francis Trochu...................... 18.50
Love, Peace and Joy. St. Gertrude/Prévot................... 5.00
The Three Ways of the Spiritual Life. Garrigou-Lagrange, O.P..... 4.00

At your bookdealer or direct from the publisher.

Prices guaranteed through December 31, 1992.

NOTES

NOTES

NOTES

NOTES